DUEL
· FOR THE ·
GOLAN

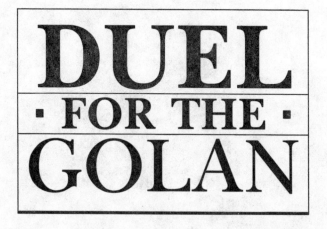

DUEL
· FOR THE ·
GOLAN

·

THE 100-HOUR BATTLE THAT SAVED ISRAEL

·

JERRY ASHER
with Eric Hammel

WILLIAM MORROW AND COMPANY, INC.
NEW YORK

Printed in the United States of America

Our thanks to Joe Bermudez,
and to Jim Stewart for his help with the maps.

LIST OF MAPS

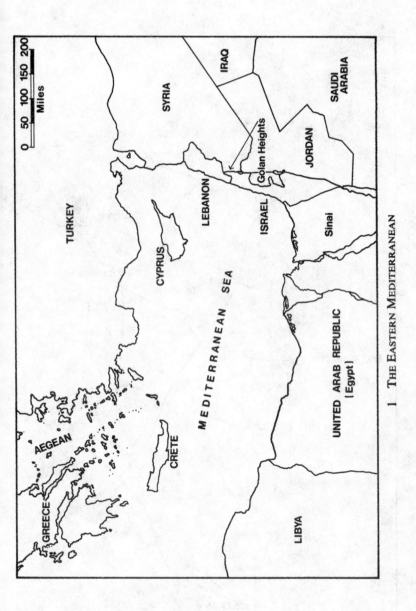

1 THE EASTERN MEDITERRANEAN

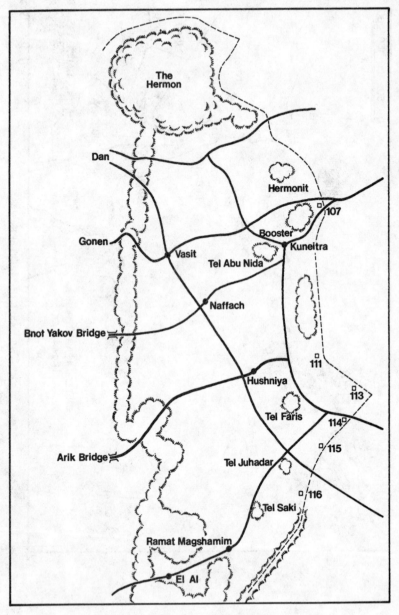

2 THE GOLAN HEIGHTS

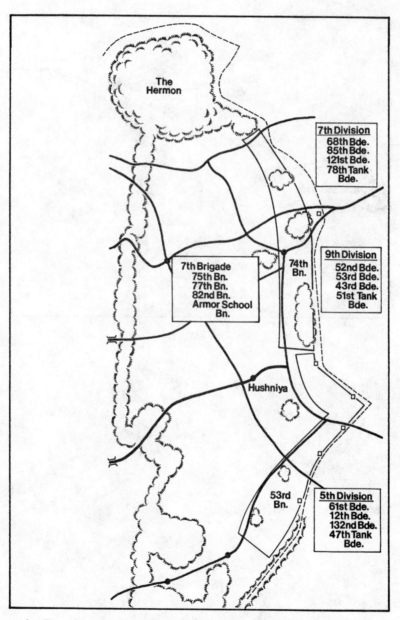

The Hermon

7th Division
68th Bde.
85th Bde.
121st Bde.
78th Tank Bde.

9th Division
52nd Bde.
53rd Bde.
43rd Bde.
51st Tank Bde.

7th Brigade
75th Bn.
77th Bn.
82nd Bn.
Armor School Bn.

74th Bn.

Hushniya

53rd Bn.

5th Division
61st Bde.
12th Bde.
132nd Bde.
47th Tank Bde.

3 The Golan Heights Deployment; October 6, 1400 hrs

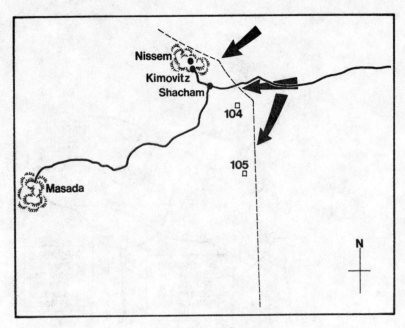

4 THE DAN ROAD

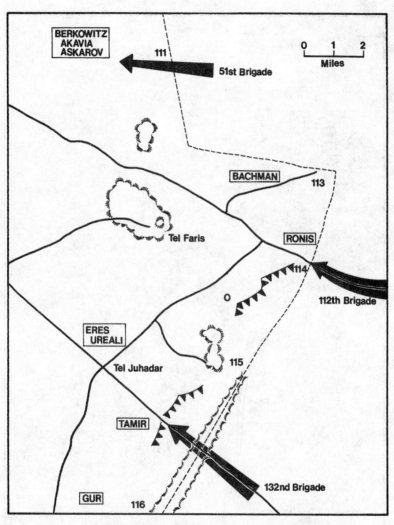

BERKOWITZ
AKAVIA
ASKAROV

111

51st Brigade

0   1   2
Miles

BACHMAN

113

Tel Faris

RONIS

114

112th Brigade

ERES
UREALI

Tel Juhadar

115

TAMIR

132nd Brigade

GUR

116

5   THE RAFID GAP; OCTOBER 6, 1700 HRS

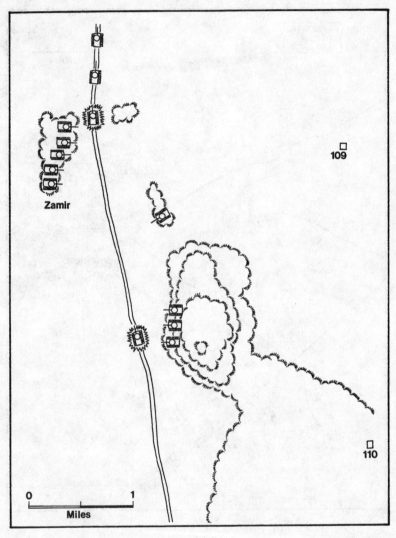

6   Zamir's Ambush

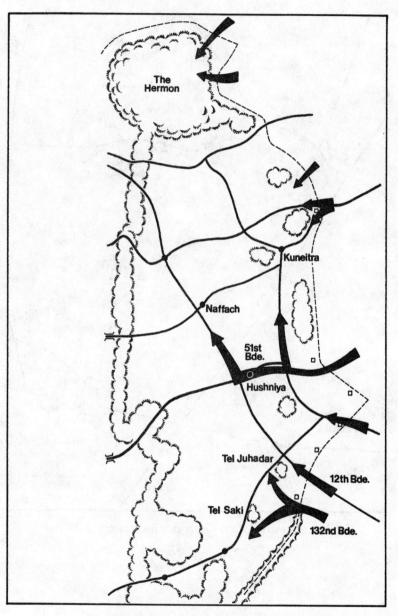

7   THE GOLAN HEIGHTS; OCTOBER 7, 0200 HRS

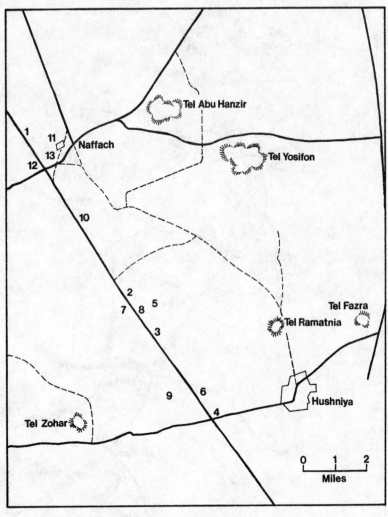

8 LIEUTENANT ZWICKA AND THE BATTLE OF NAFFACH

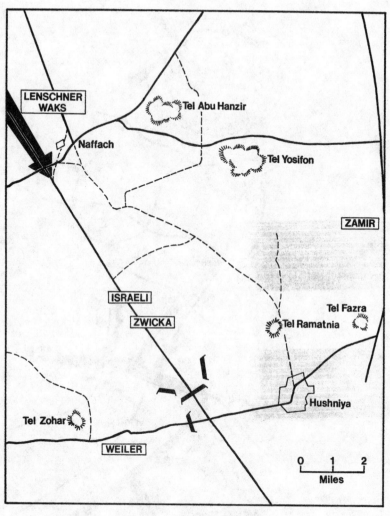

9 OCTOBER 7, 0200 HRS

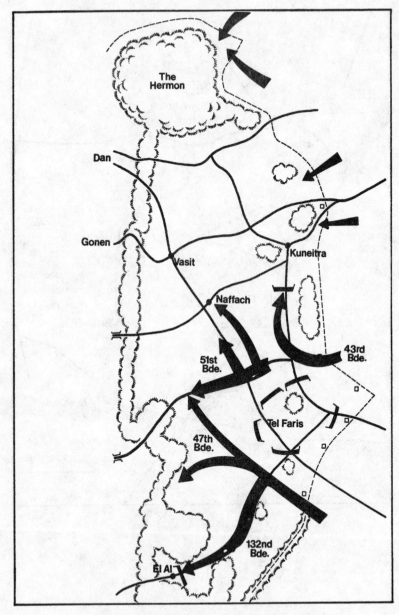

10 THE GOLAN HEIGHTS; OCTOBER 7, 1000 HRS

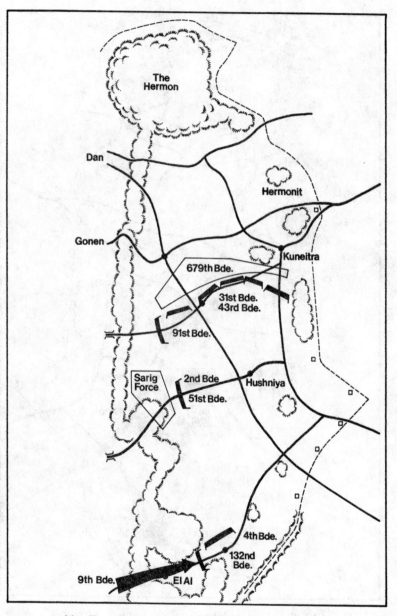

11 THE GOLAN HEIGHTS; OCTOBER 7, 1700 HRS

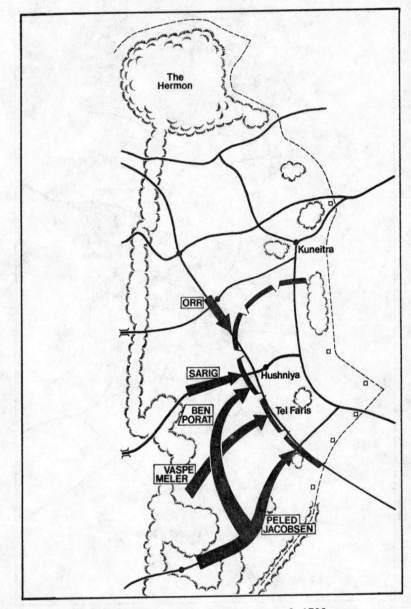

12   THE GOLAN HEIGHTS; OCTOBER 8, 1700 HRS

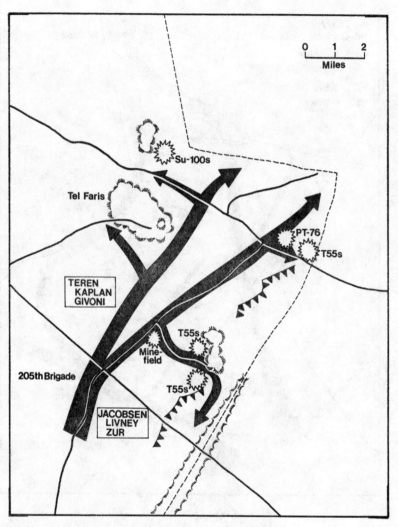

Su-100s

Tel Faris

PT-76

T55s

TEREN
KAPLAN
GIVONI

T55s

Mine-
field

205th Brigade

T55s

JACOBSEN
LIVNEY
ZUR

0   1   2
Miles

13   THE RAFID GAP; OCTOBER 9

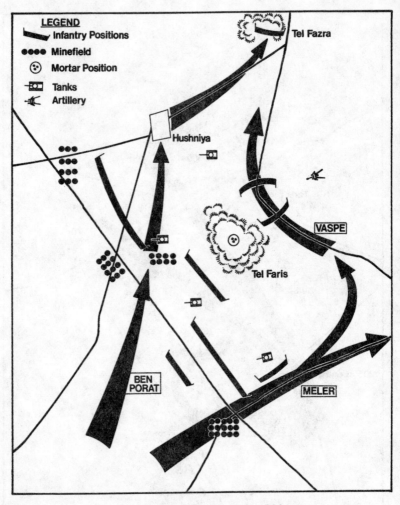

14 HUSHNIYA; OCTOBER 9, 1000 HRS

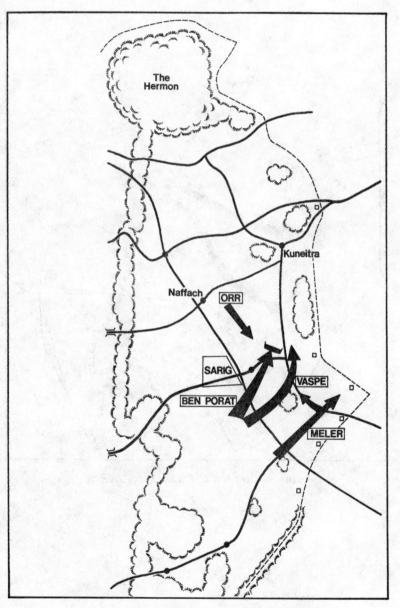

15   THE GOLAN HEIGHTS; OCTOBER 9, 1700 HRS

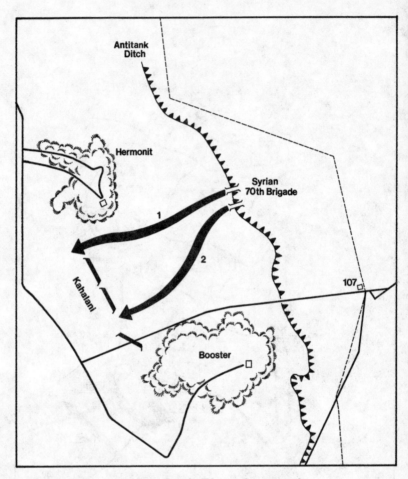

16 KAHALANI'S WALL; OCTOBER 9

PROLOGUE

The Golan: sere, stony ridges, rock-strewn volcanic hills, hardly a tree in sight. There is nothing there for Israelis to fight for and die defending. But below, within easy gunshot of the lip of the Golan escarpment, is the jewel of Israel, the Huleh Valley, the vast drained swamp with topsoil many meters deep, a breadbasket of lush grain and vegetable fields, a fruit basket of thick orchards. Farther on, but still within range of Syrian guns before June 8, 1967, is the Galil, the Israeli heartland of towns and villages and fields and orchards. Below the escarpment—you have to lean over the edge to see it—is the River Jordan, which carries the water from the perpetually snowy Hermon across the aqueduct that drains the Huleh to a vast natural reservoir, the Kinneret—the Sea of Galilee—named by ancient Jews for its shape, which is that of a harp.

Nearly everything that grows in Israel—the greenery, the livestock, the people—is nourished by the water of the Kinneret and thus of the Hermon and the three sources of the Jordan that issue from the vast mountain. Away to the north, in the very corner of Israel, is the Dan settlement, where the first faint inkling of the river-to-be bubbles up from the rocks lining the streambed. Before June 8, 1967, the Syrians controlled one bank of this narrow tributary. Upon the Golan is the second source of the Jordan, the Banias. These springs, hidden in ancient interconnected caves, were totally controlled by the Syrians before Israeli tanks and infantry crawled up the sheer walls of the escarpment and took it from them at the close of the Six-Day War. The third source of the Jordan flows out into Lebanon.

The vista over the Huleh Valley and the Galil, the pure waters issuing from the rocks at Dan, and the life-sustaining springs at the Banias—these are the reasons Israelis cling by their fingernails to the lip of the Golan. The greenery that blooms in the desert, in every valley, and upon every hillside is fed by the issue of the Hermon, which may be controlled from the Golan.

All you can see of Israel from the Golan is under your gun if you want it to be.

Even today, you may stand in a hip-deep, concrete-lined trench at the place where the road winding tortuously uphill from the B'not Yaacov (Daughters of Jacob) Bridge breasts the escarpment. Beneath your gaze are tractors tilling and reaping in the green Huleh Valley. If you want to, you can pull the pin from a hand grenade, lean out over the edge of the trench, and toss the bomb onto the roof of one of those tractors.

Farther out in the plain at the foot of the escarpment is a high earthen dam. It was built there one night in 1947 by the residents of the kibbutz behind it. It holds back no water—it was never meant to —but it did hold back a storm of snipers' bullets that were aimed for twenty years from the trenches rimming the escarpment. Just off the road, beside the trench in which you stand, are two permanent monuments to the two wars fought here: a Syrian T-34 tank destroyed in 1967, and a Syrian SU-100 gun carrier destroyed in 1973.

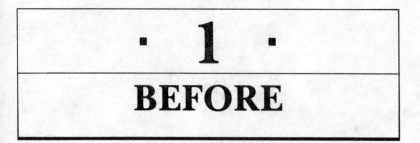

· 1 ·
BEFORE

· 1 ·

The first Saturday in October 1973, a traditional Jewish Sabbath, was to coincide with the concluding observances of the Jewish New Year, Yom Kippur. The simultaneous occurrence of the two events is highly unusual, coming only three or four times in an average lifetime.

The Sabbath is a singular weekly experience to observant Jews. All forms of labor are forbidden on that day. Work comes to a standstill, commerce is halted, even personal conveniences such as driving a vehicle, turning on a light, or shaving await the conclusion of the day mankind is commanded to rest and keep holy. It is, above all, a joyous day, set aside to reflect upon God's beneficence.

In contrast to the joy of the Sabbath, Yom Kippur is a most solemn occasion. Even the least religious Jew, comfortable with ignoring the joys and strictures of the weekly Sabbath, is drawn to prayer on Yom Kippur. It is the only day of fasting specifically ascribed to the "Law of Moses" and is further described as a "Sabbath of Sabbaths." It is widely held that God literally decides who shall live and who shall die in the coming year by sunset on Yom Kippur.

The fact that this Yom Kippur was to fall on a Sabbath was all-prevailing. But it is also recognized that all forms of work in this modern world cannot be avoided altogether. Life-sustaining services cannot cease, but they can be restricted. The demands of calendar and conscience affect both thought and behavior.

On Friday, October 5, 1973, Lieutenant Avraham Elimelech was going over plans for the religious observances when he recognized a major problem. Bunker 107, a defensive compound he commanded on the Golan Heights, had a nine-man garrison. If *ten* Jewish men gather for a religious service, the actual prayers are shorter. It is considered a *mitzvah,* a good thing, to pray and fast collectively, so Elimelech called his battalion headquarters to see if he could borrow a tenth man.

Private Avraham Lifschitz was ordered to Bunker 107 for Yom Kippur. There had been no exchanges of gunfire across the cease-fire line with Syria since January, so Lifschitz gave no thought to the danger of moving to a bunker on the border with an enemy nation. What little concern he had was dispelled when he passed prepared tank positions overlooking no-man's-land. The positions were empty, a clear indication that no trouble was anticipated. However, if the Syrians *did* mount any sort of attack against Bunker 107—or any other position screening the Golan front—the garrison would be amply protected by main battle tanks that would be positioned in such a way as to place the open, undulating ground fronting the cease-fire line under accurate fire, preregistered in interlocking and mutually supporting bands. Several tank battalions based in camps along the length of the Golan would provide the tanks as needed, and they would also mount spoiling attacks at platoon or company strength, as appropriate.

Avraham Lifschitz's arrival delighted Lieutenant Elimelech because it meant the religious observances set to begin at sundown would go well. The tiny garrison now had its own "prayerman" as well as such standard specialists as a bazookaman and a mortarman.

Bunker 107 was generally typical of Israeli positions guarding the cease-fire line. It was well constructed, capable of withstanding heavy artillery fire. Tank or infantry attacks from across no-man's-land would be minimized by a belt of mines planted along the approaches from Syria and in front of a stout barbed-wire barrier. The garrisons had light antitank weapons, chiefly bazookas, but they would also be amply protected against armored attacks by supporting armored units of their own.

There was, however, one distinct feature that set Bunker 107 apart, something its garrison tried to overlook. All the other bunkers along the cease-fire line were fronted by a continuous antitank ditch, stretching from the Hermon, in the North, to the border with Jordan, in the South. Because of the way the land lay around Bunker 107, however, it had been placed in front of the ditch by a considerable distance. The garrison was thus expected to carry on a fight against attacking Syrian forces well in front of and physically isolated from other Israeli forces. If attacked, the soldiers at Bunker 107 would have to man an exposed 360-degree defensive perimeter.

The empty tank positions that Private Lifschitz passed on his way to Bunker 107 belonged to Lieutenant Colonel Yair Nofshe's 74th Tank Battalion, a component of 188th "Barak" Armored Brigade. While all thirty Centurion tanks assigned to Nofshe's battalion were battle-ready, the crews and staff of the battalion were preparing to stand down for the holy day. As a matter of fact, the expectation of trouble coming to the Golan was so low that Lieutenant Colonel Nofshe had granted twenty-three-year-old Captain Eyal Shacham a holiday leave in honor of the young man's elevation to a company command.

While Captain Shacham was rushing home to surprise his wife and parents, Sergeant Gideon Ehrenhalt was climbing toward Mount Hermon, Israel's northern anchor on the Golan. Ehrenhalt's unit manned one of Israel's best-known military facilities, a complex of highly sophisticated electronic-warfare components spread across a ridge sixty-six hundred feet above sea level and overlooking the city of Damascus and the entire Damascus Plain south to the cease-fire line. As were most of the men posted at the complex, Ehrenhalt was a *jobnik,* a Reserve technician called up for his annual month-long stint of specialized active military service.

The vital base was guarded by less than fifteen regular infantrymen, members of 1st "Golani" Infantry Brigade.

The passages of Captain Shacham and Sergeant Ehrenhalt were typical of the normal comings and goings throughout Israel and the cease-fire lines that separated the Israel Defense Force (IDF) from the armies of Egypt, Jordan, Syria, and Lebanon. What was neither typical nor normal was the decision of the IDF chief of staff, Lieutenant General David Elazar, to order the entire IDF to a third-stage alert—Alert Gimmel (after the third letter of the Hebrew alphabet). Dado Elazar's was a momentous decision. No previous chief of staff had issued such an order so close to Yom Kippur. Alert Gimmel meant an end to both regular and special leaves for members of the standing armed forces and Reservists serving on active duty. It also meant the temporary activation of selected individual Reservists and members of several specialized Reserve units.

Alert Gimmel impacted throughout the IDF (which includes the Army, Air Force, and Navy). Brigadier General Yehoshua Saguy, commander of the Intelligence School, canceled the passes his students expected. Leave was denied the staff of the Army Broadcasting Service, which was scheduled to go off the air at sunset, the beginning of the Yom Kippur holy day. Major Yonatan Netanyahu, the veteran American-born deputy commander of one of Israel's crack parachute battalions, detained every one of his subordinates.

The "alert" portion of Alert Gimmel was coupled with movement orders for some units. Lieutenant Colonel Memshalom Carmel, of the Armor School, was ordered to draw Centurion tanks, organize his students into a battalion unit, and move to the Golan.

Colonel Avigdor Ben Gal, commanding officer of 7th Armored Brigade, Israel's premier armored unit, received his alert and movement orders with particular satisfaction, with a sense that his judgment was being vindicated. One of Ben Gal's two Centurion tank battalions, the 77th, had been detached from the brigade for temporary service on the Golan nine days prior to the alert. For over a week, Ben Gal had been quietly rotating officers from his remaining two battalions to the 77th to allow them to study the terrain. Colonel Ben Gal had had an unexplainable inchoate sense that a major confrontation with Syria was not far off, and he wanted to be ready. Readiness, in fact, was a personal trait that had marked Ben Gal early in his career for eventual high rank. Command of the crack 7th Armored Brigade was a giant step on the career path.

As soon as Alert Gimmel was issued, the entire 7th Armored Brigade was ordered to consolidate on the Golan. Its 75th Armored Infantry Battalion, outfitted with modern American-built M-113 armored personnel carriers (thoroughly refurbished to exacting IDF specifications), was to travel north from its Negev Desert training ground on its own tracks. And 82nd Tank Battalion, considered by some to be the finest tank battalion in the IDF, would transport its personnel by bus and draw Centurion tanks from reserve stocks prepositioned on the Golan.

While Colonel Ben Gal was overseeing the transfer of 75th and 82nd battalions to the Golan, Lieutenant Colonel Avigdor Kahalani was on his way to rejoin his command, 77th Tank Battalion, following a brief visit home. Kahalani had been on leave nine days earlier, putting a new roof on his home, when he had been summoned to the phone by his wife. It was Colonel Ben Gal, informing the veteran battalion commander to return to duty to lead his unit to the Golan. Kahalani had complied instantly, leaving the roofing work unfinished and his home open to the imminent start of the rainy season. Having seen to the positioning of his battalion, Avigdor Kahalani had given himself leave to return home to finish the roof. He completed the task just in time to comply with the strictures of Alert Gimmel. That was one worry out of the way for the man whose 7th Brigade tank company had led Israeli armored forces into the Gaza Strip in June 1967: his wife and child at least had a secure roof over their heads.

As soon as Kahalani arrived back at the 77th Tank Battalion command post, he was notified that the balance of 7th Armored Brigade was on its way to the Golan. Kahalani called a staff meeting and surprised his officers by issuing a new set of code designations to be used over the tactical radio net if the battalion was returned to 7th Brigade. There was vague mumbling, for the dissemination of the codes would require additional work by the already overburdened staff. One of the company commanders asked Kahalani why the new codes had to be issued. The dark-complected, black-haired battalion commander flashed the huge white smile that was his trademark and replied, "To confuse them. We've used the same code the whole time we've been here. Who knows what they know?"

In Kuneitra, Lieutenant Colonel Yair Nofshe called his 74th Tank Battalion officers together to review options for responding to just about any sort of Syrian initiative in their zone, roughly the northern half of the cease-fire line. Farther south, in Juhadar, the officers of Lieutenant Colonel Oded Eres's 53rd Tank Battalion worked on their plans.

At Northern Command headquarters in Rosh Pina, Brigadier General Rafoul Eitan prepared to form a division from the battalions and brigades that were and would be deployed on the Golan as part of Alert Gimmel. Rafoul Eitan, whose peacetime title was chief officer of paratroopers and infantry, was a close-mouthed veteran of paratroop and commando operations dating back to the late 1940s.

Only one of the two infantry battalions manning the bunker line on the Golan received word about Alert Gimmel. This was the elite, all-volunteer 50th Parachute Battalion, entirely composed of small groups of young men who had banded together in high school to join kibbutz settlements throughout the country. These groups, known collectively as *nahal,* customarily trained and served out their active-duty obligations in such elite units as 50th Parachute Battalion before being released to complete their army service at the kibbutz settlements of their choice. Thus, unlike many regular units, 50th Parachute Battalion had squads and platoons largely composed of men who had known one another before enlisting (as differentiated from being conscripted), and it was an all-volunteer unit of specially motivated young men.

When Alert Gimmel was issued, Lieutenant Colonel Yair Yaron, commander of 50th Parachute Battalion, made certain his soldiers donned their helmets and flak jackets. They were prepared, when the time came, also to don prayer shawls over the armored vests—an unusual sight, but one that would be little cause for comment.

The bunkers screening the cease-fire line were only lightly reinforced. Lieutenant Yosef Gur, commanding Bunker 116 south of Juhadar, received only three new men as reinforcements, and a six-man squad was sent to the Tel Saki position, an electronic-warfare complex overlooking the road south of Juhadar.

Alert Gimmel broke down in the case of Golani Infantry Brigade's 17th Infantry Battalion, which was responsible for manning the northern half of the Golan line. The battalion took no special precautions. Indeed, when the infantry commander of the Hermon position called the 17th Battalion command post for routine information, he was not even told that Alert Gimmel had been issued.

The alert was hardest on men denied expected leave but given no special work to do. The boredom and monotony were reaching stress levels among Major Yoni Netanyahu's battalion of high-strung paratroopers when, at 1400 hours (2:00 P.M.), the troops were suddenly and inexplicably ordered to stand down for the holy day. Brigadier General Yehoshua Saguy's students at the Intelligence School likewise heard that the alert was canceled.

These were isolated instances; as Netanyahu's and Saguy's charges scattered for home, numerous Israelis already on leave were receiving urgent orders to return to their units. Alert Gimmel had by no means been canceled. Somewhere in the chain of command, a harried or compassionate staff officer had responded to inquiries from Netanyahu's battalion and the Intelligence School more on the basis of hope than of fact.

Retired Lieutenant General Yitzhak Rabin, who had been IDF chief of staff during the Six-Day War, was at home with members of his family when a phone call canceled the leave of one of the younger generation. As with most Israelis wise to the ways of such matters, Rabin sensed that an alert was on.

All the IDF units facing Lebanon and Syria come under the control of Northern Command, headquartered in Rosh Pina.

The regional commander, Major General Yitzhak Hofi, was a parachutist, a man who had spent his entire adult life in the army. Hofi was a veteran of innumerable combat episodes, beginning in the late 1940s. He had been a charter member of Unit 101, the ultra-elite commando force that countered Arab raids and served as a model and tactical test-bed for the emerging IDF during the early and mid-1950s. It had been Hofi's mounting concern that had resulted in the assignment of Kahalani's 77th Tank Battalion to the Golan on September 27. By October 5, General Hofi felt that a major conflict was imminent.

Though Alert Gimmel ended any hope Hofi had of spending time at home on Yom Kippur, he was elated by the result of General Elazar's decision. There would be endless work, to be sure, but news that the balance of 7th Armored Brigade and the Armor School Tank Battalion—one armored infantry and two tank battalions—were to bolster the three tank battalions, one armored infantry battalion, one infantry battalion, and one parachute battalion already on the Golan was music to Yitzhak Hofi's ears. In addition to the armored battalions, the Golan rated a 30-percent increase in its artillery component. The first of the reinforcements arrived by the late afternoon of October 5; an ad hoc battalion-size force from the Artillery School reported its self-propelled 155mm and 175mm howitzers ready for deployment.

As things began picking up around Hofi's forward headquarters, at Naffach, the commanding general placed a call to Major General Dan Laner, who lived barely ten miles away, at Kibbutz Neot Mordechai. Laner had recently retired from active duty and had been designated commander of a brand-new but as-yet-unformed Reserve division assigned to Northern Command. Hofi felt Laner deserved a briefing on Alert Gimmel and what he saw as a subtly worsening situation with respect to Syria. In the course of the conversation, Hofi mentioned that he would not be going home for Yom Kippur. Laner invited his colleague to dinner, but the invitation was refused.

Dan Laner was more distressed by the refusal of his dinner invitation than he was by Hofi's frank recitation of the military situation. If Hofi was so concerned that he passed up a dinner invitation the night before Yom Kippur, Laner reasoned, things must be very serious indeed. So Laner got on the phone to key officers assigned to his division and asked them to meet with him the next morning, Yom Kippur.

Lieutenant General Dado Elazar's effort to impose his decision upon a population preparing for the Sabbath and Yom Kippur— upon institutions working toward the cessation of the normal activities of daily life—was unprecedented in Israeli history.

The chief of staff's judgment was already under considerable scrutiny for his decision to mobilize the Reserves the preceding May. Thirty million dollars had been spent on that emergency mobilization, and nothing whatever had happened. It was felt in many quarters that the money was totally wasted. So, as disturbed as Elazar was by the Arab deployments on the borders, he was not prepared to risk calling up the Reserves again.

However, his decision to transfer 7th Armored Brigade to the Golan brought Northern Command up to 80 percent of its wartime strength. If a war broke out, Northern Command would also immediately be strengthened by three Reserve brigades and auxiliary formations mustering nearly 160 additional tanks.

While the defense establishment was obliged to respond to a call by its commander, the civilian authorities were not. Elazar would have to do some heavy selling. So, while the defense forces affected by Alert Gimmel were preparing, the chief of staff moved to inform the government of his decision and the reasoning behind it.

At 0900 on October 5, shortly after issuing Alert Gimmel on his own authority, Lieutenant General Elazar joined Major General Eliahu Zeira, director of Military Intelligence, for a meeting with Minister of Defense Moshe Dayan. Zeira, the individual most directly responsible for predicting war, held the opinion that the chance of an outbreak was exceedingly remote. In his judgment, Egyptian and Syrian troop concentrations in close proximity to the cease-fire lines at the Suez Canal and on the Golan were merely conducting maneuvers that would soon end.

Elazar was uneasy with Zeira's views. Like Zeira, he saw that very heavy troop concentrations on both fronts had been in steady evidence for the entire year. In fact, numerous Syrian and Egyptian assault divisions seemed to be based permanently in close proximity to the cease-fire lines.

It was the very permanence of these deployments that worried Elazar and confounded Zeira's ability to state with absolute certainty that war was not directly in the offing.

The difference between the conclusions derived by each man from the evidence is the fruit of an age-old military dilemma.

It is axiomatic that a military response be based upon a potential enemy's *capabilities,* not his intentions, which cannot truly be gauged until after the fact.

This unyielding principle, Elazar believed, must be the basis of all Intelligence forecasting as well as military action derived from the forecasts.

The difficulty in making a clear-cut military decision—of shaping an adequate and appropriate response—on October 5, 1973, was that neither Elazar nor Zeira disputed the *ability* of the Egyptians and/or Syrians to start or wage a war. It had been evident through the year that either or both armies could do just that, and on very short notice, whenever they wanted to. In fact, a new sort of status quo had been imposed on the region: The Syrians and/or Egyptians could, as a normal matter of course, launch instantaneous war with massive forces that appeared to be permanently based right on Israel's border.

Elazar's lamented May mobilization had been based on a slight upward shift in both Egyptian and Syrian strength on the border. In fact, it had derived from only slightly increased logistical activity on the approaches to the border. Elazar had determined that the increased movement of war supplies toward the front was a final provisioning of assault units just prior to the launch of an all-out attack. This "topping off" of fuel and war materiel was deemed to be an Intelligence matter upon which decisive action *had* to be based.

Similar small ripples in the logistical preparations immediately behind Syrian and Egyptian assault divisions had again heightened the chief of staff's sense of what the enemy armies were capable of doing: They were capable of attacking Israeli frontier positions on short notice, of breaching the thinly held defense lines, of inflicting severe damage to rear-area depots, and, in the case of Syria, of both obtaining positions overlooking Israeli settlements in the Jordan Valley and interdicting the exposed approaches over which a counterattack would have to be launched and supported.

General Zeira, who had not supported Elazar's mobilization order in May, also was disinclined to agree this time. He looked at the same information as had Elazar and drew the opposite conclusion. He felt the heightened Egyptian and Syrian logistical activity close to the front was an aberration or a coincidence, just as nearly identical activity had been in May.

Elazar did not say the Arabs intended to attack; he contended that they had the capability of mounting an immediate attack. Zeira did not say that the Arabs could not attack; he argued that they did not intend to attack. Elazar felt that his duty was to complete every preparation necessary to deter or blunt the attack the Arabs could mount. Zeira felt that there was no need to prepare because no attack was going to be mounted.

Moshe Dayan listened. The nation's Military Intelligence chief rated the probability of war as low, while the nation's highest-ranking military officer had taken sound precautions in the face of manifestly awesome preparations by enemy armies; for every Israeli battalion on one or the other of the cease-fire lines, Syria or Egypt had deployed a division.

They had all been over it before. The briefing took only a few minutes. Then Dayan placed a call to Prime Minister Golda Meir and requested an immediate meeting.

• 2 •

ontrary to all of General Zeira's beliefs and convictions, Syrian President Hafez al-Assad *had* forged an alliance with Egyptian President Anwar as-Sadat, and they *were* about to go to war. The alliance was tenuous, yet it afforded each leader an opportunity that otherwise would not have existed.

Against the backdrop of rivalry and distrust permeating Arab leadership, the alliance provided both parties independence to act without undue jeopardy if the other failed to carry out his promises. For Syria, the gains stemming from the alliance were immediate, and many of those gains were not in themselves dependent upon the outcome of a war with Israel.

Assad had taken the leadership role in forging the new alliance in 1972, when he authorized a miniwar against Israel. In October 1972 and again in November, artillery, tank, and even infantry engagements were initiated against Israeli forces deployed on the Golan Heights. These "battle days" struck a responsive chord in many Arabic-speaking lands. Syrian popularity and prestige, which had been at a low ebb for years, stunningly improved with each new Syrian initiative.

There was no expression of outrage, or even surprise, by any international leader because of the onset of the new low-threshold war. Battle days were accepted by the international community—and by Israel—as normal communications between hostile states.

The Egyptians perceived the Syrian-initiated fighting as of greater consequence. Sadat quickly reacted following the first of Assad's battle days. Sadat was acutely aware that he had been upstaged and rendered politically vulnerable. Some form of Egyptian military initiative against Israel became imperative.

Sadat's one and only initiated "battle day" in 1972 resulted in no Israeli casualties.

The Egyptian minister of war opposed any immediate military action against Israel, but Sadat demanded a meeting with the Armed Forces Supreme Command. The minister of war briefed the fifteen-member body at noon on Tuesday, October 24, 1972, and concluded his presentation by stating, "The President thinks I exaggerate your problems. He wants to hear the true position from you." Later that day, at their meeting with the president, several of the officers did voice their "true position" to Sadat. Within hours, one third of the members of the Armed Forces Supreme Command, including the minister of war, had been sacked.

The extent of Egyptian unpreparedness ruled out an immediate military option. While Sadat took steps to accelerate his nation's own preparations, he paid tribute to Assad's ascending star. Though he avoided direct contact, Sadat tried through emissaries to restrain Assad. Arab associates were dispatched in November 1972 to urge Assad to halt the battle days.

With remarkable frankness, the *An Nahr Arab Report* edition of December 4, 1972, reported: "The Syrians feel that renewed fighting on the Golan will place Egyptian leadership in an extremely awkward situation and that given the international difficulties facing Sadat, Egyptian Army officers are liable to press for action along the Suez front."

The first direct Egyptian approach to Assad was made following New Year's Day 1973. Sadat sent a delegation to Damascus to seek a termination of the battle-days strategy and to offer a vague promise of war when preparations and planning had been completed. The key points of the Egyptian position can be summarized this way: Battle days with Israel were possible only as long as they were tolerated by the Israelis; sooner or later, the Israelis would over-react, and they possessed the means to inflict greater damage than could the Arab states; the eruption of a new general war in the absence of proper, thorough plans and preparations would be a disaster for all Arabs; Egypt was working on a plan and, in the future, would act decisively against Israel.

Assad's response was delivered on January 8, 1973, when Syrian Army units opened fire on Israeli positions on the Golan—the start of a new battle day. As the Egyptian envoys had predicted, Israel reacted massively to subdue Assad's desire to continue the low-threshold war. The fighting quickly escalated, eventually drawing Israeli and Syrian Air Force units into the fray.

As if alerted, Radio Damascus highlighted the fighting through-out the day. By evening, Radio Damascus was reporting 150 civilian deaths in the wake of Israeli air strikes. One Syrian mayor reported "seventy-five killed, forty-five wounded, twenty houses destroyed, twelve houses damaged, two hundred pregnant women miscar-rying, and 450 sheep and cattle killed." Next, Radio Damascus taunted Sadat and all Egyptians for not going to war against Israel. Two days later, on January 10, Syria publicly revised its report of civilian casualties upward, to five hundred dead.

Western ears might have missed the point of this frank propa-ganda exercise. The specter of dead livestock, destroyed homes, and two hundred bomb-induced miscarriages galvanized Arabs. The manipulation of such basic symbols, coupled with the allega-tion of large losses attributed to Israeli air strikes, assured the wid-est possible media coverage throughout the Arab world. Syria was perceived in the Arab world as carrying the banner for justice, while Egypt, the self-proclaimed premier Arab state, did nothing. On January 10 Radio Cairo responded to the Syrian media blitz with a quite serious contention that a courageous leader does not allow himself to be goaded into an ill-advised and premature war.

The Egyptian response would have had more weight had many Arabs then perceived Anwar as-Sadat as a "courageous leader." So many of his trumpeted "Year of Decision" deadlines had come and gone without decisions that his credibility was widely questioned and, in the case of Hafez al-Assad, forthrightly challenged.

Assad had hoped to arouse the Egyptian military with his own army's feats. Fouad Ajami, in *The Arab Predicament*, reveals the frustrations of Egypt's social and cultural leaders:

> In early January, 1973, a group of the country's most celebrated writers and intellectuals issued a public statement that [said] . . . references to the battle had confused the young . . . who worked for their diplomas only to be sent to the front "where they forget what they learned and don't find an enemy to fight." The state has to be honest "if the fog was to be cleared and people were to know what lay ahead."

Assad had won a stunning political victory. By the end of January 1973—in a space of just four months—Syria had moved from being a virtual outcast among Arab nations to the occupation of center stage with Egypt. And Assad had done it far less at the expense of Israel than of Egypt. The new Egyptian war minister, General Ahmed Isma'il, flew to Damascus and announced the creation of a joint Egyptian-Syrian command. By returning to the traditional Arab policy of "no peace with Israel" in an unequivocal blaze of glory, Hafez al-Assad had ended his nation's virtual isolation within the Arab world.

Sadat initiated one major effort to free himself of Assad's net. As with his first ploy toward Assad, it was indirect. He dispatched his national security adviser to convince the American secretary of state, Dr. Henry Kissinger, to pressure Israel into making some sort of gesture by which he could derive benefit.

Having failed to win anything from Washington, Sadat invited Assad to Cairo in late April 1973. Assad was informed that Egypt planned to go to war by mounting an attack across the Suez Canal. However, the water-crossing operation limited the timing of the attack to just three sets of dates. The earliest of these dates was in late May, and the latest was in early October.

Sadat's determination to launch a major assault across the Suez Canal placed Assad in an awkward position. Not backing his Egyptian rival would once again isolate Syria, undoing the gains he had made over the previous six months. It was clear that Syrian assistance could benefit Egypt, but Sadat's plan offered Syria very little in return for that assistance. After weighing his limited options, Assad swallowed the realities of the situation and assured Sadat that Syria would support his attack.

As Assad wrestled with the seemingly no-win situation imposed upon him by Sadat's deal, it had occurred to him that he and Syria could indeed benefit from Egypt's determination to resume hostilities with Israel. There were some old accounts to be settled with Arab neighbors. An Egypt preoccupied with launching a war against Israel would be unable to interfere in these matters, even though Syria's immediate position would be greatly enhanced and despite the fact that a positive outcome would lead to greater Syrian benefit from the upcoming general war than Sadat readily envisioned or would otherwise have sanctioned.

Within a week of his meeting with Sadat, Assad was in Moscow seeking new arms. The Soviets responded with generosity, but with the exception of aircraft, most of their assistance arrived in late May and June, after the first set of dates outlined by Sadat.

While he awaited the Soviet equipment, Assad moved to reap any advantage he could from Egypt's new focus on Israel. He had used the battle-days strategy to prove his commitment to militant Palestinians, whom he had restrained from launching attacks from Syrian soil into Israel; he had substituted his own army for Palestinian raids. The interruption in the battle days arising out of Assad's negotiations with Sadat resulted in renewed pressure from the Palestinians.

To alleviate this pressure, Assad financed a May invasion of Lebanon by the Palestine Liberation Organization. This was Syria's single most successful international initiative in modern history. Assad delivered an ideal base for continuing Palestinian warfare against Israel, and Lebanon came under increased Syrian influence. This last was particularly vital in that Syrians feel that Lebanon is part of Greater Syria, an entity that, in Syrian minds, had been fragmented at the end of World War I by Western powers bent upon curbing Syrian hegemony in the Middle East. With Palestinians (viewed by Assad as Syrian surrogates) ensconced in Lebanon (which is also to say *not* ensconced in Syria), Assad's western flank, a classic invasion route from the Mediterranean to Damascus, was more secure against Israeli attack.

At another time and under other circumstances, Egypt might have vocally objected to such a dangerous threat to stability among Arab nations. In May 1973, however, Sadat remained silent. Sadat's then-minister of information, Mohamed Heikal, does not even mention the invasion in *The Road to Ramadan.* Nor does Sadat's authorized biography, *In Search of Identity.*

To the extent that Israeli Intelligence was preoccupied with Lebanon, Egyptian military needs were met. The PLO invasion of Lebanon occurred just as Egyptian Army units were concentrating near the Suez Canal. The Israelis, who missed nothing, mobilized a Reserve division, and the Egyptians pulled back.

Ironically, the strong Israeli reaction to the concentration of forces on the canal increased Sadat's desire to have Syria contribute a maximum effort to the upcoming war. A "complete surprise" attack was perceived in Cairo as being impossible to achieve, so Sadat wanted to ensure the strongest possible second front—for the sake of drawing Israeli strength away from the canal front.

Sadat flew to Damascus to speak directly with Assad on June 12. Despite exchanges going back over nearly six months, the two presidents remained far apart. Assad had collected an unbroken string of successes over the previous ten months. Sadat, who had no matching successes, was struggling just to stay even with the Syrians. Indeed, nothing could have so brilliantly focused attention upon the relative change in the positions these two men occupied in the Arab world than Sadat's presence in Damascus. The Egyptian president was in fact a supplicant, trying to win an agreement from Assad. He ventured to Damascus to ask for full Syrian cooperation, but he offered less than full partnership in determining events. Egypt would pick the date for opening general hostilities and let Syria know.

Sadat was quite clear in his goals because he was realistic about his chances of actually reconquering the Sinai and Gaza. He sought to break the deadlock between Israel and the Arab states. Winning whatever he could on the battlefield was secondary. To fight and hold *any* portion of reconquered territory would serve Egyptian needs because Sadat was looking for a level of legitimacy that could lead to a resolution of the grinding, perpetual war with Israel through *political* means. Sadat was looking for a military opening and a political closure.

Not so Hafez al-Assad, whose imperatives were different. First, Assad could not sit out an Egyptian assault upon Israel and retain his credibility in the Arab world, nor likely keep his power—or his life—in Syria. Assad's battle-days strategy made Syria a captive of

Egyptian planning. Sadat reports that in their June discussions he told Assad, "You have no choice." Perhaps this was true on the wider plateau that Sadat felt he occupied, but it was also true that Assad in no way supported Sadat's "limited war" concept. Egypt was offering Syria an opportunity to regain the Golan Heights through direct military effort. This was Syria's national goal (as differentiated from her pan-Arab goal of liberating Palestine), and it was a goal Assad saw as being attainable. Syria's role could be realized by military means. Assad would thus be working for a military opening and a *military* closure under an umbrella of Egyptian participation—a positive wrinkle, but hardly more than a means for strengthening credibility and allowing the Egyptians to draw off the bulk of Israeli resources.

Neither president articulated his perceptions of reality, but they did accede to a clear decision to launch a war together.

3

Syria was not preparing for war with Israel solely out of an altruistic compassion for displaced Palestinians. The Syrian people—and most Arab peoples —have forever been uncomfortable with the numerous outsiders and outside influences operating in and around the Arab world. The perpetual war against Zionism is as much a war against Western influences in the Arab world as it was a war against Israelis or a war in behalf of Palestinians. At its root, Syria's dogged struggle against Israel is fueled by a determination to eradicate a Western beachhead in the Arab world.

The Syrian Army of 1973 was the greatest achievement of the modern Syrian state. Never before had the nation's resources, manpower, and energy been devoted to pursuing a single project of such magnitude.

To the extent that the composition and strength of its armed forces can be used to characterize a modern state in microcosm, suffice it to say that conscription in Syria had been haphazard prior to 1973. Individuals who did not want to serve had been able to pay to be excused or arrange exemptions to study abroad. Buying out of the service afforded the wealthy and members of some ethnic minorities with a way out of a potentially hazardous situation. Naturally, such signs of favoritism did nothing to enhance national unity among Syria's diverse ethnic elements and sharply defined social strata.

By 1973, however, conscription was universal among the young men of the nation. Of all the males in Syria age eighteen to forty-five, one in five was on active duty with the armed forces, and over 20 percent of the nation's Gross National Product was devoted to military expenditures. The typical Syrian soldier of 1973 was the best-educated in the nation's history. Born in the early 1950s, he had benefited from improvements in health, education, and the general well-being that prevailed throughout the land. He had never known a time of colonialism, nor a time of Palestine. Israel had existed throughout his life; generally the terms "Zionist" (a pejorative) or *el adu* (literally, "the enemy") were used to describe Israelis. Israelis were neither Arab nor considered to be of the Arab world (though more than half the Israelis alive in 1973 were refugees or the children of refugees from Arabic-speaking nations). Somehow, Israelis were perceived as being part and parcel of the centuries of assault upon the Arab peoples by the West—America, Europe, and Russia. Israelis were truly threatening; they occupied Palestine, holy Jerusalem, and, since 1967, the Syrian town of Kuneitra.

The Syrian military establishment had been professionalized. The troops were well led, well clothed, and well trained. Discipline was maintained; orders were obeyed. The general tensions pulling at Syrian society, ethnic and communal differences, had been institutionalized, and considerable effort had been expended to minimize ethnic and religious differences among members of the armed forces.

Soviet equipment was delivered to Syria on a massive scale. Following President Assad's May 2, 1973, visit to Moscow, 450 tanks, three hundred armored personnel carriers, two hundred artillery pieces, and over a hundred mobile antiaircraft-missile carriers arrived at Syrian military bases in under sixty days.

Simply absorbing the new equipment created a frenzy of activity throughout the Army. Modern T-62 main battle tanks replaced obsolescent T-55s in four of the Army's first-line brigades. The T-55s replaced slightly older T-54s in other brigades, and the T-54s provided for the retirement of 250 World War II-vintage T-34s from second- and third-line units.

The displaced T-34s were turned over to engineering and ordnance units. While the engineers dug defensive emplacements for 210 of the T-34s along the roads from Israel into the Syrian heartland, ordnance teams removed the turrets of forty vehicles and mounted 122mm guns on the chassis. The innovation provided the Army's artillery branch with two new self-propelled artillery battalions, which were allocated to two armored divisions.

Each of the Army's five divisions received new PT-76 light amphibious reconnaissance tanks, and two of the armored brigades were amply bolstered by new BMP armored personnel carriers. The introduction of the thoroughly modern troop carriers resulted in a flurry of training activity to familiarize officers and soldiers—including maintenance teams—with the equipment itself and the new range of tactics it allowed.

The artillery branch created a new heavy artillery brigade of thirty-six 180mm guns in addition to the two battalions created to handle the T-34 gun-carrier conversions.

The Air Defense Command was expanded to accommodate the introduction of two new weapons systems. Sixty-four self-propelled ZSU-23/4 quadruple-23mm antiaircraft gun carriers were divided among the armored divisions to provide close-in mobile antiair defenses for ground units and key sites. A large number of SA-6 antiaircraft missiles and their mobile tracked launchers were perceived as being the Soviet Union's greatest contribution to the Syrian buildup and resulting ability to wage war on better-than-equal terms against the crack Israeli Air Force.

The major combat element of the Syrian Army was the division. Five permanent divisional headquarters existed to command fifteen organic brigades. In addition, each divisional headquarters commanded such specialized units as antiaircraft and antiarmor defense, artillery support, chemical warfare, and engineering. Each divisional headquarters was sufficiently flexible in makeup to handle the attachment of virtually any sort of force in virtually any strength.

Twelve infantry, two commando, and four artillery brigades existed outside the divisional structure. The rather numerous independent brigades reflected political currents as much as military needs. There was no demonstrable requirement for more than five divisional structures. However, the Air Force officers who had come to dominate the Syrian political system were in no rush to grant the Army additional power bases or generalships. The creation of independent brigades allowed for the awarding of major perquisites to political factions or personalities while segregating each of them from a usefully stronger power base.

There was a wide range of perceptions as to the combat-worthiness of the independent brigades. Some, such as 47th and 51st Tank brigades, were well equipped and perceived as being premier units. Others, such as 141st Tank Brigade, inspired less confidence because of the quality of its equipment and personnel.

Occupying a special niche were 70th and 81st Tank brigades. This four-thousand-man force was commanded by the president's brother, Colonel Rifat Assad. A loyalty clearance was required of volunteers for these units. Officially designated the Armor Defense Force, the two-brigade establishment was commonly known as the Assad Guard. In mid-1973, the Guard was completely reequipped with new T-62 tanks and BMP armored infantry carriers mounting 73mm guns. Also under Rifat Assad's personal command was 1st Commando Group, comprising five highly trained battalions. Thus Rifat Assad commanded an army within an army.

By October 1973 there were also significant numbers of specialized independent Army-level units, including chemical-warfare specialists and the Signal Intercept Brigade. This last was responsible for the gathering of signal intelligence, jamming broadcasts, and locating Israeli headquarters and combat units by signal-traffic emissions. Signal intercept companies appear to have been deployed on the Hermon, at Hadar, and on Tel Shaar, Tel Hara, and Tel el Jaba.

While combat forces received nearly all the media attention, a well-rounded defense establishment had been created away from the limelight. Two Army coastal defense brigades backed by a naval coastal defense brigade served the Mediterranean coast, while a border guard brigade watched over much of the eastern desert. Reservists organized into independent infantry battalions had assumed home-guard responsibilities. Naturally, these forces were adjuncts to the nation's huge and growing offensive capabilities.

Though Syria's population was less than seven million, the Syrian Army could field two thousand tanks and over a thousand artillery pieces and mortars over 120mm. By way of comparison, Great Britain or Italy, each with eight times the population, could not field nearly so massive a force.

The extraordinary buildup was not undertaken by Syria alone. Soviet technicians in substantial numbers were assigned to the Signal Intercept Brigade and the Air Defense Command. Cuban technicians were housed at Kiswe Military Base outside Damascus and bore the responsibility for servicing the T-62 main battle tanks. The Soviets also assisted in another, less direct, manner. In June, Soviet ships ferried a Moroccan Army brigade to Syria. (While the thirty tanks the Moroccans drew from Syrian stocks represented an increase in combat strength of but .5 percent, the commitment of the Moroccan brigade was of enormous symbolic significance in demonstrating that the upcoming war was supported within the Arab world.)

The Syrian General Staff was almost exclusively occupied through May with preparations for handling the new Soviet weapons systems and assisting the PLO invasion of Lebanon. Detailed planning for the invasion of the Golan Heights began in June under the overall supervision of the Syrian chief of staff, Major General Yousef Chakour, and the minister of defense, Lieutenant General Mustapha Tlas. The heart of the campaign was the land offensive, and this was placed in the hands of the director of operations, Major General Abdul Habeisi.

A Vietnamese officer was once asked to describe how Americans fight in the jungle. His reply was, "The Americans do not fight in the jungle. They mow it down." This description is apropos Habeisi's operational plan; he did not so much plan on fighting as mowing down the opposition. An Israel under massive attack by Egyptian armed forces would not be capable of containing the mass and firepower he planned to commit. The essential elements of Habeisi's plan were the isolation of the Golan from reinforcement, the disruption of support and command facilities, and the overpowering of Israeli combat units deployed on the Golan before they could be strengthened.

The operational plan was dubbed, indiscreetly, Al-Owda, which literally means "Homing all the way"—a suggestive enough name to raise the interest of any Intelligence service.

Habeisi planned to open the campaign before dawn by infiltrating commando units across the cease-fire line to seize the frontier electronic-warfare posts. Of particular concern were the Israeli positions at Tel Faris, in the southern Golan; Tel Abu Nida and the Hermonit, both in the Kuneitra Gap; and the largest installation, on the Hermon. Deep raids in conjunction with these border actions were to seal the battlefield from reinforcement. These raids would be undertaken by heliborne commando units against the El Al Ridge, the Arik and B'not Yaacov bridges, and the Gonen and Dan roads. Subsidiary attacks were to be mounted against the Israeli command center at Naffach and the Mahanayim Airfield.

The war would open with the Israelis forced to react and respond to three separate surprises—air strikes, artillery bombardment, and, at critical locations, ground attack. Habeisi's plan envisaged the isolation of every available Israeli combat unit and key position. Every local commander would have to react to Syrian initiatives on all sides. Even as the Israeli commanders reacted to air and artillery bombardment, however, major ground assaults would be upon them.

Habeisi had at his disposal the equivalent of seven divisions. At the outset, following dawn air strikes and artillery bombardments, 5th, 7th, and 9th Infantry divisions would mount full-scale tank and mechanized-infantry attacks. Each of the divisions would be augmented by an additional brigade so that the equivalent of four divisions would comprise the first echelon. Two hours to the rear, deployed to exploit a successful penetration, were 1st and 3rd Tank divisions. Additional brigades could reach the battlefield within three hours and could serve as either a third assault echelon or as replacements for worn components of the first- and second-echelon divisions.

Al-Owda envisioned one of the greatest concentrations of firepower in history. It is true that the German Wehrmacht had deployed two thousand tanks for the 1941 invasion of the Soviet Union, but those tanks had been dispersed over a front of nine hundred miles. Syria planned to deploy twelve hundred tanks on a front of little more than fifty miles—along with six hundred artillery pieces of over 120mm.

Major General Habeisi enjoyed the full measure of his opponent. The battle-days strategy of the winter of 1972–73 yielded a rich harvest of information on Israeli thought and tactics. By the first week of January 1973, the Israelis had constructed new roadways for deploying their armor and had developed new tactics for countering infantry-carried Sagger antitank missiles. All this was revealed when the Syrians initiated a battle day on January 8. Analyses of the battle days convinced the Syrian planning team that the Israeli bunker line was not a serious obstacle.

Artillery could be depended upon to suppress Israeli weaponry, and maneuvering elements would neutralize any advantages enjoyed by Israeli fixed positions. Israeli bazookas and light mortars—which were known to be incorporated into the defenses of the fixed bunkers—would have a minimal impact upon armored columns as they penetrated between the bunkers. Indeed, the bunkers could be safely bypassed, and the Israelis manning them could do what they wanted. If need be, they could be mopped up after the major penetrations had been achieved.

Tanks would comprise the major combat elements of both sides. The IDF tankers of Barak Brigade were clearly the troops to beat. The Syrians even knew that the Israeli tank formations were 74th and 53rd Tank battalions. Though they did not know the tank commanders by name, they had a keen appreciation of the performance that could be expected from them.

The basic Israeli combat unit was a platoon of three tanks. Combinations of up to ten tanks were expected to be holding critical points. The basic Syrian combat unit was a company of ten tanks. The Syrians estimated that their ten company gunners could send off thirty to forty rounds per minute among them. As a result, all three Israeli tanks in each platoon would be easily overcome, and the way into the Israeli rear would be quickly uncovered. Even if the Israelis managed to destroy nine tanks from a Syrian tank company —an unprecedented three-to-one ratio—Syrian tanks would control the battlefield. Fresh tank companies could be pushed forward as needed. The Syrians would be fielding 120 tank companies on or quite near the battlefield at the outset. The Israelis were expected to have six tank companies directly on hand to meet them. By midday, the Syrians expected to have committed six hundred main battle tanks (60 companies) against an outside total of two hundred Israeli tanks (20 companies), including a very substantial allowance for reserves that might be moved to the battlefield before it was completely sealed. Fighting without additional reserves, the Israelis would simply be unable to stem the continuously reinforced rolling Syrian assault along the entire front.

The Syrian second echelon—1st and/or 3rd Tank divisions—would come into action following a successful breach in one or both of the two areas most suitable for continued armored movement, the Kuneitra and Rafid gaps.

The Kuneitra Gap, in the North, was the better route because it was bisected by the best roadway across the Golan into Israel. However, mounded lava beds to the north of the roadway form ideal defensive ground, and the southern side of the gap is shielded by the wooded height of Tel Aksa.

The Rafid Gap provided the Israelis with fewer natural defenses, but it is not a route in any way ideal for a major mechanized invasion of Israel. The best east–west road runs southwest through El Al and terminates following the steepest of several possible roadbound descents from the Golan into the Jordan River Valley. Every step westward along this diverging road would further divide the Syrian forces and decrease their ability to maneuver. The value of exploiting a penetration in the Rafid Gap was potential access to the only two north–south roads the Israelis possessed. A penetration of the gap coupled with an attack northward along the westernmost north–south road would outflank the entire Israeli line south of Kuneitra.

It was expected that between nine hundred and twelve hundred Syrian tanks would have been brought to bear upon the Israeli defenses by midafternoon. In one variation, only one of the two tank divisions would have been committed in the second wave, leaving the other as a tactical reserve for the second day's fighting, if there was a second day of battle. In a second scenario, both tank divisions would simultaneously come on, leaving the independent brigades as the tactical reserve. In any case, the second echelon was designed as a mass-maneuver force to overcome local Israeli reserves and reach the escarpment overlooking the Jordan River Valley. Each tank division, operating as a single mass, would have the power simply to crush any Israeli force still in existence. Given the restrictions on the size of available Israeli forces, the Syrian advantage always would approach a ratio of at least ten to one.

The battle would end by late afternoon of the first day. The assault forces could reorganize and revictual overnight, then sweep the Golan from end to end, beginning at sunrise. All the fighting would be over by noon of the second day. A continuous blow of thirty hours' duration would return the Golan to Syria. It would be all over except for the political end game.

The Syrians were certain that Israeli men and machines could not stop them. However, the terrain and Israeli preparations were of paramount concern. The terrain of the Golan can inhibit movement in the best of times. The lava fields, rocky outcroppings, and steep canyons dictate just how much mass can be brought to bear upon any given point. Natural bottlenecks were seen as enemies equal to the Israelis. Actual working space for the troops and their machines was at a premium.

Israeli engineers had changed the terrain to make it even more difficult to negotiate. The antitank ditch running the length of the cease-fire line was the major Israeli defensive weapon. It was possible for Syria to reclaim the Golan only if the ditch could be overcome. If the ditch could not be overcome, Syria could not benefit from the war. Bridging or filling the obstacle would require sixty to ninety minutes, both in the approach and to complete the actual labor.

Compared to the almost casual planning that had characterized Syrian efforts against Israel in 1948 and 1967—and their efforts against Jordan in 1970—this was a battle planned to the last detail. At least one method of response was prepared for every facet of potential Israeli effort. Helicopters were to transport commandos to seize bridges over the Jordan and establish roadblocks. Artillery was to disrupt communications, supply, and headquarters facilities. Tactical air support was arranged to open the first attack and to deliver pinpoint response to Israeli reactions.

The Syrian Army of 1973 appeared to be a precision instrument of unparalleled strength in its region, a weapon designed and executed to undertake its nation's most exacting venture in the field of international diplomacy.

· 4 ·

Key members of the Syrian General Staff traveled to Alexandria, Egypt, in August 1973 to present their Al-Owda plan to their Egyptian opposite numbers and to implement the coordination that would be necessary if the Israelis were to be caught off guard by simultaneous attacks on both fronts.

The conference was less an exercise in coordination between allies than in the subordination of Syrian plans to Egyptian priorities. The outcome of the conference profoundly illustrated Sadat's earlier statement to Assad: "You have no choice."

Sadat's war minister, General Ahmed Isma'il, was surprised when the Syrian General Staff officers told him they would seize the entire Golan within forty-eight hours of the start of the battle. He cautioned the Syrians against overoptimism and told them that the Golan should be taken in stages, that the Israeli forces should be destroyed in "killing areas" during each stage. More important, Isma'il rejected the Syrian proposal for a dawn attack. The Egyptians wanted to launch an afternoon assault and, moreover, would provide the Syrians with only five days' notice as to which afternoon they had in mind.

The Egyptian leadership's disinterest in coordination with the Syrians is reported by Mohamed Heikal:

> The Egyptians . . . said they were prepared to let the Syrians start at first light and to follow themselves in the afternoon. The Syrians objected that this would leave them alone in the battle for several hours and would destroy the element of simultaneous surprise on two fronts. Next the Egyptians suggested that the Syrians open up at first light on [the second day of the war]. The Syrian objection to this was that not only would it too destroy part of the element of surprise, but it would be politically wrong because it would give the impression that they were dragging behind the Egyptians [pages 13–14].

Having disputed the what, how, and when of the battle, the two allies moved on to dispute *where* the battle was to be waged. The Syrians outlined a limited air war in accordance with their needs on the Golan and with Sadat's perception of a "limited war." With the exception of portions of the Jordan River Valley adjoining the Golan, the Syrians felt that Israel should not be bombed. The Egyptians wanted a greater air effort, with the Syrian Air Force bombing Israeli bases as far south as Tel Aviv.

The meeting concluded on August 24. Operation Al-Owda was clearly unacceptable to the Egyptians. The aggressive Egyptian critique of Syrian planning masked profound weaknesses in Egypt's own plans. According to Egyptian Lieutenant General Saad el-Shazli, in his *Crossing of the Suez:*

> It was clear that if the Syrians realized that our plan was limited to the capturing of a line less than ten miles east of the canal, they would not have gone to war alongside us. My answer was that militarily I would prefer us to go it alone this time. Our success would encourage the Syrians to join us in the later rounds. Isma'il rejected that course. It had been decided that an alliance with Syria was a political necessity [pages 36–37].

Sadat undertook a journey to Damascus on August 27 to confer directly with Assad. The Alexandria meetings had been his way of keeping his word to the Syrian president that he would not go to war until a joint Syrian-Egyptian command had been established. In truth, Sadat expected little in the way of "joint" action. What he wanted, and what he actually received from Assad, was a pledge that Syria would join Egypt in an attack on Israel. Sadat also prevailed upon Assad to drop the name Al-Owda in favor of an Egyptian suggestion, Badhr.

The Syrian officers who returned from the "Supreme Joint Council" meeting in Alexandria were convinced that Al-Owda was the best plan, that all the changes favored by Egypt increased the risk to Syria. Lieutenant General Mustapha Tlas, Assad's minister of war, did not even stay to the conclusion of the meeting. He opposed any plan that precluded simultaneous dawn attacks. (Tlas is not mentioned as having been a participant in two subsequent joint command meetings.)

A severe inhibition imposed on Syrian planning for Operation Badhr was the perception volunteered by Soviet military analysts that Israel would destroy in under an hour any attempt by Egypt to cross the Suez Canal. Should Egypt fail, the Soviets added, Israel would be able to concentrate massive forces against Syria. Prudence dictated that a limited battle should not unduly enrage the Israeli leadership. A battle day was acceptable, but an all-out war was a great risk. Operation Al-Owda, mounted at dawn, had a reasonable chance to beat the Israelis on the Golan and prevent Israeli reserves from rallying; Operation Badhr, mounted in the afternoon, was by far a more profound risk.

Assad had promised Sadat his support. The nature of that support, however, did not require absolute adherence to every point discussed with the Egyptians. Contrary to Sadat's assertion, Syria had some choices. Prior to the August joint conference, it was Syria's clear intention to reconquer the Golan, period. In light of Egypt's steadfast refusal to attack at dawn, the primary goal became the insulation of Assad's regime from potential failure. The realities of inter-Arab politics surpassed in importance both the danger and the opportunity posed by the war with Israel.

The fear of failure—of exposing the regime to an uncertain future—prevented the Syrians from fully utilizing all their considerable resources for Operation Badhr. As a result, less than the full-scale attack envisaged in Operation Al-Owda would be launched. For example, the Syrian Air Force would refrain from attacking Israeli air bases in favor of concentrating on command service centers on the Golan and in the Jordan River Valley. Of particular concern were the Israeli Hawk surface-to-air missile sites near Kfar Giladi and Tiberias, and the electronic-warfare center near Rosh Pina. Except for mounting ground-support sorties, Syrian warplanes would stay behind the friendly missile barrier following an opening strike against these installations.

The Syrian decision to curtail their air force's war mission illustrates the willingness of the leadership in Damascus to place their needs above those of the Egyptians. The Syrians believed that Egypt had asked too much. In a quarter century of warfare, Israel had erected an impermeable barrier against aerial incursions. In all that time less than ten Arab aircraft had overflown Israel and survived. From the Syrian perspective, Egypt was insensitive to the probable consequences of the loss of air cover for the ground assault on the Golan. The Egyptian request that the Syrian Air Force undertake deep raids against Israel was made the more galling by the fact that the Egyptian Air Force intended to limit its air strikes to the Sinai Peninsula. In the end, the Syrians simply ignored the plan for deep strikes that they submitted to the Egyptians. Syria's 69th Rocket Brigade, a unit equipped with Soviet FROG-7 surface-to-surface missiles, was restrained by the same reasoning: Israel would perceive a rocket attack as something to which a massive retaliation had to be mounted.

If the ground attack went well, the Syrian General Staff told itself, the role of the Air Force and 69th Rocket Brigade could be escalated. If the attack went poorly, the Air Force would have been conserved as one of the major resources upon which to fall back.

The potential political repercussions arising from a basic Syrian mistrust of Operation Badhr resulted in the withdrawal of one of the two tank divisions into a strategic reserve. If the offensive collapsed, the division might be needed to defend the seat of government in Damascus—from friend or foe.

The desire for a "fail-safe" war created its own political problem. Military coups are the tested method for changing power in Damascus. If things went awry, Assad might face a tank division commander willing to try his hand at ousting him under the pretense of making peace with the Israelis. Conversely, if Assad tried to make peace, a division commander, acting under the pretense of continuing the war, might be motivated to unseat him.

The solution was to withhold Syria's very best unit, the Assad

Guard, from the attack. Thus the rigidly loyal 70th and 81st Tank brigades, with their full array of T-62 main battle tanks and BMP armored personnel carriers, would remain tied to Damascus under Colonel Rifat Assad's personal command and control.

Without one shot as yet being fired, the Syrian grand strategy for a definitive struggle upon the Golan had been scaled back by profound fear of political repercussions among countrymen and supposed allies as well as by a cloying fear of what the enemy who was to be so soundly defeated might do. By presupposing an Israeli victory, or the failure of the attacking forces to achieve all their goals, the Syrian planners and their political masters became victims of their own worst fears and prophecies. Al-Owda, a virtual blueprint for victory—the best plan any Arab state had been able to bring to the brink of execution in a quarter century of struggle with a seemingly omnipotent enemy—was replaced by a hedge that all but precluded a decisive outcome favorable to anyone but Israel.

Saddled with Operation Badhr, Syrian planners pressed on.

Engineering questions were profound. The Egyptians needed to overcome the high sand ramparts guarding the west bank of the Suez Canal and Sinai. The Syrians needed to overcome the Israeli antitank ditch to reconquer the Golan. On the one hand, the Syrians had to await the outcome of the opening Egyptian operation to know if they had a meaningful alliance and stood a chance of accomplishing the goals of their war. On the other hand, they had to await the opening operations of their own engineering units to know if they could advance into the Israeli-held portion of the Golan.

In either case, they sought the efficient use of a mass of material and men to regain the Golan before Israel could mobilize. The Israelis, in their turn, would seek to block the Syrian assault so they could mobilize in time to bolster their defenses.

Even as the Syrian military commanders were revising their plans to conform to the constraints of Operation Badhr, they maintained their belief in the efficacy of Operation Al-Owda. The Egyptian war minister, General Ahmed Isma'il, flew to Damascus on October 3 solely to inform the Syrians as to the date and time Operation Badhr would commence. He immediately found himself embroiled in a major dispute with the Syrian chief of staff, Major General Yousef Chakour, who agreed to the date only after subjecting Isma'il to a torrent of barbed comments. Chakour would not, however, submit to the Egyptian proposal that the war be launched in midafternoon.

The two presented their respective cases to President Assad, who agreed that Operation Badhr would commence at 1400 hours on Saturday, October 6.

Intent upon the last word, Chakour told Isma'il, "If there is a failure on the Egyptian front, it will be the end of the Arabs, which means the end of Syria. If there is failure on the Syrian front, this would not be the end. It is on Egypt that all our hopes are pinned."

Assad rephrased the thought to take some of the sting from Chakour's deeply held sentiments: "If Damascus falls, it can be recaptured. If Cairo falls, the whole Arab nation falls."

Assad's acquiescence to the Egyptian schedule necessitated further planning by his commanders. Little is known of what actually occurred at these final sessions, but it is clear that Lieutenant General Mustapha Tlas, Major General Yousef Chakour, and Colonel Rifat Assad were sufficiently worried by the implications of Badhr to refrain from implementing the maximum commitment envisaged in Al-Owda. The deep commando raids aimed at initially sealing off the Golan from reinforcement became a matter of controversy and were, in the end, dropped because they would involve committing units directly under Rifat Assad's command, units that would be held back in Damascus.

The requirement that the commandos be held to defend the Assad regime in Damascus both precluded a coup *and* provided the unwitting Israelis with at least a slim margin by which they might reinforce and hold the Golan, an outcome that might precipitate the danger Rifat Assad was withholding his commandos to counter.

Meanwhile, the Israelis were themselves on the brink of throwing away their best chance to win the upcoming war.

· 5 ·

Prime Minister Golda Meir first heard about Alert Gimmel at 0945 on October 5, when Lieutenant General David Elazar, Major General Eli Zeira, and Defense Minister Moshe Dayan arrived at her office to discuss the nation's preparedness in the event of war. Besides Mrs. Meir and Dayan, only one other Cabinet minister, Yisrael Galili, attended.

Elazar and Zeira launched into presentations, their second of the morning, to assert their respective opinions as to Syrian and Egyptian capabilities and intentions. But when they got to the point of discussing "this" artillery battery or "that" advanced supply base, Mrs. Meir insisted on focusing upon the larger issues. She pointedly asked, "What is the Army's opinion? What does the General Staff suggest?"

The response was that Alert Gimmel was all that could be done without a specific order from the civilian government to mobilize all or part of the defense establishment. The Army Transport Service was already seriously burdened by Alert Gimmel. Four combat battalions were already scheduled to be transported, and the men of one battalion were being moved by chartered civilian buses. It would be some time before dawn on Yom Kippur before the tank transporters would be available for any additional deployments. In the event of mobilization, two thirds of the nation's civilian buses would be requisitioned. Dayan suggested that the managers of the bus lines be contacted, and Mrs. Meir agreed.

At this point, the prime minister became the first civilian hostage to the military situation. She had planned to join her daughter for Yom Kippur but suddenly announced, "The way things are, I think I won't go to my daughter, Sarah."

A routine Cabinet meeting was already scheduled for the day after Yom Kippur, Sunday, which is a regular workday in Israel. However, Mrs. Meir decided that the danger was too great to wait. Even though most Cabinet ministers had already scattered to their homes, she tried to recall those who resided near Tev Aviv.

Ministers Shimon Peres, Haim Bar Lev, Michael Hazani, and Shlomo Hillel joined the prime minister's ongoing meeting with Elazar, Dayan, Zeira, and Galili before noon. Elazar and Zeira repeated what was becoming a stock presentation. The truncated Cabinet sanctioned the steps already taken by Elazar and Dayan as prudent precautions and adjourned for Yom Kippur. The full Cabinet would take up the issue at the regular Sunday meeting.

The stirrings in the IDF and within the government had little impact upon most Israelis on this "short Friday." Most people hurried to complete their work to gain some extra personal time. For the religious, fasting would begin at sunset. Meals had to be eaten early so that the dishes could be cleaned and put away. In a country with a six-day workweek, "short Friday" promised precious extra time for leisure, family activities, and prayer. Commerce slowed as radio and television stations joined commercial and industrial establishments in closing down for the holiday.

The chief of staff's alert order initially went unnoticed except in those families where relatives were on active duty. Alerts are normal enough fare in Israel, and there had been no recent increase in international tension. But Alert Gimmel on Yom Kippur was different. In retrospect, some people were to recall "something" about the day that set it apart.

Minister of Health Victor Shem-Tov missed Meir's ad hoc Cabinet meeting because Elazar's alert affected his family. Shem-Tov's son had arrived home on a pass early Friday morning, but he was called back to his unit after only a few hours. Instead of attending the meeting, the health minister drove the young soldier back to his unit, sensing all the while that "something was in the air."

Minister of Police Shlomo Hillel's wife thought her husband's conduct incredible. When Hillel returned home after the Cabinet meeting in Tel Aviv, his apprehension took the form of monitoring broadcasts originating in the Arab lands that surround Israel. He continuously moved the dial of his radio from one station to another, almost willing clues about Arab intentions from the ether. Finally Hillel phoned his chief deputy to discuss police responsibility in the event of an emergency. Mrs. Hillel had hoped for a quiet night; it was not to be.

Captain Eyal Shacham, who had just been promoted to command a company of 74th Tank Battalion, had decided to spend his leave at his parents' home, so he missed the order recalling him to the Golan. The news of his promotion was the surprise and delight he anticipated. His effervescent cheer spread through the family, adding a special warmth to the holiday gathering. During the evening, young Shacham took some time to speak privately with his father, a former brigade commander. "It's war, Father. I see it with my own eyes. Anyone who thinks otherwise is mistaken." The old soldier cautioned, "Leave that to the generals."

It was a very long "short Friday" for the men of 7th Armored Brigade's 75th Armored Infantry Battalion. While Police Minister Hillel scanned the airwaves and Eyal Shacham visited with his family, the soldiers of 75th Battalion were roadbound, crammed into uncomfortable military vehicles. The battalion had a lower movement priority than the tank units, so it was dark by the time the order to get on the road to the Golan was finally received.

It was a nostalgic journey for most members of the battalion. Their route took them virtually the full length of the country, and nearly all of the men would be passing near their homes.

At about midnight, the drivers began complaining to the convoy commander that they needed to sleep, that a two-hour stop would not hurt their chances of arriving on the Golan by dawn. The senior officer decided to give the troops a break.

A young officer who recognized his surroundings pulled his jeep off the road to complete a set of mental calculations. If he left the convoy during the two-hour break, he could get home, drop in to see his girlfriend, and return in time to avoid being missed. The important part was the getting home. The young man had previously served on the Golan, and he knew that he would need a parka to stay warm in the cold night air.

The young officer had not planned on awakening his parents, but his alert father heard him moving through the house and got up. The soldier explained that "something" was happening with Syria, that his unit had been ordered to move north.

There was no question but that the officer would have to awaken his girlfriend's family to see her. The girl's father was shocked by his explanation that there was an alert on and about the officer's unorthodox assignment. This was, after all, Yom Kippur; the observances were being profaned. Though highly perplexed, the father gave the young couple time to speak. Then the soldier left, returning to the battalion before it started moving north once again.

Seventy-fifth Armored Infantry Battalion began the steep ascent to the Golan just before dawn. This was to be the last reinforcement to reach the battle zone before the battle commenced.

Captain Eyal Shacham arrived back at 74th Tank Battalion's command post a short time later, having taken leave of his family while it was still quite dark. Shacham had no inkling that an alert was on, had heard nothing about it; it was simply time to begin his first day as company commander. Before Shacham could get his troops settled for the day's fasting and religious observances, events were well on the way to becoming extraordinary.

Before dawn the duty officer at IDF General Headquarters (GHQ) in Tel Aviv received an explosive report from a highly placed secret Intelligence source working in an Arab capital: Egypt and Syria planned to launch attacks later in the day.

This was clearly not the sort of information a duty officer on routine watch was expected to handle on his own. Within minutes he had called Chief of Staff Elazar, Director of Military Intelligence Zeira, and the military secretaries of the defense and prime ministers.

By 0500, Dado Elazar was sequestered with Major General Israel Tal, his deputy chief of staff for operations, and Brigadier General Benny Peled, the Air Force commander, trying to determine what should be done in response to the Intelligence report. In the first place, both Elazar and Tal agreed that the report was accurate; it fit in with Elazar's earlier surmise about Syrian and Egyptian intentions. They were inclined to place the nation on a war footing, to mobilize the Reserves. Benny Peled's contribution was to assure the others that the Air Force was fully prepared to mount preemptive strikes against Syria commencing at 1300. In keeping with his nation's tradition for handling such situations—a necessary equalizer developed in the face of overwhelming Arab numerical advantages and the need to keep the initiative in war—Elazar gave his tentative approval to the first-strike proposal and ordered Peled to mobilize the Air Force Reserves.

Eli Zeira did not agree with the chief of staff's reading of the Intelligence flash. This was the third instance in less than ten months that this particular source had issued such a dire warning. The last two had been wrong. Zeira rightly questioned the validity of this new warning. The source, which might never be revealed, responded by explaining the reasons for the earlier errors, claiming that President Sadat had changed his mind at the last minute in both cases. What, Zeira asked himself, prevented Sadat from changing his mind again? Zeira remained skeptical as to Sadat's will this third time. In any case, Israel had enough time to communicate its state of preparedness to the Egyptian president, and that might cause him to scrutinize his resolve—if, indeed, there had ever really been a firm decision to fight.

How could a senior Intelligence officer misinterpret what was so clear to a company commander such as Eyal Shacham?

A truly daunting number of details regarding Egyptian and Syrian military deployments had been accumulated. There was even detailed information that wives and children of Soviet military advisers were being evacuated from both Syria and Egypt, though neither Soviet nor Arab public broadcasts addressed the reasons behind the precipitous departures.

Once having accumulated all the data, however, Eli Zeira overlooked what he did not yet want to see. Having obtained the services of an informant who could provide a look into Anwar as-Sadat's planning processes, the Israeli director of Military Intelligence turned a deaf ear to what he did not yet want to hear.

When asked about his chief problems by the *Armed Forces Journal*

International, Zeira later provided a clue as to how his mind worked: "To underestimate. But an equally big risk is that we would overestimate. They have their own logic. Thus, we have to look hard at evidence of their real intentions in the field . . . otherwise, with the Arabs all you have is rhetoric. You [Americans] stress capabilities. That's natural for big countries. Here it is just the opposite. Too many Arab leaders have intentions which far exceed their capabilities."

Zeira went on to stress that his biggest problem lay in combating terrorism. ("You can always find three fanatics and convince them to do anything.") Finally, he treated the reporters to his definition of "normal war." What the Western world accepts as peace between the Arab states and Israel, Zeira explained, is "normal war."

Zeira turned his blind eye to a new element that had come with the predawn warning. Though the source had previously been wrong about Sadat's ultimate intentions for war between Israel and Egypt, his Yom Kippur report was the first that mentioned a link between Syria and Egypt. In fact, the foundation of Zeira's beliefs had been the assumption that Syria and Egypt were *not* working together. A unified, coordinated effort between Israel's two most dangerous neighbors should have been a red flag to him.

Ninety minutes after being awakened by his military secretary, Defense Minister Moshe Dayan opened his first meeting of the day. His entire professional staff was in the meeting room: Zvi Zur, a former chief of staff, now Dayan's assistant; Haim Yisraeli, liaison with the Cabinet; Yitzhak Ironi, the director general of the Defense Ministry; Brigadier General Yahashayu Raviv, Dayan's military secretary; and Lieutenant Colonel Aryeh Baron, Dayan's administrative assistant. Chief of Staff Elazar and Major General Tal arrived a few minutes after Dayan called the meeting to order.

Dayan's staff was uncertain if the new Intelligence report really meant that war was about to erupt. It was certainly a basis for taking steps toward greater preparedness, but was it sufficient grounds for unduly alarming the nation? Dayan was convinced that the Egyptians could not bridge the Suez Canal in less than twenty-four hours. Even if they attacked this very afternoon, the danger would remain insignificant until Sunday or Monday, a day or two hence. However, the Syrians faced no truly daunting obstacles. Their artillery, already in place, could wreak serious destruction upon Israeli villages on the Golan and in the Jordan River Valley.

At the very worst, Dayan could picture Egyptian and Syrian air strikes, artillery and tank duels, and commando raids occurring that afternoon and into the night. His vision coincided with Zeira's definition of "normal war." Dayan was convinced, as was Zeira, that plenty of time remained for signaling Israel's level of preparedness to Sadat and Assad. This method had been successful in the past. Why not now?

The meeting could not have opened on a more tragic note. Dayan's initial statement—his very mind-set—revealed the enormous gulf between his convictions and Elazar's. "Let us talk of small things," Dayan said. "What has been done to evacuate women and children from the Golan Heights settlements? We'll organize a trip for the children from the settlements and, if there is anything serious . . . we won't take them back."

Elazar certainly was comfortable with the notion of evacuating women and children, but to equate the information that Israel was about to be attacked on two fronts with the problems inherent in busing women and children down from the Golan, and to speak of "small things" and "if there is anything serious" had a devastating effect upon the naturally combative chief of staff.

There was absolutely no doubt in Elazar's mind that everything that could be done to mitigate the impact of the impending attack had to be done. He had already ordered the Air Force to disrupt Syrian plans by striking first.

Dayan was at pains to make it clear that he did not support Elazar's "first strike" decision, that it was up to the Arabs to decide if there was going to be a war. It was Dayan's view that Israel could not deliver a first-strike air attack, as it had in 1967, and expect to win any sympathy elsewhere in the world. Besides, Dayan exclaimed, if Egypt was the principal threat, a strike against Syria would be misdirected.

Elazar pressed for the immediate mobilization of the Reserves to implement Operations Dovecote and Chalk, respectively the fundamental plan for war against Egypt and the plan for an essentially defensive campaign on the Golan cease-fire line until Egypt could be brought to her knees and units on the Golan could be massively reinforced. Elazar pointed out that Chalk had particular provisions for strengthening the Purple Line—the Golan cease-fire line—with "limited Reserve units."

Dayan countered by disagreeing again. A general mobilization, he averred, was unwarranted. He did support a limited mobilization, however, and agreed to call up one Reserve brigade for the Golan and another for the Suez front.

The dispute between Dayan and Elazar revolved around timing and numbers. Two brigades could be called up in secret, by telephone and runners, while a general mobilization would require broadcasts on radio and television—on the one day in the year when both were off the air. Dayan proposed that a decision be delayed until a scheduled 0800 meeting with the prime minister. Though sanctioned, the two-brigade call-up was not immediately set in motion, though why it was not remains a mystery.

Dayan and his staff worked out a four-point agenda for the meeting with Golda Meir. The main point was how to warn the Arabs to desist from attacking.

While Dayan was rounding out his agenda, Elazar held a separate meeting at 0700 with divisional and GHQ staffers.

Major General Eli Zeira led off by asserting that *he expected war to break out that very evening.*

There it was.

In the words of Major General Avraham Adan, who was scheduled to lead a division to Sinai, "Suddenly, without any signs of emotion or embarrassment, [Zeira] predicted that war would erupt within hours."

Following Zeira's stunning turnabout, Dado Elazar summed up his differences with the minister of defense on what steps should next be taken. He and Dayan would be meeting with the prime minister, and he intended to ask Mrs. Meir for permission to order a general mobilization and authority to launch a preemptive air strike against Syria. He noted that Dayan was against the air strike and favored only a limited call-up.

The meeting among the heads of the government and the generals began at 0800. Present besides Mrs. Meir, Elazar, Dayan, and Zeira were Zvi Zur, Dayan's assistant, and the various ministers. Elazar and Dayan each stated his case—respectively for and against a general mobilization. Dayan stated, "If you want to accept this proposal, I will not prostrate myself on the road and I will not resign; but you might as well know that it is superfluous."

The critical meeting concluded with a compromise. Mrs. Meir authorized Elazar to call up a hundred thousand men, but she sided with Dayan in staying a preemptive strike.

The meeting adjourned and everyone went to work in his or her specialized area.

Major General Yisrael Tal, Elazar's operations chief, took special pains to offset what he considered to be the Cabinet's unfortunate impulse to downplay the danger. With Elazar's full knowledge, "Talik" issued orders that would set far more than the authorized hundred thousand Reservists in motion. And he contacted all senior commanders to emphasize that Israel was facing an imminent surprise attack. He noted that front-line troops would soon be subjected to extremely heavy artillery and aerial bombardment and that, as such, they were prone to call for immediate help, perhaps even magnifying the immediate danger. Whatever else might occur, it was certain that the Cabinet's dawdling had placed a premium on available Reserves. Perhaps Israel's least orthodox military thinker, Tal decided to take a direct-line approach to the general unpreparedness of the mobilizing battalions and brigades, and he advised the senior field commanders to do the same. Until manpower shortages could be reversed, platoons and companies of tanks from partially mobilized units were to be fed directly into units already at the front. Massive improvisation was vital to national survival.

The Cabinet held another meeting at noon, the last before the Syrian and Egyptian attacks were set to begin. Mrs. Meir reiterated the strong probability of an attack commencing that afternoon. She then revealed that she had informed U.S. Ambassador Kenneth Keating that Israel would *not* launch preemptive air strikes—this for transmittal to the Arab world in the hope it would serve as both a warning and a salve: Israel was prepared for war but was willing to forgo her strategic advantage if the Arabs would stand down. Finally, the prime minister informed her colleagues that a partial mobilization of the Reserves had commenced at 1000 hours.

The Cabinet became bogged down in numerous "what if" proposals and counterproposals. The fact was that, short of authorizing an eleventh-hour preemptive strike or the full mobilization that the chief of staff wanted, the civilian leaders were powerless to do more.

While many Israelis went about their Yom Kippur activities, others began to note unusual occurrences. To save time, the Air Force commander, Brigadier General Benny Peled, opted to vector aircraft by most-direct routes rather than sending them around major urban centers, as would have been customary. Thus, photoreconnaissance aircraft that overflew Jerusalem attracted attention. Helicopters and cars taking ministers and military officers to and from meetings in Tel Aviv also drew stares, ranging from the curious to the outraged.

Some things were almost automatic. A number of officers of one Reserve division were called even before a decision to mobilize their unit had been made. Their former commander, Brigadier General Moshe Peled, had recently retired from active service, but the staffers called him anyway. "We are here. Why don't you join us?" Mussa Peled was shocked to receive a phone call on Yom Kippur, but the cryptic sentences were explanation of impending danger.

Peled immediately left home. As he sped along the road to his divisional staging area, his car was spotted by a group of Orthodox youths, who decided that such profane behavior required an instant remedy. In time-honored tradition, the young men threw stones at the general's car. It says a great deal about Mussa Peled that he stopped the car and walked over to the youths to explain that there was a military alert and that soldiers were required to travel. Peled arrived at his divisional command post at 0900 and resumed command of his unit. He ordered all those on hand to prepare for mobilization.

Major General Dan Laner was not an Orthodox practitioner of Judaism. As was the case for many kibbutzniks, Laner was not drawn to prayer even on Yom Kippur. It was Sabbath, however, and he was taking his turn at working at the kibbutz swimming pool when, at 0930, he was ordered to report for duty. As his divisional staff was already assembling, Laner drove the short distance to meet Major General Yitzhak Hofi at the Northern Command headquarters bunker.

Even after Hofi's detailed briefing, Dan Laner was uncertain that he was facing his fourth war. As he drove to his division's staging

point, the general mused over what might happen if no battle occurred. What, he thought, if this is just one of the alerts that comes
to nothing? He decided to return home to pick up a bathing suit. If
nothing else happened, Laner reasoned, he could at least go swimming.

Gradually more and more people were affected by the government's decisions. Throughout the land, the command to report for
duty overrode religious tradition. Street scenes soon began taking
on a bizarre quality. On one Tel Aviv street, a uniformed soldier was
seen walking with his pack slung. Over his shoulder was draped his
prayer shawl, and in his hands was an open prayer book. He obviously chose to walk to his assembly point to avoid, as much as
possible, a desecration of the holy day.

Doron Levy, a medic who had been married for but five days,
returned to his parents' home following his brief honeymoon,
where he received his mobilization order. His wife and parents
escorted him out to the street and lovingly sent him on his way.

The nature of the secret mobilization differed sharply from place
to place. A single phone call received in a small village or kibbutz
settlement had more impact than a hundred calls in the larger towns
and cities. When Amos Ben David, a Reserve tank company commander, was ordered to report, he phoned his close friend Moshe
Waks, who lived in Haifa and who knew nothing about the alert.
Waks no sooner cradled his phone, however, than it rang again with
his call to report for duty. He gathered up his military gear, waved
good-bye to his wife and two children, and left home. He was in
good humor, but he refrained from kissing his wife or one-week-old
child for reasons his wife could not fathom.

Almost the entire Shapiro family had gathered for the day at
Louie and Hetla's home in Haifa. As Louie looked out the window,
he noticed the unusual traffic on the streets. The phone rang a few
minutes later with orders for Louie's daughter-in-law to report to
her unit. Louie's two sons, both paratroopers, stood by their parents
as the girl left; only she had been called.

Individuals making their way by car or on foot slowly coalesced
into groups and rudimentary formations. Paper organizations were
slowly becoming flesh-and-blood entities.

By 1700, Major Yoni Netanyahu, deputy commander of the crack
18th Parachute Battalion, could watch large portions of his unit

reassembling to draw arms. The unit had been placed on alert at 1000 the day before, but after only four hours, the troops had been given holiday leave. Soon the battalion was nearly back to fighting trim, but Yoni Netanyahu felt that the whole rush could have been avoided by consistent decision-making at the top.

Tranquillity remained in many regions of the tiny country. In too few places, peace still reigned because of preparedness; everything was ready, so there was nothing to do but wait and, because this was Sabbath and Yom Kippur, pray.

The order to evacuate women and children from the Golan was producing havoc. A "small thing" to Moshe Dayan was devastating to the people involved. Mobilization orders moved individuals, so it affected only those people and their families, a normal enough event in Israel. The evacuation order, however, dissolved whole communities, and it was not taken too kindly by all the civilians. At Mevo Hamma and Meran Golan, it was thought that the army was being manipulated by an unsympathetic government. The people's distrust of the minister of defense was sufficient for them to dispatch a delegation to argue with the military authorities. So, in the midst of one of his most intense days as commander in the north, Major General Yitzhak Hofi had to drop everything to meet with irate civilians and convince them of the gravity of the situation.

The hours-long Yom Kippur religious service at Ramat Magshimim was interrupted by the evacuation order. The rabbi had to decide how best to carry out his religious duties in the midst of an emergency evacuation that he could not ignore. There was no standing procedure for this particular turn of events. Riding in a vehicle was bad enough, but the work involved in packing and carrying was an outright abomination. The rabbi quickly adjusted, authorizing travel by bus and stipulating how much water could be taken and what clothes it was permissible to pack and carry.

The men of combat units arrayed across the Golan were by no means exempted from the shock that was sweeping the nearby villages. Lieutenant Colonel Yair Nofshe, commanding 74th Tank Battalion, spread his unit across its sector and spent the best part of the day visiting his platoons and the infantry-manned bunkers they were set to guard. It was Nofshe's task to convince the tank crews and bunker garrisons to break the fast and make ready for battle. Nevertheless, Nofshe personally found his duty odious.

Lieutenant Colonel Avigdor Kahalani's day began when he was awakened by an old friend, Major Gideon Weiler, who had just arrived on the Golan with the Armor School Tank Battalion. Kahalani was delighted to see Weiler but was surprised to hear that the ad hoc battalion had been assigned to the Golan. Later, as Kahalani made the rounds to check on his 77th Tank Battalion, he was stopped by Sergeant Ami Bashari, a tank commander, who asked, "When are we going to stop shooting at barrels?"

A Golani Infantry Brigade staffer neglected to send the required fourteen-man infantry section to reinforce the defenses around the electronic-warfare installation on the Hermon. Other bunkers, however, were reinforced. Bunker 107, where Private Avraham Lifschitz had been sent as the "prayerman" the day before, received a seven-man squad, which, though it terminated Lifschitz's special status, bothered him not at all.

There is probably no other nation in the world in which the activities running their course in Israel would have been considered in any way normal. The tragedy is that, for Israelis, the mobilization was an essentially normal experience, made different from other such alerts only by the gravity of the holy day. Israeli minds focused on everyday matters such as bathing suits and leave-taking among family members. Jan Boger, an Israeli paratrooper, later wrote, "It is a heavy price each generation has to pay again and again to live in Israel. . . . To the Israelis who do not know differently, who never knew peace, it does not appear to be the sacrifice it really is."

Even military personnel on active duty could not focus on the significance of Dado Elazar's Alert Gimmel, for they shared with Eli Zeira the concept of "normal war." Lieutenant Colonel Yair Nofshe thought in terms of a few days of heavy artillery bombardment. Sergeant Gideon Ehrenhalt and the garrison of the Hermon bunkers were told to expect some shelling. Lieutenant Yosef Gur and the men in the bunkers mixed flak jackets and prayer shawls. Israelis associated with what they knew, and they knew peace and peaceful pursuits only through the prism of war.

* * *

The noon meeting of the Israeli Cabinet was careering along from question to question, accomplishing little more than the provision of a pastime for ministers awaiting word of the imminent war. At 1355, as the honored members of the government were trying to decide if they had taken adequate steps to ensure the IDF's ability to mount a counterattack, the door to the Cabinet room suddenly opened. All eyes were on Brigadier General Yisrael Leor, the prime minister's military secretary.

"The news is that the war has begun."

From outside, the ministers could hear the wailing of air-raid sirens.

· 2 ·

ASSAULT

· 6 ·

An artillery officer assigned to the north of Nofshe's battalion, high on the slopes of the Hermon, spotted a flurry of Syrian activity at 1355 hours. He yelled, "Look there! Just look!" as Syrians pulled camouflage netting from their guns and tanks. The first shell landed seconds after the artilleryman's shout, and its blast bowled over the officer and the other three members of his forward observer team. None of the Israelis was wounded and, as soon as they sorted themselves out, all four scrabbled for the more-protected parts of their position.

Lower down, several alert soldiers manning one of the bunkers guarding the Purple Line spotted Syrians across the way rolling up the netting that camouflaged their tanks and artillery. The report of the sighting swiftly made its way up the command chain. On the strength of the report, Colonel Yitzhak Ben Shoham, commanding Barak Brigade, ordered his tank battalion commanders, Lieutenant Colonel Yair Nofshe and Lieutenant Colonel Oded Eres, to deploy their nearly seventy Centurion main battle tanks in prepared battle positions.

Nofshe was not surprised by the timing of the Syrian bombardment. He had been stationed on the Golan long enough to have discerned a pattern: The Syrians usually initiated incidents at about 1400 hours to prevent a massive Israeli retaliation during the few hours remaining until sunset. This was a little different, however, if the reports about tanks so near the front were to be credited.

Nofshe was at his Kuneitra command post when Colonel Ben Shoham, reached him on the tactical radio net with orders to deploy his tank platoons and move his vulnerable headquarters vehicles to safety. Nofshe no sooner signed off than he ordered everyone out of town, tanks forward, and soft vehicles back.

Moments later, Eres reported that his 53rd Tank Battalion was on the front line, guarding the southern sector. His forward command post was on Tel Juhadar, at the intersection of the Petroleum and El Al roads.

Aran Zamora, of 75th Armored Infantry Battalion, was studying his maps when he heard the sound of approaching jet engines. If war broke out, Zamora's unit was to wait until nightfall, then cross into Syria to lay markers that would be used to guide Israeli Air Force jets against preselected targets. If all went well, the pathfinders would return to friendly lines at daybreak. When Zamora's mind focused on the high-pitched whine overhead, he looked up from his maps to see what was going on. By so doing, he probably became the first Israeli to see the Syrian jets. Zamora knew the meaning of what he saw: The fight was on. He returned to his studies.

Less than two minutes later, the first jets were spotted by a farmer, who also saw the first bombs as they were released over Israel. The man shouted the news to fellow villagers, "They're bombing Kiryat Sh'moneh! It's war!"

More than one hundred Syrian aircraft took part in the opening strikes. They targeted all the IDF encampments on or near the Golan. The majority of the sorties struck at installations and defensive positions along the twisting road leading to the plateau from the B'not Yaacov Bridge. Antiaircraft missile batteries in the Jordan River Valley and electronic-warfare centers throughout Northern Command also received considerable attention.

The regional forward command center at Naffach, where Brigadier General Rafoul Eitan's divisional staff was headquartered, was a primary target and bore the brunt of attacks by at least twenty Syrian

UNITED NATIONS/Y. NAGATA

U.N. observation post at OP ROMEO in the northernmost area of the Golan Heights

A Syrian soldier

UNITED NATIONS

Syrian "SCUD" missiles hit Kibbutz Goat.

**Israeli soldiers take a lunch break
on the Golan Heights.**

UNITED NATIONS

A Syrian pilot captured by IDF forces

UNITED NATIONS/Y. NAGATA

A Syrian P-55 tank with mine-clearing wheels operating
near UNTSO Patrol Base 44 (*in background*)

■

**Israeli personnel carriers heading toward
Pitulim Peak on Mt. Hermon**

**Israeli artillery moves into
position near Qnaitra.**

jets. But the Syrian pilots missed an unanticipated opportunity. Colonel Avigdor Ben Gal, the 7th Armored Brigade commander, had ordered a briefing of his officers at precisely 1400 hours. All of the brigade senior staff officers and battalion commanders, plus General Eitan's staff, were present when the first strike arrived. The Syrians apparently were locked into flying a predetermined course with a predetermined release point. Either their aiming point was fractionally off or their speed and altitude were slightly over or under the desired. For whatever reason, most of the bombs narrowly missed the camp at the base of Naffach Hill and exploded in an unoccupied gully. No one was injured.

Lieutenant Colonel Avigdor Kahalani, the curly-headed, dark-complected son of Yemenite Jews, had been the first Israeli officer to cross into the Egyptian-held Gaza Strip in June 1967. Today, though he heard the planes, he did not see them. He had just stepped from his jeep when a bomb exploded close to where he stood. Kahalani's first thought was to seek cover, a natural enough impulse for even so well-blooded a combat officer, and he ran to the lee of the nearest building. As the attack continued, however, he decided to return to the 77th Tank Battalion command post. He hurtled into his jeep and drove back up the asphalt road, certain that he was presenting the Syrian pilots with the largest target on the whole Golan.

The Syrian pilots encountered little opposition. Individual soldiers fired their personal weapons in reaction, and several tank commanders manning turret machine guns tried to track the swift aircraft, but little or no damage was inflicted. Most soldiers simply sought cover. Gunners manning the only antiaircraft gun battery deployed on the Golan, at Tel Abu Nida, reacted smoothly to the sudden aerial assault, but their four guns made little impression on the first waves of warplanes.

Considering the numbers of aircraft and the utter surprise they achieved, the Syrians had little to show for their attack. Damage and casualties on the ground were minimal. Not one tank or artillery piece was disabled.

Israeli pilots reacted sluggishly to the Syrian attacks. Nearly every war since World War II has begun with an attacking air force striving to knock out the bases and disrupt the communications of the opposing air force. IAF personnel assumed that they would be the first and primary target of Syrian air strikes, so as soon as the air-raid sirens sounded, Israeli fighters scrambled to protect their bases. They ignored the Syrian bombardment for nearly thirty minutes, thoroughly faked out by the Syrians, who ignored the air bases.

As it became evident that Syrian aerial operations were hitting only ground targets near the front, the Israeli airmen began shifting their emphasis to meet the unexpected threats. By nightfall, Israeli ground patrols were combing the Jordan River Valley in search of the crews of eight Syrian jets that had been shot down.

For most of the Israelis on the Golan the war arrived in the form of the Syrian artillery bombardment. The coordination between the Syrian Air Force and the artillery brigades was flawless. Once the Syrians opened with bombs, the shells followed, and most Israelis felt no letup.

United Nations cease-fire observers on neutral ground between the lines logged the opening rounds. Their records show that the entire Israeli front was taken under fire between 1356 and 1403 hours.

The workhorses of the Syrian bombardment were 153 artillery batteries equipped with 122mm, 130mm, and 152mm weapons. The 152mm was capable of getting off only four rounds per minute, and it had the shortest reach, 12.4 kilometers. The 122mm could be fired at a rate of about eight rounds per minute at distances of 15 kilometers. The 130mm guns could hit targets 27 kilometers distant at a rate of about six rounds per minute. The Syrians had also emplaced several 180mm batteries, which had a reach of about 29 kilometers but which were capable of firing only one round per minute. Rounding out the artillery envelope were some five hundred rocket launchers, mortars, and dual-purpose antiaircraft guns.

In all, Syria had more weapons of 122mm or above than Israel had men deployed in the bunkers screening the Purple Line. There were actually more individual weapons on hand than there were legitimate military targets for them. Even with all the crossroads, command and service centers, bunkers, and tank and artillery positions under fire, the Syrians had guns to spare. Their legitimate choices were either to withhold the fire of a number of their guns or to double up on many targets. They chose, instead, to direct the surplus against civilian villages.

Mahanayim, Ayelet Hashachar, and Shamir were all shelled. The

Syrians also directed fire against a civilian airfield just south of Mahanayim on the excellent notion that it could be put to good use by light military aircraft.

Moshe Dayan's most important "small thing," the evacuation of women and children from the Golan villages, had proceeded well. However, one bus had broken down on the way to the Golan, and it reached Ramat Magshimim only in the early afternoon. The children and their mothers were lined up, ready to board the vehicle, when the first rounds impacted. Everyone broke for cover. The bus was damaged, but no one was hurt.

Just to the east of Ramat Magshimim, at Bunker 116, Lieutenant Yosef Gur was participating in Yom Kippur prayers when the shelling began. In the hope of divining a pattern, Gur manned an observation post as the shells continued to land. One salvo dropped into the bunker compound every four minutes.

To the northeast, at the military camp at Hushniya, the opening salvoes sent Israeli tank crews scrambling into their armored vehicles. The tanks surged toward prepared positions at the front, but the Syrian gunners followed them along the roads. It was clear that the Syrians had the road net zeroed in, so there was no alternative but to breast the fire. One Barak Brigade tanker "had the feeling that they could see us exceptionally well. Either that, or the force of their artillery could cover the whole of the Golan. Wherever I looked, shells were falling. We simply stopped paying attention to them."

One of Nofshe's 74th Tank Battalion platoons was near the Vasit crossroads when the Syrian jets went after Tel Abu Nida. The three Centurion crews watched the attackers depart before climbing aboard their tanks and starting up. The battalion commander radioed orders to drive forward to prepared revetments on the bunker line. The three Centurions moved out in a cloud of dust, driving only a kilometer before coming under large-caliber artillery fire.

Nofshe himself had managed to drive a mile from Kuneitra before the Syrian artillery barrage crashed down around him. Nevertheless, he radioed the Barak Brigade command post before 1400 hours with the news that 74th Tank Battalion was ready for combat and that he was manning a forward command post on a ridge north of the B'not Yaacov road known as "Booster."

The fifty-five-man garrison manning the Hermon bunkers went through the standard drill. Everyone who had no need to be outside assembled in the central hall, where roll was taken and personal weapons issued. Then the technicians sat around to await the outcome of the Syrian bombardment. After a time, several became adept at picking out the distinctive sound of bomb bursts against the general cacophony of a torrent of artillery rounds.

The fifty-five-minute barrage was just long enough to allow the Israelis time to overcome the shock and fear that sweeps the ranks of even blooded veterans at the onset of an artillery bombardment. By the time the fire slackened, or shifted to targets farther back, the troops on the front, the ones who would bear the brunt of the ground assault, had regained their composure. To the extent that most of them had been able to determine a pattern to the firing, they felt more in control of the situation. (By comparison, the Egyptian bombardment on the Suez front lasted only twenty minutes, and the leading Egyptian assault waves broke upon Israeli defenders who were still very much in shock.)

Major General Yitzhak Hofi, the commander of all IDF forces on the Golan, was in Tel Aviv when the shooting began. His light courier plane attempted to land at the Mahanayim strip but was held off by the Syrian barrage. It was precisely this sort of disruption that the Syrian bombardment had been engineered to inflict. Interestingly, Hofi thought the fire directed against the airstrip was FROG surface-to-surface missiles.

The confusion at the airstrip was greater than it might have been. Hofi had planned to direct the anticipated battle personally. The actual outbreak of the fighting had caught him in the wrong place at the wrong time, and he was forced to fly around nursing a rising frustration. Brigadier General Rafoul Eitan, the sector commander, had been in control at Northern Command headquarters at Rosh Pina when Hofi ordered him to Mahanayim to pick him up; the drive could be used to discuss options. With Hofi circling the airstrip and Eitan stuck on the ground awaiting Hofi's arrival, command of the Golan front devolved to Colonel Yitzhak Ben Shoham, a tall, slim, dark-haired, Turkish-born professional, aged thirty-nine, who was manning the Northern Command forward command post at Naffach.

Ben Shoham had four battalions deployed along the main line of defense, the so-called Purple Line. Two battalions—17th Infantry and 50th Parachute—manned fixed positions along the border. On their flanks and rear were two tank battalions, 74th and 53rd, both of which were components of Ben Shoham's own 188th "Barak" Brigade. Along with support and administrative units also deployed on the Golan, these combat units were part of 36th Armored Infantry Division, a paper organization scheduled to come into being in the event of war. The Regular components of 36th Armored Infantry Division would be augmented by a Reserve armored brigade and two Reserve mechanized brigades. The division commander was the district commander, Brigadier General Eitan, for whom Ben Shoham was standing in.

Eitan's mission was simple: to repulse any Syrian effort to cross the cease-fire line. Most of the tanks were committed to fighting from ingeniously prepared positions around the fixed bunker complexes. Until Reserve units began appearing, only twenty tanks were available for assignment to a reserve pool from which maneuver elements could be drawn. Fortunately, Lieutenant General Dado Elazar's Alert Gimmel had marshaled considerable tank and armored infantry reserves at the last minute. Colonel Avigdor Ben Gal's entire 7th Armored Brigade—77th and 82nd Tank battalions and 75th Armored Infantry Battalion—and Lieutenant Colonel Memshalom Carmel's Armor School Tank Battalion also were available. Thus, even without the Reserves, Northern Command could count upon 80 percent of its allotted wartime strength.

Israeli tank experts had long since come upon a clever system for optimizing the positive features of the tank in defense. This was not the role tankers prefer, but a decade of "normal war" had forced the Israelis to use tanks—or, more significantly, tank-mounted guns—in what might have been seen as unorthodox settings in other parts of the world.

The key to the defensive system on the Golan was a line of ramparts built to cover the shallow valley that separated Israeli defenses from the Syrians. In the main, the ramparts were along the low ridge on the western side of the valley. They were three-tiered gunnery platforms providing superb, often interlocking fields of fire as well as excellent cover and observation.

The first, lowest step of the rampart was at or just above ground level. The tall Centurion tank could sit on this step, completely unobserved by Syrian forward observers. On the second, middle step, the Centurion would be "hull down," which is to say that the body of the tank, but not the turret, would be behind the earthen barrier. The top step, protected in most places by a low berm, provided a higher platform for the tank, and the hull, but not the treads, would be exposed to fire from across the way. A tank sitting on the top step could sufficiently depress its main gun to fight tanks or infantry at close quarters. The forward slope of the rampart was uniformly steep, thus obviating direct assault by Syrian tanks.

The most distinctive feature of the Israeli fixed-tank system was gunnery training. There were fewer Israeli tanks available than there were Syrian, so a heavy emphasis on exacting gunnery training was made to equalize the Syrians' numerical advantage. The Israelis had mounted 105mm guns on their Centurions and World War II-vintage Shermans to counter the 105s aboard the Syrian T-55 and T-54 tanks, and the 115mm guns aboard the T-62s; indeed, the Israeli tank guns outranged the Syrian tank guns by several hundred meters. Since the Israeli tank gunners would enjoy an advantage in height and, therefore, range, the very best Israeli gunners had been designated to carry out long-range harassment fire.

It was extremely difficult for the Centurion gunners or forward observers to whom they were linked by radio to see the advancing Syrians through the dust and smoke of the artillery barrages. So, while Colonel Ben Shoham authorized his tanks to open fire at 1415, the ranges were too extreme for any but the very best. In all, less than a dozen Israeli tanks actually fired. Nevertheless, the Israelis were encouraged and the Syrians discouraged by this puny response. Some Israeli tank gunners put out rounds as far as four kilometers.

Despite the heavy incoming fire, the Israeli defenders were positively uplifted by the tank gunnery. Cheers went up whenever a hit was perceived, and there were more and more of those as the ranges closed and the gunners settled in.

The Syrians attributed the increasingly accurate fire to some new American technical device acquired by the Israelis. But the feat was one of training and will. The Syrians quickly learned the right response: Keep moving.

Most of the initial sightings and firing were in the northern sector, manned by 17th Infantry and 74th Tank battalions. Captain Avner Landau, a 74th Battalion company commander, reported Syrians advancing near the Hermonit and the Dan Road.

This was clearly no mere battle day.

· 7 ·

While Israeli tank gunners sniped at distant Syrian tanks, and Israeli bunker garrisons wrestled with final preparations for repulsing the very heavy Syrian attack, Captain Avner Landau had to strain just in the hope of seeing his enemies in the northern sector of the Kuneitra Gap. Before seeing even one Syrian tank, Landau intuitively understood that his force of seven Centurion tanks soon would be engaging an enemy ten times its size.

A few miles to the south of Landau's holding position, Lieutenant Colonel Yair Nofshe also was straining for a view through the dust thrown up by the Syrian artillery preparations. Nofshe had moved his 74th Tank Battalion into the middle of the defensive gap near Kuneitra and had occupied the Booster position, one of the keys to the Golan. To Nofshe's left was Landau's company; on the right was Captain Zvi Rocks's company. In tactical reserve to the rear of the Booster position was Captain Eyal Shacham's company of ten Centurions. Whatever the Syrians had moving toward Nofshe's thin line would have to be held off until no one knew when. There was, Nofshe knew, very little chance that his battalion would be reinforced before nightfall, still three hours away.

Fortunately, Nofshe's battalion was able to move into prepared battle positions with neither personnel nor equipment losses. As the Israeli tank commanders awaited the onslaught, they dropped down into their turrets and pulled their hatches shut to avoid unnecessary casualties in the unremitting rain of shell splinters.

Almost due east of Nofshe's command post, Major George Mayes was experiencing none of the visual problems bedeviling the Israeli defenders. An Australian, Mayes was serving with the United Nations Truce Supervisory Organization (UNTSO) on the Syrian side of the cease-fire line. It was as though he were in the eye of a hurricane. Great clouds of dust rose and swirled and eddied and flowed to the east and west of the U.N. position, but the post was untouched, its vistas unblocked, a strange island of calm befitting of its function in the hands of peace-keepers.

Mayes was stunned by the size of the Syrian force. Thundering past his observation post was a gargantuan assemblage of armor and supporting arms. It first struck Mayes that he was looking at a parade large enough to incorporate the whole of Australia's army. Then he thought that within his line of sight was a collection of arms far exceeding anything his nation could put into the field. Sometime later, Mayes tried to find words to convey to a group of news reporters what he saw this afternoon: "It wasn't like an attack. It was like a parade-ground demonstration."

This was the moment of the Syrian 7th Infantry Division's greatest vulnerability. The attackers were formed in a giant, teeming hourglass, as the scattered armored formations, picking their way toward the former no-man's land, came together for a short approach march, then split again into definable combat formations to head for their individual objectives. The IAF should have been on station to disrupt and destroy this assemblage. Israeli artillery should have been answering the frantic calls of forward observers, raining fire upon the immense mass of an armored division on the move. But Major Mayes saw no such thing. It was as though the Israelis were *unable* to react.

The Syrian column split in plain sight of the UNTSO post, its moment of greatest vulnerability past. Eighty-fifth Infantry Brigade struck due west on the road to Gonen, and 121st Mechanized Brigade continued southwestward, toward Kuneitra.

For all they impressed Major Mayes, the Syrians had made a major, perhaps decisive, error. In their rush to battle, the armored units had raced ahead of the engineers. The tanks arrived at the deep Israeli antitank ditch before the means for crossing could be set up.

The 85th Infantry Brigade assault column reached the Israeli antitank ditch before its officers noticed that the engineers were not in the vanguard. The only recourse was for tank crewmen and mechanized infantrymen to dismount and rush forward on foot to improvise crossings. This substitution had three immediate impacts upon the Syrian column: It brought the advance to a grinding halt in full sight of the Israelis; it exposed defenseless men to Israeli fire; and it channeled whatever progress could be made into clearly defined killing zones.

The waiting Israeli tanks opened fire, and Israeli artillery forward observers ordered up a few registration rounds from batteries safely deployed to the rear. The toll was raised yet higher as footborne Syrians and the lead Syrian armored vehicles moved into Israeli minefields fronting the antitank barrier.

Quite aside from the ample satisfaction of destroying an enemy bent upon destroying them, Israeli tank gunners were at least in part motivated by a tradition that had evolved during the many confrontations with Syrians over the years. Each time an Israeli gunner knocked out a Syrian tank, he received a bottle of champagne. Israelis are among the world's least enthusiastic drinkers, but the bravado of the tradition spurred Nofshe's gunners to greater glory. One of the gunners described the emotive force of the bottled recognition: "I suddenly saw a considerable number of armored personnel carriers and Syrian tanks moving toward us. We began to fire, and we set some of the tanks ablaze. We counted them and shouted about champagne."

As 85th Infantry Brigade was stalemated at the forefront of the assault, the outpaced Syrian engineering units pushed forward past stalled assault vehicles. They soon came under direct Israeli observation and began suffering casualties as Israeli officers redirected fire from the Syrian vanguard against what they immediately grasped as the Syrians' best hope for pushing their assault forward once again.

One Israeli tanker, among many, watched the Syrian engineering vehicles cross into view from behind a hill. Bridging tanks and soft vehicles, including trucks and auxiliary vehicles, were sitting ducks in the Israeli gunner's sight. He fired at the first bridging tank he saw and hit it. Then he quickly shifted fire to the next nearest bridging tank. It, too, was stopped. A third bridging tank fled from sight.

Sergeant Doron Gelber, whose Centurion was positioned in the Hermonit area, also felt that the bridging tanks were the most important targets to be found that afternoon: "When such masses of tanks as these approach you, you are likely to hit each tank you shoot at. You have to decide in seconds which tank is most important to get. It was obvious that we had to first destroy all the bridging tanks."

Still, there were too many targets for too few Israeli gunners.

The first close combat erupted in the northernmost portion of 74th Tank Battalion's sector. By an utter fluke of terrain and deployment, the thirty-tank Moroccan Brigade was the first Arab unit directly to engage the Israelis on the Golan.

Ahmed Ashan was in the first Moroccan tank to penetrate the Israeli line. He was about to fire at several oil tanks in Tel Shaeta when he saw a Centurion fire at a comrade's vehicle. Quickly, Ashan traversed his turret and fired, hitting the Centurion. Two Israelis bailed out of their burning tank and ran for cover as Ashan tried to hit them.

Lieutenant Avner Kimovitz, leading a Centurion platoon that had been detached northward from Captain Avner Landau's company to guard the Dan Road, found his three Centurions under heavy pressure. As the Moroccans moved from the north against Tel Shaeta, a Syrian battalion closed from the west along the Dan Road.

Landau noted the threat against Kimovitz, but his force of seven Centurions was facing a greater threat in their sector. He reported what he could see to Lieutenant Colonel Nofshe, adding that he was unable to reinforce Lieutenant Kimovitz.

Nofshe decided to delegate the area north of the Hermonit to his deputy, Major Yosef Nissem, and to reinforce the sector with Captain Eyal Shacham's company. After briefing Nissem, Nofshe requested and received Captain Moshe Rosenwig's company of the Armor School Tank Battalion as a tactical reserve. Thus, in less than forty minutes of action, every Barak Brigade Centurion in the northern Golan had been committed.

Upon assuming tactical control of 74th Tank Battalion's northern sector, Major Nissem directed Shacham's company to reinforce Kimovitz's platoon around Tel Shaeta and the Dan Road. This area, however, was less important than the open stretch just south of it, which could provide easy access to the northern slopes of the Hermonit. Nissem ordered Shacham's deputy, Lieutenant Asaf Sela, to cover that area with one platoon.

As Nissem deployed Shacham's company, Kimovitz's platoon was able to stabilize its front. The Moroccans continued to fire at Tel Shaeta, but they did not advance. And the Syrian battalion column heading westward along the Dan Road was stymied when its leading vehicles were destroyed on the roadway.

After briefly milling about on the Dan Road, the Syrian battalion commander ordered his unit southward, to try for a penetration between the Dan Road and the Hermonit bunkers.

Without knowing it, the Syrians advanced between Captain Shacham's force to the north and Lieutenant Sela's to the south. The two Centurion units quickly adjusted to spring a trap. Both Shacham and Sela were particularly impressed with the obvious care the Syrians had exercised in fitting out the assault column: Each spotted bridging tanks, bulldozer tanks, main battle tanks, and armored personnel carriers. In addition, they saw several BRDM armored anti-armor missile carriers, which had proven highly effective in recent battle days.

Shacham's and Sela's Centurions opened fire just before 1500 hours. The Syrians deployed to the sound of the fire, but the Israelis, whose 105mm guns could outreach all the Syrian tank armaments, held superior positions from which they fired whenever a target presented itself, pushing back attempted envelopments and direct assaults. The Syrian battalion withdrew in a little more than two hours, leaving behind its bridging tanks, a bulldozer tank, two BRDMs, and six main battle tanks. Shacham's company lost two Centurions.

A short time after the bulk of the Syrian battalion withdrew, just before nightfall, Shacham spotted three SU-100 gun carriers and a truck close to Major Nissem's position. The Syrians had selected their route well, for Nissem was unable to engage them from his prepared positions. However, he was able to order Lieutenant Sela, who could not see the Syrians, to intercept. Directed by Nissem and Shacham and accompanied by one other Centurion, Sela maneuvered to the rear of the Syrian detachment and opened fire. All the targets were caught between two hundred to three hundred meters from the two Centurions and destroyed.

Two Syrian bridging tanks succeeded in crossing the open ground to the antitank ditch in the unguarded stretch south of Major Nissem's sector. It was far later than envisioned by the Syrian planners, but the way west finally was opened. Immediately the stalled Syrian tank companies moved to exploit the breach in the man-made obstacle and rushed forward toward the ditch in the communal hope of overwhelming the thin Israeli line. It was already dusk, the best time for the Syrians to cross the ditch and plunge into the darkened Israeli rear. There would be no better opportunity to sow confusion among the defenders. Upon learning of the successful bridging effort and impending crossing, Lieutenant Colonel Nofshe ordered Captain Avner Landau's truncated company to counterattack.

A Syrian tank company quickly crossed the bridge and deployed to guard the vital treasure. These first Syrian tanks were still trying to locate the best defensive positions when Landau's Centurions hit them. It took only a half hour for the desperate Israelis to seal the bridgehead and destroy the Syrian vanguard company and bridging tanks.

The vast majority of Israelis stationed on the Golan were not in combat during the afternoon of October 6. Nevertheless, many men tried to find useful pursuits to fill the time. The 77th Tank Battalion medical section found an excuse to argue over paperwork when they rushed to treat the battalion's first casualty, an unfortunate soul who injured his hand while playing around with a machine gun. A discussion of major import was soon under way over whether the bloody member should be treated as a training accident or a combat injury. This was truly momentous, as the outcome would determine which form was to be filled out.

On the other hand, the commander of Golani Infantry Brigade's

17th Infantry Battalion found that he had some idle troops who might be put to use, a platoon with six jeep-mounted 106mm recoilless rifles. Sending this unit into action was one of those things that seemed to work well in practice, where the jeeps took up position, fired a few rounds, then drove off to find a new position before the enemy could return fire. But the Syrian artillery bombardment was so dense this afternoon of real combat that steel slivers flattened the jeep tires and rendered the recoilless rifles immobile. There was no way to keep up with the demand for new tires.

Lieutenant Avraham Elimelech's worst nightmares had come true. Bunker 107, the only Israeli strongpoint east of the antitank ditch, was quickly bypassed by the Syrian battle columns. Almost as soon as the Syrian ground assault began, Elimelech and his subordinates helplessly watched as seven Syrian tanks moved directly toward their stronghold. All the bunker commander could do was call for help and hope for the best.

Six Israeli Sherman tanks—part of a local home-guard unit that had been formed only days before the war and that was acting entirely on its own initiative—arrived after a brief, heart-stopping interval and took the Syrians under fire. The Israeli crews were untrained or, perhaps, rusty or unfamiliar with their equipment; certainly the gunners did not show the same mastery of their trade as did the 74th Tank Battalion gunners they were supporting. Rather, the two tank forces stood off and traded fire across the antitank ditch for nearly twenty minutes without scoring a single hit. Though they sustained no damage, the Syrians broke off the action and withdrew. Most likely, they had run out of ammunition; all Israeli tanks were capable of carrying up to twenty-one more rounds than any of the Soviet-supplied T-54s and T-55s, a critical difference. Hard-pressed along his entire front, Colonel Yitzhak Ben Shoham could hardly afford to assign even a poorly trained company of sorely needed tanks to guard the outpost, even a vital outpost, and he pulled the Shermans to more fruitful ground, leaving the bunker garrison to fend for itself.

The Syrians returned just before nightfall. Lieutenant Elimelech again asked 74th Tank Battalion to bail him out, but this was the most critical period in Nofshe's defensive effort: The Syrians had breached the antitank ditch in the extreme North. All available tanks were moving to beat back the threat. Nofshe had to refuse the request.

A lone Syrian tank approached the bunker complex to provide direct support while a Syrian armored personnel carrier picked its way through the minefield before stopping to disembark a squad of riflemen, who in their turn fanned out and headed for the wire surrounding Bunker 107.

Private Yosef Zadak was by far the section's least-willing soldier. Although most Israeli junior officers, including Lieutenant Avraham Elimelech, are disposed to putting up with unsoldierly "individualistic" behavior from subordinates raised in an egalitarian society, it was all Elimelech could do to overlook Zadak's studied reluctance, which was just a shade short of outright insubordination. In an army that prizes volunteerism, Zadak was comfortable with never doing one bit of work beyond what he was ordered to do.

The section's only bazookaman was Private Zadak, and he was on the side of the bunker farthest from Elimelech, farthest from the advancing Syrian tank and armored personnel carrier.

For the first time in his service career, Yosef Zadak moved of his own volition, utterly without supervision—without even the suggestion of supervision. He worked his way through the trench system knitting the bunker complex together, all the way to the best possible position for impeding the assault. Then, to the total astonishment of his comrades, who already had more from him than any ever expected to get, Zadak moved into the open to engage the threatening tank, which he blew to pieces.

Sergeant Nissan Avidan took advantage of the shock of the tank's demise to shift positions, and he caught the exposed Syrian infantry squad as it continued to grapple in the open with the perimeter wire. Five Syrians fell in quick succession as Avidan opened fire with his light machine gun. The survivors broke off the attack and, with their armored personnel carrier racing them for cover, disappeared from sight.

The Syrians launched one gambit that might have been decisive. Under cover of the intense air and artillery preparation, four troop-carrying helicopters approached Tel Abu Nida, the highest peak in the area, with the intent of disrupting vital Israeli electronic-warfare capabilities.

Unhindered, the Syrian commando platoon reached the tel and disembarked. One section launched an immediate assault against the electronic-warfare installation while another went for the outlying antiaircraft battery, the only Israeli antiaircraft unit stationed on the Golan. The defenders hurled hand grenades at the superior Syrian force and fired back with their Uzi submachine guns, MAG light machine guns, and FN assault rifles. The attackers sought cover while the antiaircraft gunners ran for the main bunker.

It was touch-and-go for a while. The bunker was cut off until Captain Yosef Sarig's company of the Armor School Tank Battalion counterattacked up the tel and drove the Syrian commandos away at nightfall.

In the southern sector of the Kuneitra Gap, as elsewhere, the Syrian air and artillery bombardment set the armor of both armies in motion. An Israeli Centurion company moved forward to engage a column of 121st Mechanized Brigade T-54s. The Israelis spread out as they moved, taking what advantage they could of the broken, undulating terrain. As the tanks moved beyond the line of prepared positions held by Israeli infantry, the ground trembled from the heavy Syrian bombardment. Numerous near-misses made it clear that the T-54s had been able to register on the route the Israelis had chosen, so the Centurions changed course and raced to positions from which they could engage the oncoming Syrians with a modicum of protection. The tank-vs.-tank duel commenced, thirty Syrians against ten Israelis.

Three crucial advantages enjoyed by the defenders played a role here. First, the British-made 105mm guns in the Israeli tanks were more accurate at greater ranges than the Soviet-made tank guns. Second, the Centurions each carried up to fifty-four rounds, while each Syrian tank stocked only thirty-three. Finally, the taller Centurions could depress their guns several degrees farther than could the T-54s and T-55s. Thus, on undulating ground such as was being fought over, the Syrian tanks had to expose themselves on hilly crowns or even forward slopes to fire at the Centurions, which could return fire or spring ambushes "hull down" from steeper reverse slopes.

One of the Israeli tank commanders recounts, "It is a strange feeling to see people who crossed into our territory to destroy us turn into burning targets over two thousand meters from us. We saw their crews run in every direction."

Another, larger wave of T-54s drove into sight. There were at least sixty, impossible odds but for the fact that the Israelis were slightly higher than the Syrians, had the better view, and could reach their targets with greater ease. The ten Israeli tanks charged, firing as they went, to within fifteen hundred meters of the oncoming T-54s. Within minutes, many of the Syrian tanks were funeral pyres.

Lieutenant David Eiland, a platoon leader in Captain Zvi Rocks's Centurion company, was rapidly moving along the Kuneitra Road, the other two tanks of his platoon following in his wake, when he spotted a Syrian bridging tank at four kilometers. To Eiland's deep surprise and keen satisfaction, his gunner hit the target. First blood!

Shortly after destroying the Syrian bridging tank, Eiland's platoon was flagged down by Lieutenant Oded Yisraeli, the deputy company commander, who was stopped by the side of the road in the company's command APC. Yisraeli placed Eiland under his direct command and led the platoon farther south. As they drove, Yisraeli told Eiland that Syrian tanks and infantry had crossed the antitank ditch near Bunker 109.

The undulating ground prevented the onrushing tank crewmen from seeing what might be in the way or on the flanks. They topped a ridge and found fifteen Syrian tanks and several more armored personnel carriers less than four hundred meters away. Oded Yisraeli no sooner ordered Eiland's platoon to attack than his thin-skinned APC came face-to-face with a Syrian infantryman armed with an antitank rocket launcher and steady nerves. As the Syrian tracked Yisraeli's APC in his sights and before Yisraeli's driver or machine gunner could react, David Eiland caught the movement out of the corner of his eye. It was a matter of seconds but seemed a lifetime before Eiland could get his gunner to traverse the turret and fire. The brave Syrian soldier fell. The Israelis kept up an intense, rapid fire, moving south all the while, thoroughly defeating the Syrians.

As Eiland's Centurions crested another small rise, Lieutenant Yisraeli spotted two Syrian tanks parked in a gully about 150 meters away. There was no time to lose, so Yisraeli radioed orders to the tank gunners to traverse and fire on the run. Both Syrians were destroyed.

Next up was a thoroughly alerted force of tanks and armored personnel carriers, all deployed to bar Yisraeli's force from access to Bunker 109. Yisraeli ordered his tanks to engage the superior force. As the APC and Centurions swept forward, Captain Rocks arrived with seven Centurions, the balance of his company, which had been heading for Bunker 109 along a converging route.

As always when a pure tank force comes up against infantry or infantry and tanks, the infantry proves more elusive and, therefore, potentially more harmful than the tanks. If infantrymen facing tanks are brave and steady, they have a good chance of defeating the armor. Inasmuch as Rocks, Yisraeli, Eiland, and nearly all Israeli tank commanders considered it both a point of honor and more efficient to fight while standing exposed in their turret hatchways, the Syrian infantry they faced could, if well led and well motivated, be of particular danger.

David Eiland was advancing with his platoon up a small hill when he saw one of his tank commanders, Sergeant Nimrud Khochavi, suddenly slump forward. A sniper had inflicted the first casualty on Eiland's platoon. Khochavi died instantly and his crew withdrew down the hill, not stopping until their undamaged Centurion reached Kuneitra.

In the meantime, the Syrian force was dispersed with heavy losses.

Though the company was still well short of Bunker 109 and despite the loss of only one of his tanks, Rocks decided to hold onto the ground he had gained rather than continue his advance.

Lieutenant Eiland felt okay about the way things were going. He had lost a tank commander and, by extension, one third of his platoon, but he had weathered his first combat with some significant contributions to his credit. When Captain Rocks ordered Eiland to direct his fire against scattered approaching targets, Eiland complied with the assurance that he could and would prevail.

The Syrians advanced across broken ground in increments of twos and threes. Eiland's gunner fired whenever he had a clear target, but he scored no hits.

Suddenly three Syrian tanks burst into view a mere fifty meters away, right in front of Eiland's Centurion. There was no time to call for help and barely time to scream a warning to his gunner, who had still less time to get even one of the approaching targets in his sights.

CrackBOOM! . . . *CrackBOOM!* . . . *CrackBOOM!*

Three rounds, three burning Syrian tanks.

And so it went.

At sunset Captain Rocks directed his company to prepared battle positions around Bunker 109, where the area was far from secure. Syrian infantrymen armed with antitank weapons were combing the broken ground, keeping pressure on the tired Israeli tank crews. Movement by tanks was fraught with danger both from roving Syrians—tanks and infantry—and edgy friends. Tankers, by nature a paranoid lot, are doubly so at night.

Zvi Rocks felt an overwhelming urge to see that his company was amply resupplied, for the startling afternoon successes had depleted ammunition and fuel. It is a hallmark of Israeli leadership, though sometimes misguided, to seek personal danger before ordering others to take risks. Rocks pulled his tank from its position and set off down the road to Kuneitra, the nearest reprovisioning point. Startled crewmen working in and around the other tanks were sure they were witnessing Zvi Rocks's last ride.

The lone Centurion zigzagged across the broken, undulating ground. Gunfire from unseen assailants sought to reach it, but none did. In due course, Rocks arrived at the 74th Tank Battalion resupply point in Kuneitra, tired and triumphant. Half the trip, at any rate, was over.

While his crew loaded ammunition, Captain Rocks sat and listened to the crew of Sergeant Nimrud Khochavi's tank. The shooting and killing were stupid, one averred. Another asked who benefited from Nimrud's death, then answered that not even the Syrians benefited, for the tank was still in fighting condition. It was all stupid, they agreed. So why go back? Why die? Zvi Rocks just listened. Finally, when it was time, he stood up. "I'm going back." He mounted his waiting Centurion and rode back into the night. Later, at Bunker 109, he found the missing tank, in position and ready to fight.

Nowhere in the Kuneitra Gap was it easy. But along the dark line, the tank crews, infantrymen and parachutists in the bunkers, gunners manning the artillery batteries to the rear, supply and support troops, tank repair teams, communicators, and medics—all the tired, frightened defenders—knew they had held against what ought to have been overwhelming odds. The victory, however long it was destined to last, was itself a confidence-building tonic for what might then have been the world's most confident army. The night air carried the sweetness of respite; it was relatively safe to rearm, rest, adjust to total war.

Forty-nine Syrian tanks lay burning on the approaches to and within the Kuneitra Gap. Others—no telling how many—had been damaged, perhaps disabled. Farther to the north, along the Dan Road, another ten Syrian tanks had been destroyed.

Lieutenant Colonel Yair Nofshe had overseen a model defense. The northern Golan front had held.

· 8 ·

At the same time Nofshe's 74th Tank Battalion was holding its line in the northern Barak Brigade sector, Lieutenant Colonel Oded Eres's 53rd Tank Battalion was facing battle in the brigade's southern sector.

Initially the components of 53rd Tank Battalion were deployed in accordance with previous experience in fighting Syrians on the Golan. The key points on which earlier Syrian raids had concentrated were the Hushniya, Rafid, and Petroleum roads.

Eres, who had been on the job for less than two weeks, chose to direct his sector's defense from Tel Juhadar, which provided a central observation point overlooking the Rafid and Petroleum roads. To the north was Captain Uri Michael Akavia's tank company, which deployed a platoon each at Bunkers 110, 111, and 113. South of and parallel to the El Al Road was Captain Avi Roni's company, broken down into platoon increments to defend Bunkers 114, 115, and 116. The battalion deputy commander, Major Shmuel Askarov, was in charge of the reserve, Captain Uzi Ureali's company.

Syrian pressure was first exerted on Bunker 111, where observers reported approaches by Syrian tanks four times within the first hour of the attack.

According to one Syrian, "At the exact time as planned, all of our tanks moved fast and started positioning the bridges under fire. We were able to accomplish this because the enemy was surprised. It was hard to position the bridges, and required a lot of talent, because they had to be placed diagonally due to a sand embankment on the other side. We began firing as soon as we [crossed the bridges and] moved into the enemy area."

Captain Akavia moved his tank up to support the platoon deployed around Bunker 111. In Akavia's first report to Eres, he estimated that his four Centurions were facing between forty and sixty tanks and armored personnel carriers, and he asked for some help.

Akavia waited until the Syrians were about a mile from his position. His own tank was perfectly situated, so he decided to control the target acquisition. Long-range fire accounted for four tanks of 9th Infantry Division's 53rd Infantry Brigade, a mixed tank–mechanized infantry unit.

Eres gathered from Akavia's initial report that Bunker 111 was the target of a major Syrian thrust, so he dispatched Major Askarov, with one of the platoons held in reserve. Askarov's component arrived in time to take part in the destruction of six more Syrian tanks, for a total of ten. When there was a moment's lull, Askarov reorganized the defenses and, in doing so, found that the tank platoons around Bunker 111 had suffered no losses in men or equipment.

The Syrians then threw twenty tanks at the Israeli force, and the Israelis again fired only on direct orders from their senior officers, who assumed responsibility for target selection. Though each Israeli tank had started with fifty-four rounds of ammunition, mainly antitank rounds, it was standard procedure to husband the supply to the extent possible. In time, as the Syrians neared the bunker complex, the gunners naturally picked up the pace and, in time, a free-for-all developed. At this point one of the platoon leaders' tanks was hit and the young officer commanding it was killed.

Captain Akavia decided to change positions in the hope of getting a better view of the developing action. The command Centurion was just below the crest of a small hill when it was hit in the turret. Akavia was killed.

As the battle raged around Bunker 111 and with the overwhelming force of Syrian tanks striving to sweep westward, a Syrian shell ignited Sergeant Zvi Mizrachi's Centurion. Another tank commander, Sergeant Tsion Charbari, ordered his own driver to pull up alongside the stricken vehicle so he could help evacuate the crew. Major Askarov saw Charbari's tank disabled by three hits in quick succession, which killed Charbari.

It was getting dark. Though they had inflicted grievous casualties upon the Israelis, the Syrians pulled back, leaving thirty-five armored vehicles burning or abandoned between Tel Kudna and Bunker 111.

The moment the pressure eased, Major Askarov set about reorganizing his defenses. He was surprised that his command was down to just three Centurions armed with only sixty-nine antitank rounds. He was sufficiently concerned to direct his tank commanders to fire their remaining 105mm rounds solely at other tanks; armored personnel carriers were to be engaged only with heavy machine guns. That done, Askarov then ordered his driver to run the command tank back and forth to raise dust, in the desperate hope of bluffing the Syrians into believing that reinforcements were arriving.

Though Askarov had won the first round, he remained apprehensive about continuing the action into the night. The Centurion crews had accounted for the first ten Syrian tanks without loss, but attacks by the next twenty-five had resulted in the deaths of two Israeli officers and two enlisted tank commanders. As always, he would have to assure that the surviving crews husband both their ammunition supplies and their extremely and increasingly valuable lives.

Askarov was certain that two Syrian tank battalions had been involved in the attack, a total of sixty or seventy tanks against his small force of eight. Notwithstanding the crushing odds Askarov had overcome, he found himself admiring his adversaries: "They fought bravely, they were determined, and constantly tried to penetrate our lines. They did not pull back from the fire we put on them."

Meanwhile, Akavia's deputy commander, Lieutenant Boaz Tamir, was initially in command of the company's main body of six tanks strung out along the Petroleum Road. He soon realized that stopping the Syrian attack was going to be difficult.

A Syrian tank column rapidly thrust toward Tamir's sector and, in a matter of minutes, lost the two leading tanks. Unexpectedly, the following Syrian tanks bypassed the leaders and kept on coming. The Israelis continued to score hits at ranges of under three hundred meters, but the following tanks just kept grinding forward in what seemed to Lieutenant Tamir to be inexhaustible numbers. Still, he refused to believe that he was standing against anything more than a raid-in-force by unusually determined Syrian tank crews—despite the fact that his six tanks were whittled down to two effectives by sunset.

While following Askarov's fight near Bunker 111 on the tactical radio net, Lieutenant Colonel Eres kept his attention riveted on the two roadways the Syrians were sure to prize the most, the Rafid–Kuneitra and Petroleum roads. Despite calls for assistance from several bunker commanders in his sector, and news of mounting losses, the 53rd Tank Battalion commander maintained the bulk of Captain Uzi Ureali's company in reserve.

Captain Avi Roni was with his company's forward tank platoon on the Rafid Road and, like Captain Akavia and Major Askarov, took responsibility for target acquisition and spotting for individual, designated gunners. Roni appears to have been the first Israeli officer to recognize the magnitude of the Syrian assault; he pointedly told Eres that this was not a raid but an assault, not a battle day but a war. Roni was killed before nightfall when, just like Captain Akavia, he sought to move his well-situated command tank to an even better position.

In contrast to the fighting along miles of front to the north, Lieutenant Oded Bachman's Centurion platoon was not attacked, or even directly harassed. Bachman sighted large Syrian infantry formations, but these almost invariably shied away from presenting a direct threat, or a direct target. The only challenge in Bachman's sector came from a group of Syrian infantrymen who moved to set up antitank weapons directly opposite the Israeli tank platoon. Bachman laconically called for direct artillery support, then watched as the accurate fire disrupted the Syrians' efforts.

* * *

Lieutenant Yosef Gur, commanding Bunker 116, spotted a Syrian armored column to the southwest and asked for air support. He was gratified to get it and highly impressed by the way the Israeli pilots timed their attacks to coincide with the completion of the Syrian bridging efforts. Gur noted, however, that the tireless Syrian engineers went to work repairing the bridges as soon as the Israeli jets flew from sight. The Syrian advance near Bunker 116 soon was back on track.

It fell on Lieutenant Netaniel Aharon, deputy commander of Captain Avi Roni's company, to stem the Syrian assault near Bunker 116 with Lieutenant Yoav Yakir's platoon and his own command APC. Aharon commanded the southernmost Israeli tank force on the Golan. As had most of his fellow commanders, he chose to open with long-range fire by designated gunners at targets he called out. He climbed into the turret of one of Yakir's Centurions to do so. Unlike similar stands to the north, Aharon's tiny force succeeded in keeping elements of 5th Infantry Division's 61st Infantry Brigade in check at distances of two or three kilometers from his rampart position. Aharon's tank was hit and rendered inoperable during the long-range exchanges, but no one was hurt and the Israeli platoon observed the destruction of eight Syrian tanks before the sunlight faded.

While perhaps not quite as intense as the fighting in Nofshe's northern sector, Lieutenant Colonel Eres's 53rd Tank Battalion had fought a model defensive stand. Nearly sixty Syrian tanks had been destroyed in the southern Golan before nightfall, as had a goodly number of Syrian armored personnel carriers. Unlike Nofshe's battalion, however, Eres's had taken a beating. A dozen of its precious tanks had been knocked out, though only a few were totally wrecked, and two of three company commanders were dead.

Reinforcements were urgently required.

⋅ 9 ⋅

Major General Yitzhak Hofi managed to land at the Mahanayim civilian airfield during a lull in the Syrian artillery bombardment in the late afternoon. He was greeted there by a frustrated and anxious Brigadier General Rafoul Eitan, with whom he drove to the Naffach forward command center to assume control of the defense from Colonel Yitzhak Ben Shoham.

The Israelis had initially deployed for a "battle day" with a force less than 30 percent of what they felt was called for in the event of all-out war. By the time Hofi and Eitan reached Naffach, it was clear that the sixty-five Centurion tanks of Barak Brigade were in danger of being overwhelmed and that Northern Command could not contain the massive Syrian onslaught without dipping into the General Headquarters units already on the Golan. Immediately, Hofi issued orders committing the 105 Centurions of Colonel Avigdor Ben Gal's crack 7th Armored Brigade. Thus Hofi moved from a "battle day" to "war." However, he was a day late in deploying, and his total force, including thus far uncommitted units, was only 80 percent of what the learned consensus believed was adequate for a full-scale war.

Hofi's dispositions clearly illustrate Israeli understanding of the military geography of the area. The northern sector of the Golan, which is bisected by the Kuneitra Gap, was crucial, while the southern sector was of less significance. Hofi thus ordered Ben Gal to assume command of the vital area from Bunker 107 northward. This placed the key Kuneitra Gap within Ben Gal's domain. At the same time, Barak Brigade's responsibility was narrowed to the southern sector already occupied by Lieutenant Colonel Eres's 53rd Tank Battalion.

No time was lost in reshuffling positions; Hofi merely swapped units between the two brigades. Lieutenant Colonel Yair Nofshe's 74th Tank Battalion was operationally transferred from Barak Brigade to 7th Brigade. In return, Hofi ordered the transfer of the entire newly arrived 82nd Tank Battalion and two companies of the newly arrived 75th Armored Infantry Battalion from 7th Brigade to Barak Brigade.

The decision to return Lieutenant Colonel Avigdor Kahalani's 77th Tank Battalion to 7th Brigade was particularly noteworthy in that it reflected Hofi's critical concern for the northern sector. Kahalani and his tankers had worked for over a week with Ben Shoham's brigade, and they knew the terrain. On the other hand, with the exception of a company commander and several other officers, 82nd Tank Battalion, which went to Barak Brigade, was totally unfamiliar with the roads, hills, and other terrain features of the area. This meant that Ben Shoham would be covering his sector with a force quite a bit smaller than Ben Gal's, and one in which fewer officers and soldiers knew their way around the battlefield and rear areas.

Ben Gal's 7th Armored Brigade had had a relatively quiet afternoon as it sat, waiting, behind the main defense line monitoring the radio traffic among Barak Brigade units and Ben Shoham's command post. As Ben Gal mulled over the anticipated commitment of his brigade, he recognized a basic weakness in his tactical organization that he still had time to correct. Inasmuch as he controlled two first-rate battalions he thought would eventually have to be committed to the fight, the brigade commander decided to create a personal reserve by attaching one company of 82nd Tank Battalion to 7th Brigade's headquarters. It was a good guess, for 82nd Tank

Battalion was transferred to Barak Brigade within the hour. Ben Gal was bending the rules by withholding the company, but he had a definite and long-standing fixation on keeping something in reserve.

Like Ben Gal, Lieutenant Colonel Oded Eres recognized the need to withhold a reserve for as long as possible. Unlike Ben Gal, however, he had not had a quiet afternoon in which to reflect on the matter. Two of his company commanders were dead, and there appeared to be no letup in the Syrian attack. Through it all, however, Eres instinctively kept Captain Uzi Ureali and two Centurion platoons out of the fight.

The leading elements of the fresh 82nd Battalion arrived at Tel Juhadar just before 1600 hours. Eres immediately noted that one third of the battalion was missing, but that was nothing to the concern he registered when he learned that the battalion commander also was missing. The battalion's deputy commander, Major Dan Pesach, thought the officer was back up the road. He reported that he was not in radio contact with him, however. Frantic calls to Naffach and the battalion's former bivouac both indicated that the 82nd Battalion commander was en route, but a search through the radio frequencies failed to get a response from him or anyone who knew where he was. Eres waited nearly thirty minutes for information pertaining to his whereabouts; then Eres simply assumed command of the fresh tank companies and directed Major Pesach to take Captain Dan Levine's company south to Ramat Magshimim.

With great reluctance, Eres ordered his reserve, seven Centurions under Captain Ureali, to bolster those already in action in the central portion of his battalion sector, along the Petroleum Road. Then he personally led Captain Eli Geva's 82nd Tank Battalion company on the first part of a sweep along the Rafid Road. Eres soon left Geva to his own devices in favor of stopping to reorganize the remains of Captain Avi Roni's force.

Lieutenant Boaz Tamir, who was overseeing the defense of the Petroleum Road, was certain that his six-tank unit would eventually be reduced to nothing in the face of sheer numbers and volume of fire. But Tamir's negative thoughts dissipated as soon as Captain Ureali brought up 53rd Tank Battalion's former reserve—just as it seemed certain that the Syrians were indeed achieving the break-through they sought.

Until Ureali's arrival, Tamir and his crews had been frustrated in their attempts to form a coherent response by the need to rush up and down the road, firing a few rounds here and a few there to blunt Syrian thrusts. One tank after another had been hit, a total of four.

Ureali's force, with Tamir's two tanks appended, swiftly advanced into the teeth of the Syrian assault. When the Israelis spotted bridging tanks crossing the antitank ditch on the back of another bridging tank, the lead gunners destroyed two.

The Israelis next spotted Syrian infantry, an easy enough adversary to overcome. But Lieutenant Tamir had an uneasy feeling about this batch of footborne invaders. The tanks opened with their machine guns, and the Israelis watched numerous Syrians fall or take cover. But the Syrians came on, seemingly oblivious to the consequences, rising and falling in no apparent order, doing nothing to save themselves in the face of massed fire.

Tamir's biggest problem was choosing a target for his tank's 105mm gun from among twenty oncoming Syrian tanks. He could not see more than two or three Syrian vehicles at a time in the rolling fields. Hit in the head earlier, Tamir's problems in target acquisition were deepened by a steady trickle of blood into his eyes. This last was remedied when one of his crewmen passed a water bottle up to the turret every few minutes so he could rinse his face.

There was nothing for Tamir to do but fight on. To stop would be to die.

Captain Geva's attack near the center of the southern sector, which had begun with Lieutenant Colonel Eres in charge, made its way rapidly up the Rafid Road. The company reached the Purple Line within an hour of reporting to Eres, one Centurion lost for twenty Syrian tanks and armored personnel carriers. Geva requested permission to continue the counterattack.

Geva's report was easily the high point of Eres's day: An Israeli company in good condition was poised on the border, its commander seeking permission to attack into Syria. However, if Geva's and Ureali's counterattacks made matters in the center look better than they had in hours, it was also true that Eres's defensive efforts on the flanks were disintegrating.

* * *

Major Dan Pesach's force was speeding southward along the El Al Road when it ran headlong into a Syrian ambush. The Israeli crews quickly overcame the initial surprise and crushed the barrier before resuming on to Ramat Magshimim without further incident. On reaching the village from which Israeli women and children had been evacuated under the opening Syrian artillery salvoes, Pesach deployed Captain Dan Levine's company in positions that would deny the advancing Syrians access to the strategic El Al Ridge. The position was significant but somewhat removed from the battlefield, so as soon as Pesach reported in, Eres ordered him to split the force and have Levine retrace his steps to Tel Juhadar.

Though he had encountered Syrians along the road to Ramat Magshimim, Levine assumed the route would have remained clear. Eres's order had conveyed such urgency that in the interest of speed Levine declined to put out scouts and flankers. The result was the worst disaster ever inflicted upon Israel's armored corps.

A fresh Syrian force had reached the roadway in plenty of time to set up antitank weapons in concealed positions. Levine's tank was among the very first hit, and control was never regained. All ten Centurions were destroyed or disabled in under two minutes.

Neither Pesach, Eres, nor Ben Shoham was sure what happened to Levine's force once it was reported long overdue.

Within a very short time of turning command of the fighting over to Generals Hofi and Eitan at the Naffach command center, Colonel Yitzhak Ben Shoham learned that the 82nd Tank Battalion commander was out of contact, that Captain Uzi Ureali had mounted a successful counterattack, that Captain Eli Geva had overcome a large Syrian force and was poised to mount an attack into Syria, and that Captain Dan Levine's company had vanished. It became clear, as the news arrived, that Naffach was not the right place from which to read the battle or control events in the southern Golan. So Ben Shoham decided to abandon the command center and move closer to the battle with his mobile forward command group, to place himself where he might be able to exert more personal control over events he had been training to meet all his adult life.

Upon reaching Tel Juhadar, Ben Shoham found Eres's forces being hard-pressed. The most immediate need was for illumination on the battlefield, for Eres was being forced to accept unremitting battle in almost total darkness.

Following are extracts of conversations among Ben Shoham, Eres, Hofi, and Major Benny Katzin, the Barak Brigade operations officer:

ERES:	I need artillery on [Bunker] one-eleven and south of Rafid.
BEN SHOHAM:	Wait. We have other problems.
HOFI:	We can't let [Bunker] one-eleven fall.
BEN SHOHAM:	We have to put something on Petroleum [Road]. I must have artillery illumination.
ERES:	I have made a lane near [Tel] Juhadar. Am awaiting artillery.
BEN SHOHAM:	Light near [Tel] Juhadar. We hit one [tank]. We need light.
KATZIN:	You'll get it.
ERES:	I have already hit three [tanks] at short range. We must have light.
BEN SHOHAM:	We need light. It's an emergency.
KATZIN:	You'll get it.
BEN SHOHAM:	We need light. Eventually they'll get us.
ERES:	Is there any way to get more forces?
BEN SHOHAM:	Negative. I have some getting ready. It will take time. Light. One kilometer east.
KATZIN:	You'll get it.
ERES:	Put it eight hundred [meters] east.
KATZIN:	We don't have enough light.
BEN SHOHAM:	I know. I know.

About ten minutes after completing these radio exchanges, Ben Shoham found his command post under artillery fire. It is reasonable to assume that radio signals monitored and analyzed by the

Syrian signal-intercept unit at Tel Al Jaba had been the cause of the artillery probe. Wherever Ben Shoham went for the rest of the night, his communications emissions were monitored, and artillery soon would begin falling around him.

While constantly wiping blood from his eyes, Lieutenant Boaz Tamir strained to find targets in the pitch-black night. Suddenly a Syrian tank loomed from out of the darkness and raced directly toward Tamir's Centurion. It was the closest a Syrian had gotten to Tamir, but he hardly gave it a thought and directed his gunner onto the onrushing shadow. The first round slammed into the Soviet-built vehicle but did not stop it. The next round stopped the Syrian only fifteen meters away, and a round from the tank next to Tamir's also hit it. That was enough for the Syrian crewmen. One of the hatches on the rounded T-55 turret popped up, and two Syrians popped out. Both men were instantaneously dropped by Tamir's machine gun. It was the first time he was able to see the faces of men at whom he shot.

The most successful Syrian unit throughout the afternoon and early evening was 5th Infantry Division's 132nd Mechanized Brigade. Major Dan Pesach, of 82nd Tank Battalion, had overcome the unit's first penetration while on the way to Ramat Magshimim, but Captain Dan Levine's company had been obliterated by 132nd Brigade infantrymen manning antitank weapons.

The 132nd Mechanized Brigade tank battalion met stiff resistance. When Lieutenant Yosef Gur, at Bunker 116, had first spotted the armored vanguard in the late afternoon, he had directed telling air strikes, which had destroyed two bridging tanks. However, only limited support could be offered by the hard-pressed IAF, and the Syrians soon breached the barrier in force.

Lieutenant Netaniel Aharon, of 53rd Tank Battalion, had stood off a portion of 132nd Mechanized Brigade's tank battalion for nearly two hours with long-range fire, but his tank was knocked out before nightfall, leaving defense of the area around Bunker 116 to two Centurions under Lieutenant Yoav Yakir.

Three 132nd Mechanized Brigade tanks and two armored personnel carriers advanced on Bunker 116 just after sunset. The leading tank broke through the perimeter wire and advanced on the main bunker before being stopped by a bazooka round. Lieutenant Yosef Gur knocked out the second tank, which had followed the first into the bunker compound, with antitank rifle grenades fired from only twenty meters away. The crews of both tanks were killed by grenades and machine-gun fire as they jumped to the ground. The third tank withdrew, leaving both armored personnel carriers, which the Israelis destroyed with bazooka fire.

As soon as the shooting ended, Lieutenant Gur ordered the perimeter bolstered with mines. It was a wise precaution, for an advancing tank soon was disabled by the newly sown explosives.

The Syrians next brought up a recoilless rifle, which badly damaged the walls of the main bunker. With the Israelis reeling from this blow, five tanks mounted an assault, which ran headlong into an artillery concentration Gur managed to direct in the nick of time. The Syrians pulled back, but three of the tanks immediately returned. These were forced to withdraw in the face of Gur's precisely directed artillery fire.

As the pressure on Bunker 116 continued to mount, Lieutenant Yoav Yakir battled across the darkened countryside with the last two Israeli tanks in the area, his own and that commanded by Sergeant Nir Atir. About sixty Syrian tanks were combing the area around Bunker 116.

When Atir's gunner reported that he had fired the last of his 105mm rounds, Atir engaged the rapidly moving shadows he could see with the .50-caliber machine gun mounted in the Centurion's turret. Unbelievably, a lucky round ignited the fuel of one of the Syrian tanks, and the resulting conflagration convinced the Israelis that hope remained.

The jubilation was short-lived, for Lieutenant Yakir's Centurion was hit and the platoon leader was wounded. A quick check revealed that the damaged Centurion could still get around, but its 105mm gun was inoperable. The driver of the damaged vehicle followed Sergeant Atir's tank all the way to Bunker 116, fortunately without meeting any other Syrians.

The Syrians attacked Bunker 116 while the Israelis were frantically shifting ammunition from Yakir's tank to Atir's. However, illumination rounds fired by the bunker's 81mm mortar allowed Atir to destroy three Syrian tanks in the stark, magnesium brightness.

By this time, Sergeant Atir had had enough, so he requested

permission to pull back from Bunker 116 to join Major Pesach's small Centurion force near Tel Saki. The request was approved by Lieutenant Colonel Eres, though Lieutenant Gur certainly was displeased with being abandoned when he was just getting the feeling that he had a chance of holding against renewed Syrian attacks.

The Syrians mounted yet another attack soon after Sergeant Atir left the bunker compound. Lieutenant Gur called for artillery support, but it failed to materialize. The 81mm mortar damaged another Syrian tank and the attackers pulled back again, this time for good. They left seven tanks and two armored personnel carriers burned out or abandoned in or near the Bunker 116 compound.

Sergeant Atir managed to reach Major Pesach's scratch force at Tel Saki without incident, raising Pesach's command to five Centurions. After sharing out all the 105mm rounds available, Major Pesach moved his force from the tel right into an area controlled by 132nd Mechanized Brigade infantrymen armed with RPGs. Pesach managed to get through the block, but three of the Israeli tanks were hit. Atir's tank was not hit, but it stopped when the crew found itself surrounded by Syrians. The Syrians must have assumed they hit the stalled Centurion, for they left it alone. Atir's crew lay doggo, observing and trying to figure a way out of its predicament.

Other Syrians pressed on toward Tel Saki. The three or four APC-mounted squads of 50th Parachute Battalion defending the position were certain they faced a full battalion of Syrian infantry, and they asked for an immediate artillery barrage to replace the support they had lost when Major Pesach drove off into the night. No artillery was available to stop a lone Syrian tank, which closed on the tel and poured round after round into the Israeli position. In very little time, nearly all the defenders were wounded.

The bunker commander made a frantic plea for medical assistance and artillery support. An APC was dispatched to evacuate the wounded, but when it neared the compound, the driver reported that a Syrian artillery curtain had descended on the approaches and he could not safely advance through the fire.

At length, Lieutenant Binyamin Hanni volunteered to mount a second attempt to relieve Tel Saki. He collected a dozen soldiers in two half-tracks and drove off. Some hours later, after picking their way across the treacherous landscape, the two Israeli vehicles were stopped by 132nd Mechanized Brigade infantrymen. Unable to withdraw or advance, Hanni ordered everyone to the ground and established an all-around defense. The Israelis were found four days later in a tight defensive circle, facing outward, dead.

In the meantime, the Syrian assault on Tel Saki petered out, leaving the wounded Israelis in peace, but terribly isolated and untended but for rudimentary first aid. One of the Israelis attempted to contact Syrian outguards left to monitor the tel, but he was shot dead. The remaining members of the garrison elected to sit tight and see what daylight might bring.

The destruction of virtually every Israeli tank in the Tel Saki area had opened a significant hole in the Israeli defenses. One Israeli tank on the El Al Road, Sergeant Nir Atir's, still was operable. Though unable to get himself moving, Atir was willing to fight. He was actually tracking an oncoming Syrian tank, ready to fire, when his headphones crackled with a message that ten other Syrian tanks were right behind his target. He opted for continued silence.

Just to the north, several large elements of 9th Infantry Division were presenting Barak Brigade with the most dangerous threat of the night.

· 10 ·

At almost the same time Lieutenant Colonel Eres was launching his counterattack in the center of the Barak Brigade sector, his deputy commander, Major Shmuel Askarov, in the North, was confronted by nearly a hundred armored fighting vehicles near Bunker 111. Askarov commanded eight operational Centurions.

Major Abdullah Qablan, commanding the lead tank battalion of 9th Infantry Division, looked on as the Israelis destroyed his mine-clearing tanks that had been posted in his column's vanguard. Qablan balked when he reached the edge of the Israeli minefield. The 9th Infantry Division commander, Colonel Hassan Tourkmani, moved to the head of the stalled column to confer with Qablan.

Unlike the Syrian assault divisions on either of his flanks, which were launching multipronged advances, Tourkmani had opted to count upon just one massive thrust. He could not afford to stop because he lacked a few specialized vehicles; the entire advance in his sector hinged on movement through the minefield. Tourkmani was willing to pay whatever price success required, so he peremptorily ordered Major Qablan to resume the advance, with or without mine-clearing vehicles.

Qablan, who had been directing the advance from his command armored personnel carrier, dismounted and climbed into the turret of a nearby tank. He personally led what was left of his battalion into the minefield. Nearly all Qablan's tanks were disabled, but the battalion commander's tank made it through, only to have its turret sent flying through the air by a direct hit from one of the Israeli tanks under Major Askarov. Qablan managed to bail out before the resulting fire touched off ammunition and fuel.

Colonel Tourkmani coolly watched the immolation of Major Qablan's battalion. When he had seen what there was to see, he ordered the tank battalion following Qablan's to exploit the path that had just been "cleared."

Three Israeli tanks were lost to Syrian fire, but Major Askarov sparked a spirited defensive effort until he was badly wounded. Askarov had been the tiny holding force's only officer and, as is often the case where a strong leader exhibits superior command presence, his loss had an immediate and telling effect upon the crews on the firing line.

No officer was in the area to take Askarov's place, for even the lieutenant commanding nearby Bunker 111 had been combed from the Israeli ranks. The bunker's defense was in the hands of Private Ezra Tsion, a very junior ranker but with the personality and will needed to win instant respect. Command of the tank force fell to Sergeant Daniel Berkowitz.

Upon assessing the situation, Berkowitz ordered all the wounded tankers and infantrymen taken inside the bunker. Then he placed an urgent call for an evacuation attempt. One APC made it through the Syrian fire, but the crew reported that the road to the rear had been closed behind.

Berkowitz radioed the Naffach command center, from which only an hour earlier General Hofi had admonished Colonel Ben Shoham, "We can't let [Bunker] one-eleven fall." With Berkowitz's report, however, it became clear that the defensive force was spent. Northern Command authorized Berkowitz to withdraw.

Though Colonel Yitzhak Ben Shoham had learned that Major Askarov was seriously wounded before he left Naffach for Tel Juhadar, Ben Shoham apparently did not recognize how serious a loss his brigade had suffered. He had even passed just a few miles to the west of the bunker without entertaining the idea of checking in.

After attempting for two hours to navigate through the pitch blackness, Sergeant Berkowitz gave up and returned to the bunker complex, where all available hands pitched in to retrieve and share ammunition from the bunker stores. Two snooping Syrian tanks that approached too close for Berkowitz's liking were destroyed. However, "Berkowitz Force," as it had been designated by Colonel Ben Shoham, remained less a viable combat element than a group of survivors waiting for sufficient light in which to find a safe route away from the perilous front.

For the most part, Israeli and Syrian artillery fought wars somewhat removed from the swirling tank battles. Adhering to the traditions and experience of their Soviet trainers dating back to World War II, the Syrians' artillery doctrine emphasized massive saturation fire. In contrast, Israeli artillery doctrine called for precision firing at specific targets. The difference lay in both the quality of training and the availability of arms. The 153 Syrian batteries expended more rounds in the first hour of the war than the IDF's two 160mm mortar batteries, two 175mm gun batteries, and seven 155mm gun batteries fired in the first *eight* hours.

At 2200 hours, members of a self-propelled gun battery deployed near Tel Faris spotted the first Syrian tanks of Major Farouk Ismail's 452nd Tank Battalion, a part of 9th Infantry Division's 51st Independent Tank Brigade, which had just bypassed Bunker 111. This was the first direct challenge to an Israeli forward artillery position.

It took another thirty minutes for the Syrian crews to spot the Israelis and for a fight to erupt. However, Ismail's intent was to the west, so he led his battalion in that direction. After exchanging fire with the Israeli artillery, Ismail's battalion cut right through the Hushniya military base and proceeded toward the Hushniya–Petroleum crossroads.

When a supply column comprising fuel tankers and half-tracks laden with tank ammunition making its way up the Petroleum Road from Naffach arrived at Tel Juhadar, Colonel Ben Shoham stopped it and warned the convoy commander not to go farther along the dark and unsecured roadway. Then the brigade commander suggested that Lieutenant Colonel Eres infiltrate his 53rd Tank Battalion Centurions to the rear to resupply dwindling fuel and ammunition stocks. Eres, however, was committed to the last tank and dangerously close to being overrun in several sectors; he was afraid to pull any of his tanks off the line, even for fuel and ammunition. Ben Shoham saw Eres's point but nonetheless countered with advice that the tanks be released one at a time. Eres vetoed even this modest suggestion.

Minutes later, when Ben Shoham noticed a darkened tank moving alone along the Petroleum Road, he radioed Eres to ask if he had changed his mind. Eres averred that he had released none of his tanks from the front, so Ben Shoham ordered the resupply convoy commander to stop the armored vehicle and order its crew back to the front after resupplying and refueling. The captain jogged onto the roadway and yelled to get the attention of the driver, who by now had driven to within ten yards of the brigade commander's command half-track. The captain had said only a few words when it dawned on him that the tank was Syrian. The lost enemy crewmen, as confused and horrified as the Israeli officer, battened down their hatches and roared off into the night.

Ben Shoham ordered the ammunition convoy to remove its volatile burden from the congested area, so the fuel trucks and half-tracks started back up the Petroleum Road toward Naffach.

The convoy commander halted his column just south of the Hushniya–Petroleum crossroads to allow a tank force to pass. An artillery officer who was guiding the resupply convoy looked on for a time but began doubting that Israel had as many tanks deployed on the whole Golan as he was watching in the passing procession. He mentioned his doubts to the convoy commander, who readily agreed. Then both men clammed up, feeling it was far more prudent simply to wait than to draw the only weapons they had, Uzi submachine guns, against at least a battalion of tanks.

The supply convoy sped off toward Naffach as soon as the tank column had cleared the crossroads. The convoy commander radioed Ben Shoham to report that a very large concentration of armor, perhaps fifty tanks in all, had been encountered.

What he had witnessed was the unchallenged passage of Major Ismail's 452nd Tank Battalion.

* * *

Once Ismail's column passed the Israeli supply convoy, the battalion commander halted his tanks to conduct an odious piece of business.

Al-Owda, the original Syrian attack plan, undoubtedly had provisions for prisoner collection and treatment, but Badhr apparently did not. Thus, according to Israeli accounts, Major Ismail oversaw the execution near the Hushniya–Petroleum crossroads of eleven Israeli prisoners of war his battalion had scooped up during its lightning advance beyond Bunker 111.

Once beyond Bunker 111 and Hushniya, 51st Tank Brigade had what appeared to be a clear run through the Israeli rear.

However, Lieutenant Uri Kushinari, a 75th Armored Infantry Battalion company commander, took advantage of the darkness and confusion on the battlefield to demonstrate how APCs could fight tanks—contrary to everyone's opinion and all standing orders.

Parked off to the side of the road when 51st Tank Brigade moved through Hushniya, Kushinari jumped from his vehicle and walked down the roadway. He climbed up onto one of the Syrian tanks, pulled open a turret hatch, and dropped in two hand grenades. Then he jumped clear and walked back to his darkened vehicles. He arrived just as the tank exploded. With that out of his system, Lieutenant Kushinari ordered his APCs out of the area—for, as everyone knows, APCs do not engage tanks.

The Hushniya area was filled with Israelis using the cover of darkness to get to safety. One, Mordechai Oakvi, fought the loneliest battle of all.

Oakvi was a medic who had been left behind when his tank company went into combat. He spent the entire day alone, often under shellfire. But once the shelling slackened off at nightfall, Oakvi began wandering around the ruins of his position. He was accosted in the dark by a man gesturing for a light for his cigarette. The two peered at one another for a moment longer, then ran in opposite directions. They were, after all, enemies.

As Oakvi rested in a garbage dump, Syrians searched all around where he hid. Later, when the hubbub died down, he stalked off in the direction of his battalion headquarters. Morning found him hiding in a barn in the abandoned village of Nahal Geshur.

As soon as their brush with the tanks of Major Ismail's 452nd Tank Battalion abated at about 2300 hours on October 6, the Israeli gunners arrayed north of Tel Faris resumed firing on targets to the east. However, in view of the Syrian penetrations, it was decided that the precious self-propelled guns would have to be withdrawn. The move began at 0200 hours on October 7.

A half-track led the way for the four self-propelled guns, another half-track, and an ammunition truck. When the officer in the lead half-track saw tanks in a night laager, he assumed they were friendly and proceeded through their encampment. The lead half-track and one of the self-propelled guns were able to get back to Tel Faris, but the remaining guns and vehicles were destroyed, fifteen Israelis were killed, and eleven Israelis were wounded.

From the moment Colonel Yitzhak Ben Shoham learned that Syrian tanks were passing the Hushniya–Petroleum crossroads, he did all he could to arrange for counterattacks. The complete absence of reserves in the Barak Brigade's sector didn't help.

Upon hearing that four disabled 53rd Tank Battalion Centurions were on the way to Naffach for repairs, Ben Shoham called his deputy, Lieutenant Colonel David Yisraeli, and told him, "I want Zvika. One vehicle or two."

"Zvika" was Lieutenant Zvi Greengold, and seven hours earlier he had been safely at home at Kibbutz Lochamei Hagetot, near the coastal city of Haifa. Greengold had just been released from service with Barak Brigade and was on a two-week leave preparatory to beginning a company commander's course. He was one of the first unattached personnel to make his own way to the battlefield, having donned his uniform and hitchhiked to Naffach. When he got there, he greeted the brigade commander, who was just departing, then sought out the Barak Brigade operations officer, Major Benny Katzin, and asked if there was any chance of his getting a command. There was nothing in the offing, so Zvika volunteered to help with the wounded who had begun pouring into the camp.

As soon as Lieutenant Colonel Yisraeli concluded his conversation with Ben Shoham, Yisraeli called Zvika aside and told him that the brigade commander wanted him to sweep along the Petroleum Road toward Tel Juhadar. Any tank at Naffach that could be armed and moved was to be designated Zvika Force.

Zvika first helped with the removal of two corpses from one of the tanks, then put together scratch crews from among numerous displaced tankers who had made their way to Naffach. Only two of the four Centurions could be made to run, so at 2100 hours on October 6, Zvika climbed aboard one of them and led the way out of Naffach along the Petroleum Road.

The Petroleum Road is a strange testament to the reality of the Middle East. It is nothing more than an access road between tall wire fences and runs a few feet to the east of the pipeline that has for years been carrying Arab oil through Israeli territory to ports on the Mediterranean. The Israelis are paid royalties for maintaining the pipeline and monitoring the flow of its precious contents. Indeed, though war had been raging for hours, the flow of oil had not ceased, nor would it.

At about 2120 hours, Zvika spotted a solitary Syrian tank on the road about four kilometers outside Naffach and only ten meters from his own Centurion. Zvika tapped his gunner, and the Syrian burst into flames. Fearful of being seen or set ablaze in the horrendous flash of burning fuel and munitions, Zvika ordered his driver to back up fast. Then he found that he had no way of communicating with the other tank nor even of speaking with his own crew. The shock of the explosion of the Syrian tank had jolted out the radio and intercom circuits. Zvika jumped down to the roadway and stalked over to the other Centurion, ejecting its commander and motioning him to climb aboard the defective tank. "Watch me," he cautioned the other man, "and do as I do, if possible."

Zvika Force resumed the drive southward on the Petroleum Road. Somehow, the second tank went astray in the darkness. After advancing several kilometers, Zvika spotted three tanks with sidelights ablaze as they roared out of the otherwise perfect darkness. The intruders belonged to 51st Independent Tank Brigade, and they were feeling their way into the Israeli rear, seeking to exploit the breakthrough. Apparently they had turned on their sidelights to see better, to gain speed. .

Zvika ordered his driver to stop. The 105mm gun at the young lieutenant's feet was trained out, and the first of the approaching targets was tracked. Three shots rang out, and all three targets were set ablaze in quick succession. They continued to burn until after sunrise.

The lone Centurion pulled over to the side of the road and went hull-down behind a tiny hummock. The four-man crew waited for nearly thirty minutes before spotting at least thirty tanks and numerous trucks sweeping up the roadway. It was as if the main body of Major Ismail's 452nd Tank Battalion was on parade, so perfectly aligned and spaced was the column.

Zvika waited until the lead tank was only twenty meters from where he was hunkered down. The first shot stopped the first target and stalled the entire column.

Zvika knew there was no way to win if he stood still, so he ordered his driver to poke around in the eerie gloom of firelight while he directed the gunner.

The Syrians were extremely bewildered by the single shots that kept hitting their tanks from all along the roadway. At length, several switched on searchlights to try to find a target. This gave Zvika's nerveless gunner unmistakable targets. Ten armored vehicles were destroyed or severely damaged before Major Ismail ordered the survivors to turn tail. The Syrian major had no idea that his efforts to sweep the road had been thwarted by four Israelis thrown together by pure chance.

Colonel Ben Shoham had left Tel Juhadar shortly after the resupply convoy that had first discovered Ismail's penetration. After driving cross-country in search of an adequate vantage point, the colonel had found the Gamla Rise, a lonely spot overlooking the Kinneret, a clear outlook on the road leading up to the Golan from Ein Gev. His brigade headquarters was one tank and a communications half-track. With these meager facilities, he had been calmly running the battle to save the southern Golan, speaking soothingly to rattled troop leaders as they called in on the tactical net, quietly arranging for artillery support and illumination, patiently attempting to master the eerily lighted or altogether darkened chessboard that was his area of responsibility. The brigade commander had been catching snatches of Zvika's reports almost from the time the eager young kid with red hair and freckles had left Naffach. He finally had to cut in at about 0200 hours on October 7, asking the "task force" commander how many tanks he had used to seal the Petroleum Road to the enemy brigade.

"My situation isn't good," Lieutenant Greengold admitted, "but I can't tell you how many."

The brigade commander accepted the answer, perhaps understanding both the gravity of Zvika's situation and the magnitude of his accomplishment in light of it.

Rather than continue up the Petroleum Road alone, Zvika chose a good defensive position and waited. He did not know it, but help was on the way.

· 11 ·

The summons of veteran crews to man the IDF's Reserve brigades had begun in mid-morning.

The Reservists were older than the conscripted crewmen manning the 7th and Barak Brigade Centurions, and there was little joy about being back in uniform. Some, like Amos Ben David, took the time to phone friends before leaving home. Others just said their good-byes and went off to their mobilization centers. For most, the juxtaposition of Yom Kippur observances and the mobilization imbued this call-up with a unique character.

The mobilization had a rhythm all its own. The armored infantrymen were called up after the tankers. This frustrated David Givati, who had to stand by at the window of his apartment and watch trucks arrive to pick up men with higher priorities. Givati decided to kill time with a nap, but he soon found himself pacing again. At last, there was the by-now welcome knock at his door. Another armored infantryman, Benjamin Sheskapovits, was at least as impatient. After waiting for hours, he declared to his wife, "If they don't come soon, I'll go myself." He was summoned a short time later.

Some men mobilized themselves. When Ehud Dafna heard of the mobilization, he telephoned around to locate "old buddies." He found they were on the way to the Golan, so he ventured from home on his own to join them. Giora Bierman, a staff officer, was in a hospital being treated for jaundice. He decided that his comrades needed him more than he needed perfect health, so he discharged himself to make his way to his depot. Each individual wrestled with problems and passages. Many talked and speculated as they waited for transportation at the pickup points. On the other hand, Sorial Birnbaum ignored the talkers as much as possible to concentrate on the observances of Sabbath and Yom Kippur that this great hubbub had interrupted.

A piece of paper, a phone call, or a verbal message does not begin to make a civilian a soldier, nor even a soldier a combatant. The man must leave his home with whatever necessary equipment he stores there, get to a pickup point, be transported to a depot, be recorded as present, and told what to do by the professional soldiers comprising his unit's permanent cadre. Where the system is working, the arriving Reservist finds all or most of his equipment neatly layed out, perhaps piled on the floor of a building, aligned with piles of equipment awaiting the arrival of the other members of his platoon or company. Personal weapons and ammunition must be issued from the armory, with all the required paperwork. Vehicles must be located, and last-minute provisioning and servicing must be undertaken. Where men are late or ill, or where there are unfilled gaps because of transfers or incomplete expansions, substitutes must be found and incorporated into vehicle crews or service and support units. Slowly the individuals are married to their organizations, and the organizations are rebuilt into cohesive fighting units. Within hours, commanders such as Moshe Waks, now Captain Waks once again, are able to declare, "The company's ready."

Naturally, the news that war had actually erupted added a great sense of urgency to what was, for many, a maddening interruption of the holy day observances or just plain real life. Somehow the government was replaced in evil mutterings by the many names Israelis have for their enemies.

Lieutenant Moshe Nir's company commander was vacationing outside Israel, so Nir was made acting company commander. While issuing orders, Nir was approached by one of his men, who clearly needed reassurance. "Do you know," the man asked, "there is a war?"

In an army where authorities habitually "look the other way" when men "organize" jeeps, half-tracks, and even tanks, improvising was second nature. For example, Lieutenant Shimon Ryan could not find his jeep, though he searched high and low through his unit's depot. Finally he went to his company commander and admitted failure. The company commander left Ryan, but returned only minutes later with a brand-new jeep he had stolen. (The owner found Ryan a month and a war later and, of course, demanded that he return the vehicle.)

Amos Ben David, Moshe Waks, Giora Bierman, Moshe Nir, and Shimon Ryan had no inkling that the hundreds of tiny decisions they made in those first, critical hours would substantially reverse the course of the war. They hurried through the familiar process because there was a war on, but they were not fully aware of the ultimate importance those preparations were becoming to senior commanders.

Out of the chaos of thousands of individual arrivals, Northern Command anticipated that three fully constituted Reserve brigades —the 679th, the 9th, and the 70th—and two separate Reserve battalions would deploy on the Golan before nightfall of October 7. As it turned out, this was about twenty-eight hours after the onset of the war. The 159 tanks assigned to the Reserve units would nearly equal the number of tanks Northern Command had been able to deploy on the Golan at the moment the war started.

There were considerable differences among the Reserve units. Colonel Gideon Gordon's 70th Armored Infantry Brigade was a unit that time had forgotten. Indeed, there were plans to disband it because it was equipped with unmodified World War II–vintage Sherman tanks and equally ancient M3 half-tracks. The troops still wore old football-type helmets rather than the modern plastic headgear that had been issued almost universally throughout the IDF armored and mechanized units. All things considered, the brigade was a perfect snapshot of a 1963-vintage formation. It was thought that 70th Brigade could be called upon to defend prepared positions or guard lines of communications, but no one believed the unit could be effectively or even safely employed in the attack.

In sharp contrast, Colonel Mordechai Ben Porat's 9th Armored Infantry Brigade, also equipped with Shermans, was perceived as being a useful striking force. The Shermans had been upgunned and extensively and expensively modernized, and the troops were younger than the veterans of 70th Brigade. Moreover, 9th Brigade had long been a stalwart fighting force, nearly always operating in Northern Command. Most of the officers and troops had trained on the Golan and knew their way around.

Colonel Uri Orr's 679th Armored Brigade, a relatively new formation, was equipped with early-model Centurion tanks that had been scheduled to be upgraded over the next few years. The crews were composed of younger men. In all, 679th Brigade was considered to be only marginally inferior to Barak Brigade.

The two separate Reserve battalions—71st Armored Infantry Battalion, under Lieutenant Colonel Yoav Vaspe, and an unnumbered tank battalion directly attached to Northern Command—were perceived as absolutely first-rate units. Seventy-first Battalion, which featured two organic tank companies and one APC company, was earmarked for direct attachment to Barak Brigade. The Northern Command Tank Battalion, commanded by Lieutenant Colonel Uzi More, was equipped with thoroughly updated Centurions; officially it was to operate as a weapon of opportunity under the direct control of Northern Command headquarters. Both of the separate Reserve battalions had trained specifically for assignment to the Golan.

Brigadier General Rafoul Eitan was emerging as the sparkplug running the Israeli engine of war. A parachute officer, Eitan had trained for many years in the art of instant assessment of battlefield puzzles and the fine art of rapidly moving troops and equipment to solve them. While fellow paratrooper Major General Yitzhak Hofi kept his attention riveted to the larger panorama, and his ear glued to the phone linking him with the chief of staff and the government, Eitan focused his energies and powers of concentration on the shifting events and fragmentary reports from the hard-hit bunkers and tank battalions.

At length, his observations caused him to place an urgent call to the Reserve tank unit whose depot was nearest the Golan. He asked that a force—any force, really—be immediately dispatched to the heights.

Colonel Ran Sarig, who was supervising the mobilization of the separate tank battalion, was more surprised by the locale to which the troops were to be sent than he was by the immediacy of Eitan's request.

The mobilization was proceeding more rapidly than usual. If crew integrity and unit cohesion were disregarded, men and machines could be made available to Eitan.

Colonel Sarig, a highly skilled professional armor officer well schooled in *his* branch's doctrine of applying mass on the battlefield, asked Eitan if it was indeed desirable to divide even the few tanks he could then scrape together. Eitan confirmed his feelings that in this case it certainly was.

At that moment, Sarig could field just eight Centurions to meet Eitan's requirements. If no tragedy befell it, the stopgap force would reach the front sometime early Sunday morning.

The dispatch of the first group of eight tanks was yet another pressure on the Reservists still mobilizing. The yelling and prodding were not part of the time-honored exercise of hurry up and wait. The troops fully comprehended the urgency of the orders and oaths. They felt needed. The Syrian breakthrough near Hushniya showed them just how crucial their presence on the battlefield might be. Colonel Yitzhak Ben Shoham had succinctly stated his priorities: "One tank or two."

Under the direct leadership of the separate battalion's commander, Lieutenant Colonel Uzi More, the eight Centurions ascended the Golan escarpment to Vasit and then proceeded southward along the Petroleum Road to link up with Zvika Force.

By the time More reached Zvika, a second group of fourteen Centurions was on the way up the escarpment. They were under the command of More's deputy, Major Baruch Lenschner, and Captain Moshe Waks. General Hofi considered Lenschner's force—Baruch Force—"a big force." The commanding general felt it was what he needed to confront the Syrian breakthrough at Hushniya.

Colonel Ben Shoham requested the use of "More Force" in an immediate counterattack against the Syrians holding the Petroleum–Hushniya crossroads. In Ben Shoham's reading of the battle, time was a greater factor than mass. As he told Hofi, "What we can do now, we might not be able to do later." As Baruch Force was well on the way, Hofi sanctioned Ben Shoham's immediate night counterattack with More's eight Centurions.

As soon as More was briefed by Zvika, he decided to attack in two columns. Zvika would have four tanks in the right column, and More would lead the other five on the left.

The attack commenced immediately. The first tank in Zvika's column was set ablaze by a rocket-propelled grenade.

When Zvika saw that the road ahead was blocked by Syrian tanks equipped with searchlights, he took a short break to think things through. Then he ordered one of the remaining tanks forward to rescue the crew of the burning Centurion, and he positioned his own tank to cover the flank.

Both tanks—Zvika's and the rescue tank—were hit. Zvika's gunner was injured, and the lieutenant felt the shock of the blast and a searing pain. He pulled himself out of the turret and clumsily somersaulted to the ground. Zvika lay flat for a moment and collected his wits, but the realization that he was next to a burning tank that might explode at any moment was sufficient to goad him to his feet. He unthinkingly ran straight toward the Syrians, then cut back to the last tank in his column. He had been wounded in the upper left arm and the left side of his face, but he felt no need to be evacuated. He climbed aboard the last battleworthy Centurion in his column and ordered its commander to turn around and leave the vicinity of the fight.

Unbeknownst to Zvika, the Syrians had redeployed following his abortive attack. He had found them roadbound, lined up in column preparatory to moving. The attack had been misread by the Syrian 452nd Tank Battalion commander, Major Farouk Ismail, who assumed he had faced a more significant enemy force. Ismail decided to wait for daylight before moving on, and he ordered his troop leaders to establish defensive positions along a front of two kilometers.

Lieutenant Colonel More's five-tank attack followed Zvika's by a lengthy interval. It did a great deal to confirm Ismail's convictions, but the initial contact upset More, who reasoned that his attack was based upon faulty information with respect to the Syrian disposition and, it appeared, the composition of the Syrian force. In the heat of his brief, sharp fight, Zvika had not observed the mechanized infantry accompanying Ismail's tanks.

More's tanks were hit and disabled, one at a time. When the battalion commander saw a Syrian aim an antitank rocket at his command tank, he grabbed hold of his free machine gun and opened fire. But the machine gun jammed and the Syrian grenadier let fly. Uzi More lost an arm and an eye in the blast.

Zvika emerged from the dark, standing erect in the turret of the only Centurion to survive his column's abortive attack. He reached Colonel Ben Shoham by radio and reported the destruction of More Force.

For his part, Ben Shoham acknowledged that what could not be done immediately would have to be done later. He raised Eitan on the command net and told him of the failed counterattack, suggesting that Baruch Force be split to reinforce Zvika on the Petroleum Force. The balance of Major Lenschner's tanks would establish defensive positions on the Sindiana Road.

At this stage of his holding battle, Eitan discarded specific limited counterattacks to establish a coherent defensive line through the southern Golan. What Eitan proposed was a considerable undertaking in light of the numbers and dispositions of men and equipment and the complexity of moving them through the darkened battle area. Eitan laid out a new defense line from Bunker 110, on the east, through Tel Yosifon to the Kuzabia crossroads, on the west. The line was then extended southward, through the waterfall area to Tel Bazak and on to the El Al Ridge. The forces involved were not large, but they incorporated Regulars and Reservists in six distinct movements and concentrations.

The southern anchor of Eitan's new line was manned by Lieutenant Colonel Yair Yaron's 50th Parachute Battalion, which still could field several APC-borne infantry squads in the vicinity of Ramat Magshimim and Tel Saki.

In addition, Yaron unknowingly and quite temporarily received some assistance in the form of several jeeps and APCs manned by Israeli border patrolmen. Without bothering to inform their own headquarters, much less Yaron's, the inquisitive patrolmen had simply gravitated toward the sound of the guns. In time, they bumped into Syrian tanks. Amid the heated exchange of gunfire and crude

Arabic epithets on the El Al Ridge, the border patrolmen did the sensible thing and fled.

Slightly to the north of Yaron, on a dirt trail known as the Waterfall Route, was Colonel Ben Shoham, with his command tank and communications half-track. Nearby, at Tel Bazak, artillerymen who had been forced to give way earlier were at work on a new battery-site. To Ben Shoham's northwest was the Arik Bridge, the southernmost Jordan crossing in the Golan sector. The route from the bridge was the most direct from the Jordan Valley to the Hushniya area, so Eitan used it to dispatch Major Gideon Weiler's force of Centurions from the Armor School Tank Battalion to establish a blocking position dominating the Tel Zohar–Kuzabia crossroads. Northeast of Weiler's position was Baruch Force, fourteen Northern Command Tank Battalion Centurions deployed to cover the two roads leading from Hushniya.

Paralleling Ben Shoham's and Eitan's concerns for time and movement, Colonel Hassan Tourkmani's 9th Infantry Division sought to exploit the Hushniya breakthrough. Checked to the north and west by the Northern Command Tank Battalion, Tourkmani ordered the 43rd Mechanized Brigade tank battalion to advance up the Rafid–Kuneitra Road.

This movement was spotted by Israelis manning a nearby outpost, and a highly accurate report claiming an attack by forty Syrian tanks was flashed to General Eitan. Tourkmani had managed to find the one approach that the Israelis had not covered.

Eitan wrestled with finding a way to block this new threat. The Reservists were too far to the west to be of any use in countering Tourkmani's new thrust, and Ben Shoham had absolutely nothing left to spare. Eitan called Colonel Ben Gal of 7th Armored Brigade and ordered him to assume responsibility for the Rafid–Kuneitra Road.

Ben Gal earlier had kept back Captain Meir "Tiger" Zamir's company of 82nd Tank Battalion as his unofficial reserve. He now ordered Major Eitan Kauli to use Zamir's company to stop the Syrian advance.

Tiger Zamir deployed two tanks abreast Bunker 109 as a rear guard, two more tanks on the same hill but farther south, and a single Centurion on a small hill across and overlooking the roadway. The deputy commander was given four tanks and sent to another small hill a mile to the south, from which he was to trigger the ambush Zamir had in mind.

When all the tanks had been deployed, Tiger returned to the position abreast Bunker 109 in his own tank and ordered all crews to shut down and wait in total silence for the approach of the Syrian column and the illumination of his deputy's searchlight.

The Syrians rolled down the road oblivious to the waiting Israelis. Though Tiger had planned to contain all the Syrian tanks between the ends of his ambush, he had to allow a dozen of them to pass through the head of the ambush before the last of them passed the deputy commander. The gunners were losing their minds, so great was the tension of having to wait with so many good targets so easy to reach.

The searchlight snapped on, followed by the instantaneous bark of a 105mm tank gun. Every Israeli gunner had been tracking targets, so all opened fire within a matter of seconds. Beneath their seats, to the right, the well-drilled loaders rammed home fresh antitank rounds and hit the gunners to let them know they could resume firing. Load, fire, train, load, fire, train. The gunners and loaders worked in superb harmony as the deputy company commander illuminated the roadway.

The Syrians returned fire, but the Israelis were hull-down, virtually impossible to spot—except for the deputy commander, whose searchlight drew heavy fire. Suddenly the light snapped off. Zamir first feared that his gunners would be unable to acquire targets, but there was more than enough light from blazing hulks.

When nearly twenty-five Syrian tanks had been destroyed, Tiger reorganized his company and led it southward to get at the survivors. To his surprise, his entire company still was operational, including the deputy commander's tank. This last both relieved and upset Zamir, who asked the lieutenant why he had shut off the light. The man mumbled that it was dangerous.

The lieutenant was both right and wrong. Zvika earlier had used Syrian searchlights to acquire targets, and Tiger's ambush certainly had been successful because the roadway was amply lighted by burning tanks. However, Tiger felt that his deputy had given in to his fears before the company could safely do without the light. As an officer, Tiger reasoned, his deputy had a prime responsibility to the mission and only secondarily to himself.

Eitan's calculated maneuvering and the timely introduction of the first tiny Reserve formations had contained the Hushniya break-through, but a threat to the north still had to be eradicated with the resources at hand.

Brigadier General Omar Abrash committed his 7th Infantry Division's 78th Tank Brigade in the northern sector of the northern Golan at 2200 hours, about the time Lieutenant Zvika Greengold was blunting 51st Tank Brigade's advance.

Abrash was hours behind schedule, but he expected to make up the lost time if 78th Tank Brigade could reach and secure the Kuneitra–Masada Road, four and a half kilometers west of its starting line. If the road could be secured, the Israeli defenses in the northern Golan would certainly collapse.

The Syrian government had been at pains to ensure the success of their fighting units, seeing to it that the assault brigades were equipped with the latest and best equipment available from the Soviet Union.

Since their introduction in France in 1916, tracked armored fighting vehicles have been extremely vulnerable in night actions, particularly night actions orchestrated to break into an enemy position rather than merely move along a single axis of advance. Night, like built-up areas, further reduces the limited visibility of drivers, gunners, and commanders of armored fighting vehicles, and especially when, as with the Syrians, the vehicles operate while "buttoned up." The advantage is with the infantryman equipped and trained to fight tanks.

The resources lavished upon 78th Tank Brigade typified the care with which the Syrian planners had gone about the commitment of their resources. Each of the brigade's ninety-five T-55s was equipped with a specially designed infrared nightscope, purchased and installed to extend the effective combat hours during which a 78th Tank Brigade tank could be used. Even given the presence of these special tools, however, General Abrash's decision to commit 78th Brigade to a night attack was a bold one.

The Israelis were the acknowledged experts of post–World War II armored warfare, and they were conservative in comparison to the Syrians, who designed 78th Tank Brigade and its night-fighting mission. The Israeli tanks were in no way prepared to mount night armored attacks. However, though they were about to be technically outmatched, the Israelis were equipped with something the Syrians lacked, and that is the years and years of training and, more important, direct experience in developing and utilizing armored warfare tactics.

There is no name for the defensive strategy the Israelis employed on the Golan, but in many ways its precepts were even more radical than the Syrian notion of equipping a first-line brigade specifically to fight a night break-in battle. Both by default and design, the Israelis had adopted the principle of employing the tank as the main instrument of defense in darkness. The primary drawback to the Israeli defensive strategy was the limited night-fighting capability of their tanks and crews.

With the exception of the bunkers and village defensive positions, the entire Israeli defensive force was capable of movement. Tanks, self-propelled artillery, infantry, and armored infantry were all in motion, or could be on short notice. Artillery batteries moved, set up, fired, rested, moved, and fired again in no particular sequence. A tank company could move, attack, and move again within minutes of receiving an order. While fixed by a foundation of bunker complexes, the entire firepower of the Israeli battle force could move from one fulcrum to another in an infinite variety of combinations.

An attacker could never be certain just what combination he might encounter. It was a strategy based upon mobility and the paramount Israeli requirement that the expense in men and equipment be minimal.

The soldiers of Colonel Avigdor Ben Gal's 7th Armored Brigade were aware that they were disadvantaged by the Syrians' use of "cat's eye" equipment. However, the confrontation was to take place in bright moonlight.

Seventy-eighth Tank Brigade crossed through the Israeli minefields and over the remains of the antitank ditch. Protected by concentrated artillery fire, the T-55s moved up the valley between the Hermonit and the Booster position just 2.5 kilometers from the Kuneitra–Masada Road.

To compensate for the Syrian advantages, Colonel Ben Gal had to divert his meager artillery resources from fire missions to illumination. In addition, the Israeli artillerymen were told to remain silent until the Syrians were well within range, to maximize the shock as well as the accuracy of the fire.

The Syrian tanks were within eight hundred meters of the Israeli defensive positions by 2200 hours.

All battles are confusing to the participants, and night battles are the most confusing. Syrian and Israeli tank commanders and drivers strained to see the next obstacles. Simply handling armored vehicles in off-road conditions requires unparalleled concentration, exceptional sensitivity, and constant adjustment. Driving a tank cross-country in the dark creates enormous mental strain.

The Syrians and Israelis lost vehicles just moving toward one another in the dark. Captain Yair Sweet, one of Lieutenant Colonel Avigdor Kahalani's 77th Tank Battalion company commanders, was under orders to move to the Booster position to reinforce a 74th Tank Battalion unit there. Sweet lost two of his precious Centurions to the terrain. One crew was able to extricate its tank and use it to pull the second one free, but the delay drove Kahalani to distraction. Lieutenant Ami Doron, deputy commander of another of Kahalani's companies, spent hours retrieving two Centurions that became stuck just south of the Hermonit. A tank from Captain Menachem Albert's company fell into a shell crater on the eastern outskirts of Kuneitra and had to be abandoned. Sergeant Ami Bashari moved into a prepared position at the base of the Hermonit at twilight, but two of the six tanks with which he had moved were by then out of the battle, hung up on rocks.

Sergeant Bashari first spotted the oncoming T-55s of 78th Tank Brigade, at a range of fifteen hundred meters. Bashari's gunner and the others took up a methodical, paced fire, destroying one Syrian tank after another as they closed to within three hundred meters.

After Bashari had directed his gunner to destroy ten of the T-55s, he was himself killed by shrapnel. His body fell from the open turret hatch into the tank, scaring the gunner and loader into believing the tank had been hit. The two abandoned the vehicle, though it was otherwise in fighting trim. The driver was ordered to withdraw to the Vasit crossroads but became lost in the dark and ran the Centurion off the road. He abandoned it, leaving Bashari's body.

Lieutenant Colonel Yosef Aldar, commander of 75th Armored Infantry Battalion and responsible for the area penetrated by 78th Tank Brigade, was wounded during the fight, so Colonel Ben Gal ordered Lieutenant Colonel Kahalani to assume responsibility for standing against the oncoming T-55s. At that moment, Kahalani's companies were scattered across seventeen kilometers of front, between the Hermonit and Bunker 109.

Captain Yair Sweet's company had only just completed its tortuous deployment along the ridge between the Hermonit and Booster at 2200 and had yet to locate adequate fighting positions. Kahalani, who had accompanied Sweet from the Booster, was unable to see enough to run the local fighting. So, utilizing the darkness, he ordered Sweet and Lieutenant Ami Doron to shut off all engines and lights. After a while, however, the battalion commander noticed a light. He contacted his officers to be certain they had obeyed his order. They reported that their tanks were shut down, as ordered. Kahalani was annoyed because he could still see the light, but both officers continued to avow their innocence. At last, Kahalani entertained the notion that he might be witnessing a Syrian tank—or a lost Israeli tank that had not received his order to shut down.

There was only one thing to do. One of Sweet's tanks was ordered to flick on its searchlight while Kahalani's own gunner brought his 105mm gun to bear on the light. At Kahalani's order, the searchlight picked out a T-55, which was destroyed.

A second T-55 moving around the first was caught in the glare of the fire and knocked out by one of Sweet's gunners at under a hundred meters.

Next, two T-55s passed right through Lieutenant Doron's position, just to the south of the Hermonit. They were spotted in plenty of time, but Kahalani decided to let them pass to prevent the larger force of Syrians to the rear from locating his waiting Centurions. The two intruders returned through Doron's line in about an hour. No other Syrians had followed them, leaving the Israelis with the impression that the two had been lost.

Elsewhere, a Syrian antitank unit sought to advance down the B'not Yaacov Road—right in front of Bunker 107. When Sergeant Nissan Avidan saw the roadbound column heading right for him—it was evident the Syrians did not know the bunker was occupied—he opened fire with his heavy machine gun and flamed two trucks. A nearby Centurion platoon was drawn by the action and contributed to the carnage. After a brief interval, the surviving Syrians retreated on foot after abandoning all their equipment.

For the time being, at any rate, 78th Tank Brigade and supporting units hunkered down. Night-vision apparatus or not, unexpected resistance was taking too great a toll.

· 13 ·

The small Israeli garrison at the Hermon compound—technicians and infantrymen—buttoned itself inside the bunkers when the Syrian artillery bombardment began at 1400 hours on October 6. After a while, the station commander, Captain "Haggai," and his deputy, Lieutenant David Nachliel, went outside to observe as much as possible. Within minutes, the two were forced to return to the safety of the bunker, explaining, "No one can stay outside; it's certain death." Thus the position dubbed "the Eyes of the State of Israel" was rendered sightless.

Israeli observation outposts on the Hermon reported in quick succession that helicopters were approaching from the Syrian Hermon.

The Hermon bunkers had been constructed largely with the help of Druse villagers living on the Golan. Colonel Hikmat Shahabi, chief of Syrian Military Intelligence, had sent a letter in April 1970 through Sergeant Major Nozi Tewfik Aba Saleh, a Syrian Druse, to Kamal Kanj, a respected Golani Druse leader and a former member of the Syrian parliament whose brother, Nur el Din Kani, was a general in the Syrian Army. Saleh, who was also related to Kanj, crossed the border on foot to make the delivery. The letter asked Kanj to forward details pertaining to Israeli defensive positions, a proposal to which Kanj readily agreed. He carried out his mission until arrested by Israeli Military Intelligence in May 1971. (Kanj was pardoned in June 1973.)

Elements of the Syrian 82nd Parachute Regiment planned and mounted a precisely detailed heliborne assault of the Israeli Golan, employing data collected through Kamal Kanj.

Four Soviet-built MI-8 helicopters had been airborne for nearly two hours before being spotted by Israeli observers on the Golan. After lift-off near Damascus, the helicopters had flown west into Lebanon and circled until forty-five minutes into the massive pre-assault bombardment on the Golan. The aircraft then headed southeast to commence the long approach on the Israeli complex.

If the Israelis had pinpointed the flight, it is certain they would have linked it to the Syrian war effort and launched fighters to destroy the easy prey. As it was, however, no Israelis spotted the four helicopters until nearly 1500 hours, when the outpost at Har Dov and then a three-man team at the ski lift a mile from the electronic-warfare bunker reported their sightings.

The Israelis at the ski lift fired at the helicopters, but the big machines soon flew from sight as they continued downslope. At this juncture one of the big MI-8s inexplicably blew up in midair.

While the assault teams aboard the helicopters closed on the Israeli Hermon, the bulk of the 82nd Parachute Regiment assault force, under cover of the artillery bombardment, climbed the last few hundred meters toward the Israeli compound. These crack soldiers had been at it nearly all day.

Captain Jassam al Salah, commanding the point company, found "the door to the Israeli position wide open."

The Israelis manned their fighting positions, certain they would be facing, at most, a few dozen heliborne commandos. However, they found themselves confronting Captain Salah's company and the many, many Syrians behind it.

The Israelis could bring to bear the firepower of but one heavy machine gun and one automatic rifle, plus the short-range Uzi submachine guns in the hands of the Golani Brigade infantrymen. The machine gunner was among the first casualties, and two other fighters had to be released to carry him to the aid station. Unbelievably, one of the men who went with the dying gunner was the bunker commander, Captain Haggai.

Much of the initial fighting took place around the observation point. Captain Salah and Captain Mahmoud Ma'aleh, commander of the second Syrian company, were both wounded, but the speed and mass of the Syrian drive, together with the parachutists' superb fire control, soon gained the upper hand. The Syrians were dressed in dusty-brown commando uniforms, which blended so perfectly with the rocky landscape that their positions could, in the words of one defender, "be gauged only by the flare of their gunfire."

The Israelis were forced deep into the bowels of the bunker complex after only forty-five minutes of fighting. This provided the Syrians with complete access to the area on top of and around the Israeli bunkers. In time, the invaders cautiously probed into the first-floor rooms of the complex, discovering that they had been abandoned.

The game by nightfall was cat-and-mouse. Each time an Israeli entered a corridor, he was driven back by massive Syrian gunfire. Sometimes the Syrians combing the upper floor would drop a hand grenade down one of the air vents. Most important, the Israelis had lost their cohesion. They had taken refuge in a number of rooms, and each little group was utterly isolated from the others. When they learned they could not venture from their rooms, they passively sat in the dark concrete crypts.

It is one of the Israeli Army's great strengths that every man, no matter what his rank or station, may contribute to discussions impacting upon common problems. This trait is paramount in Israeli society and, while officers are ultimately responsible for making decisions, everyone and anyone who has an opinion is encouraged to voice it—indeed, to defend it as vocally as possible in the face of conflicting opinions.

It remained clear through the early evening that the only real hope lay in a successful Israeli counterattack from the Golan. No one in the bunkers had any notion as to the massive tank battles being waged just to the south. In time, however, the various discussions focused upon what must be done. Some thought it best to wait for help. Others were not so sure help would come. Several optimists ventured that the bunkers had been cleared of Syrians, that it might be safe to leave the locked rooms. Others brought up the idea of surrender, but this suggestion was parried by serious questions regarding the potential sincerity of any Syrians who might accept surrenders. A small core thought aloud of breaking out, and these men turned their attention to technical details, chiefly the definition of a route down the darkened mountainside.

While the Israelis debated, the Syrians strove to secure the entire complex. When Captains Salah and Ma'aleh were wounded, command of the assault force fell to Lieutenant Naif al-Aqual, who oversaw the seizure of all the outer buildings and encirclement of the compound as well as the ongoing cat-and-mouse maneuvers within the bunker complex. Lieutenant Ahmad Rifai Jojo, leader of the helicopter assault, oversaw the occupation of the upper ski lift and the securing of the upper approaches to the bunker complex.

It was bitter cold on the Hermon that night, so the Syrian soldiers were thankful for the fine Israeli blankets that fell into their hands. Overall, the Syrians enjoyed high morale, both as a result of their relatively cheap partial victory—the Israeli electronic-warfare capability had been negated—and because the information they had received in great detail was entirely accurate.

Captain Haggai decided to break out. He knew a bit more than the Syrians about the layout of the bunker complex, so managed to lead twenty men to the outside. The group immediately spotted three Syrian soldiers, but everyone crawled past their position without making a sound. The fence surrounding the compound had been breached in several places during the Syrian assault, and one of these portals was used as an exit.

Haggai deliberately led his men upslope in the hope of eluding sentries no doubt expecting a breakout on the downhill side of the compound. He managed to reach the upper level of the ski-lift terminus within about ninety minutes. It was nearly midnight when Haggai ordered his men to head downslope.

The long, silent line was suddenly riddled by gunfire put out by commandos under Lieutenant Jojo.

Some of the Israelis fell to the ground to escape the gunfire. Others died where they stood or fell. Lieutenant David Nachliel did the unexpected by opening fire with his Uzi submachine gun and charging Syrians who were firing at him.

Doron Sharfman, who was wounded in the initial outburst, was helped away from the killing ground by another soldier. The two met up with David Nachliel, and all three continued downslope. They were joined by Captain Haggai moments before being ambushed once again by Syrians. The four broke free and continued their flight down the mountain. Haggai assumed responsibility for Sharfman, at times literally dragging the injured man across the rough, steeply sloping ground. They were fired on once more in the dark—by a jumpy Centurion tank commander.

A fifth member of the escape party joined Haggai in safety soon after. Three others reached the Israeli settlement of Nevi Ativ, and two more arrived at another Israeli-held position. A lone straggler came in much later. All told, eleven of the twenty survived and reached safety. The other nine died on the ski slope.

Golani Brigade commander Colonel Amir Drori had the tally by midmorning of October 7: Thirty-four of his countrymen were as yet unaccounted for in the Hermon Bunker. A position had fallen and the commanding officer had left subordinates behind, an altogether miserable performance.

It is true that Haggai's defense force was badly understrength and that 17th Infantry Battalion had erred, perhaps fatally, in failing to dispatch the reinforcements required by the Alert Gimmel plan. Haggai did the best he could for the men in his care, most of whom were noncombatants, specialists with little training in self-defense. There were not enough weapons to go around, and too few of sufficient caliber to serve as a basis of a serious defensive effort. Haggai had ordered everyone inside during the bombardment, a decision for which he can be only partly faulted; he had no more idea he was facing total war than did thousands of his countrymen locked in massive tank battles on the Golan. He had, however, left his fighters without his guidance when he helped convey the mortally wounded machine gunner to the aid station. That was foolish. He had led all the men he could find in a reasonable bid to escape, an act that would no doubt have been seen as courageous had it come to less grief. Certainly his devotion to saving the life of Doron

Sharfman was exemplary in the extreme. But, when all was said and done, Haggai's public fate was sealed by just four words uttered by one Israeli soldier and believed by most Israelis: "The officers ran away."

· 3 ·
BREAKTHROUGH

· 14 ·

olonel Hassan Tourkmani, commanding 9th Syrian Infantry Division, strove mightily through the first night of the war to exploit the breakthrough of 51st Independent Tank Brigade near Hushniya. In rapid order, 9th Infantry Division units had bypassed Bunker 111, secured one crossroad on the Rafid–Kuneitra route, overcome the Hushniya military camp, and secured another crossroad on the Petroleum Road. The fact that all of these accomplishments had been planned in advance did not detract from the actual performance. Tourkmani's tanks and mechanized infantry had secured the only road into the Israeli rear open to any Syrian, had split the Israeli defensive forces, and now threatened the command center at Naffach.

The failure of 5th and 7th Syrian Infantry divisions to secure roadways in their sectors shaped the continuation of 9th Infantry Division's thrust.

Shortly after midnight, an Israeli radio operator began broadcasting orders to units in the area between the El Al and Arik Bridge roads. Syrian Intelligence believed the broadcasts to be deliberately misleading and that no significant forces were operating in that particular area. In fact, since 5th Infantry Division still had to grapple with achieving access either to the Rafid or the Petroleum Road, it fell upon Tourkmani to secure his own flank. Thus 9th Infantry Division reconnaissance units began probing south and west toward El Al shortly after dawn.

This was one of the most exhilarating assignments drawn by Syrians during the entire war. It became apparent as they fanned out that the area was devoid of organized Israeli tank forces. The radio broadcasts had indeed been a hoax. The first Syrians to reach the escarpment had a breathtaking view of the Kinneret and the Jordan Valley. The natural splendor of the lush green fields and deep blue waters was enhanced by the realization that retaking the Golan was within their grasp.

With his southern flank secured, Colonel Tourkmani detached fifteen T-55s to secure the only roadway necessary for the defense of 9th Infantry Division's western flank. This element of 51st Independent Tank Brigade moved almost due west on the Hushniya–Arik Bridge Road until it spotted an Israeli blocking force between Tel Zohar and the Kuzabia crossroads. The Syrian commander led his tanks off the roadway and quickly downslope across broken fields. The Israelis—a four-tank platoon led by Major Gideon Weiler of the Armor School Tank Battalion—got off only a few rounds before the Syrians were out of sight. Once beyond range, the Syrians veered back to the roadway and rapidly advanced toward their objective.

Meanwhile, Israeli Colonel Ran Sarig, with Major Giora Bierman and Captain Amos Ben David, led the very last tanks of the Northern Command Tank Battalion across the Arik Bridge. Sarig planned to lead these Centurions in a counterattack directly against the Syrians at the Hushniya–Petroleum crossroads. However, Sarig was not informed of the brief clash at the Kuzabia crossroads, so he set off unknowingly into the teeth of the fifteen advancing Syrian T-55s.

As Sarig's tanks advanced, they "acquired" with the help of a senior officer a jeepborne infantry reconnaissance company. Thus was born "Sarig Force."

By the time Sarig Force reached the escarpment, at about 0520 hours, the fifteen T-55s from 9th Infantry Division's 51st Independent Tank Brigade had advanced over six of the twelve miles it needed to control the bridge route.

The two forces nearly collided before either was aware of the other. Gunfire broke out spontaneously, and both columns deliberately unraveled onto the roadway, the shoulders, and the fields on either flank.

Ran Sarig reported to Northern Command headquarters at 0520 that he had been engaged by Syrian tanks in a small valley at sea level just three miles east of the Arik Bridge. Headquarters staffers were utterly shocked by the news. Tourkmani's tankers had come close to attaining the ultimate coup of the war.

Sarig Force made short work of the fifteen T-55s, destroying all of them in proximity to the Kuzabia crossroads.

The long hours of darkness had worked as Israel's ally, but they also contributed to Israeli illusions. Major General Yitzhak Hofi's Northern Front headquarters had firmly believed that Sarig's tanks would be able to seal the 51st Tank Brigade penetration at dawn.

Just after 0600 hours, less than thirty minutes after Sarig's awful report, Lieutenant Colonel Oded Eres of 53rd Tank Battalion shattered what few illusions remained at headquarters by reporting that the Centurions he had deployed along the frontier in the Rafid Gap were incapable of holding the line any longer. He offered to concentrate his waning tank force at Tel Faris to maintain a limited defense, or to wage a fighting withdrawal. In no event, he avowed, could he hold where he was, because his limited forces were spread too thinly.

Eres had begun October 7 in a positive frame of mind, even in view of all he and his battalion had endured through the previous afternoon and the long, bloody night. His first act, when the sun came up, was to request an immediate air strike against Syrian tanks threatening to overrun his lines. The request was fulfilled almost immediately by a flight of four A-4 Skyhawk fighter-bombers. But the heartening arrival of the Israeli jets was dampened when the telltale streaks of surface-to-air missiles crisscrossed the dawn sky, testifying to the destruction of all four of the Skyhawks. Two other Skyhawks from a second four-plane strike were shot down minutes later.

As if to clinch the matter it became apparent at about the same time that Lieutenant Colonel Yair Yaron's 50th Parachute Battalion could not hold the El Al Ridge.

* * *

By daylight, Lieutenant Boaz Tamir was commanding the only Israeli tank remaining on the Petroleum Road near the Purple Line. When he saw a fresh formation of sixty Syrian tanks coming right at his lone Centurion, he contacted Lieutenant Colonel Eres on the tactical net and asked for all the help the battalion commander could muster. Eres detached one Centurion and a half-track.

Both Tamir and Eres realized the absurdity of this token reinforcement, and Eres asked Northern Command for permission to withdraw the remnants of his shattered battalion. Tamir's response was to send the half-track back to relative safety and prepare his two tanks for a final stand.

Tamir's tank was hit within moments. Then hit again. And again. And yet again. Incredibly, it could still function despite the death of the loader. Tamir directed his gunner in firing several more antitank rounds before a fifth hit rendered the battered Centurion useless. The accompanying tank also was hit several times, but it, too, continued to fire. Tamir traded places with the other tank commander and ordered the man to withdraw with Tamir's tank. The second tank was hit again within minutes and had to be abandoned. Boaz Tamir helped a wounded crewman to a nearby Israeli position and collapsed with a deep sigh. The Syrians had bludgeoned an opening on the Petroleum Road.

Enter Moshe Dayan.

Virtually every Israeli officer and soldier on the Golan had grown to manhood in the defense minister's long shadow. The young soldiers had been children when the man with the black eyepatch, then chief of staff, had led his nation's army in the breathtaking sweep across Sinai in 1956. As teenagers in June 1967, they had seen the minister of defense in ecstatic prayer at the Wailing Wall, the center and symbol of a reunited Jerusalem. Dayan was a man whose life spanned the birth of modern Israel; to most Israelis he was a symbol of the living nation.

If ever there was a moment for Moshe Dayan to weave his magic, this was it.

But Dayan had no magic, no word of insight or encouragement. He had, less than twenty-four hours in a distant past, presided over a crucial meeting with his mind engulfed by "small things," the evacuation of women and children from the Golan settlements. The women and children were safe, but their homes had been abandoned and, in some cases, destroyed by Syrian artillery fire.

The defense minister understood at once that the key to holding the Golan was now the Israeli Air Force. No time could be wasted on the niceties of convention, so he placed a direct call to Brigadier General Benny Peled, the Air Force commander, and told him to send his warplanes into immediate, continuous action against the Syrian tank formations that had breached the Israeli line. He emphasized that only Peled's force could possibly stop the Syrian advance.

Dayan's call to Peled set off a command crisis that almost surpassed in noise the cacophony of the Syrian attacks. The defense minister had supplanted Chief of Staff Dado Elazar by imposing an operational decision upon the IAF. Moreover, Dayan had gone over the head of the regional commander, Major General Yitzhak Hofi.

Before leaving Tel Aviv for the Golan, Dayan had specifically questioned Elazar as to the fitness of parachutist Hofi to oversee an essentially armored conflict. Elazar had made it abundantly clear that he supported Hofi, but Dayan remained unconvinced that either Hofi or Elazar fully grasped the reality of the Syrian penetration. Dayan was also upset that Elazar—who was, after all, running a war on two fronts—was not sufficiently concerned to fly to the Golan with him for an on-site inspection. Shocked by what he found, Dayan simply bypassed Hofi and Elazar and appealed directly to Peled.

Dayan's action, as much as his insensitivity, provoked Elazar. It was a clear-cut dispute. As chief of staff, he, and not Dayan, was authorized to issue direct orders to the military forces.

Elazar chose to forget that when he had been Northern Front commander six years earlier, in June 1967, he had accepted a direct order from Defense Minister Dayan to conquer the Golan and that then Chief of Staff Yitzhak Rabin had not been brought into the decision-making process. Indeed, the Israeli Cabinet had not been party to Dayan's 1967 decision. Nonetheless, Elazar had not hesitated in 1967 to employ Dayan's authority to launch an attack he had been begging to launch for nearly a week.

Now, on October 7, 1973, the resolution of the dispute rested less upon either man's contentions than upon the prime minister's judgment as to whose perceptions she should trust. Dayan bombarded Mrs. Meir with questions through the first afternoon and night but emerged second to Elazar after seventeen hours of heated exchanges.

The first skirmish between the two men ended by 0700 hours on October 7. Dayan had by then sown havoc at Northern Front headquarters. But Elazar asserted his leadership and countered the defense minister's pessimistic demeanor by allocating one Air Force squadron to assist on the Golan. He made it absolutely clear that General Hofi and not Dayan was the on-the-spot decision-maker and that he, Elazar, was not anticipating a withdrawal from the Golan.

Hofi and Dayan entered into a discussion over the morality of bombing the Tel Faris area, where pilots would have difficulty distinguishing between friend and foe. Major General Issacar Shadmi, one of many retired Israeli generals who had no assignment but who turned up to help in any way he could, felt that the discussion was getting nowhere, so he interrupted to say: "Leave the decision to bomb or not bomb to Mordechai Hod [a former Israeli Air Force commander, now serving as Hofi's air operations adviser]. The question is what will be tomorrow in the Jordan Valley. There are no Molotov cocktails in Degania."

Shadmi's reference to Kibbutz Degania was poignant on numerous levels, for Degania is Israel's oldest kibbutz. The first child born there was Moshe Dayan, and Mordechai Hod also was a son of that kibbutz. Syrian tanks and infantry had been stopped at the kibbutz gate in 1948 by defenders hurling Molotov cocktails. Indeed, the battle for the kibbutz had turned to Israel's advantage only when a force incorporating the first artillery battery in the young Israeli Army had arrived. The relief force's commander had been Lieutenant Colonel Moshe Dayan.

The debate stopped upon Shadmi's words. Hofi ordered Shadmi to assume command south of the Kinneret: "Go down and organize a second line. Organize the Jordan Valley." Shadmi's command was the least desirable he could have imagined, for, if it became active, the fate of his nation might depend upon his success.

* * *

While Dayan and the generals struggled to impose order upon the command chain and their options, the battle hinged upon the actions of four men: Lieutenant Zvika Greengold, Major Baruch Lenschner, Captain Moshe Waks, and Captain Meir Zamir.

Tiger Zamir had nine operable tanks from 7th Brigade's 82nd Tank Battalion moving into position to take on the remainder of the tank column he had ambushed near Bunker 111 before dawn. Thus he was poised upon 7th Infantry Division's right flank, which ran along the Rafid–Kuneitra Road.

Colonel Hassan Tourkmani's major 9th Infantry Division thrust along the secondary road linking Hushniya to Naffach through Sindiana faced just seven Northern Command Tank Battalion Centurions under Major Baruch Lenschner and Captain Moshe Waks. The Israelis were deployed in a dry streambed—a wadi—a mile south of Sindiana.

Zvika commanded eight Centurions on Tourkmani's left, including seven detached in the night from Baruch Force.

The Syrian 43rd Mechanized Brigade tank battalion was barely moving on the Rafid–Kuneitra Road. It had been whittled down by over 60 percent in its predawn confrontation with Tiger's Centurion company, and the surviving T-55s were pretty much stopped by the necessity of scouting the area for Israeli armor. They turned northward only after spending precious time without finding Tiger, who had moved south immediately after his "searchlight" ambush.

Tiger hit the bobtailed Syrian column from the rear, destroying five more T-55s in the opening round and obliterating the cohesion of the rest of the battalion. The survivors attempted to form a defensive laager in an abandoned Israeli artillery position but were all destroyed.

No sooner had Tiger's company finished drawing the teeth of 43rd Mechanized Brigade than one of his tankers spotted a Syrian supply column approaching from up the road. This was too good to pass up, so Tiger quickly deployed his company and attacked the soft supply vehicles from the rear. The head of the column turned northward, toward Kuneitra, and then fled eastward, back into Syria.

Captain Zamir reported in to Colonel Ben Gal, with whom he did not get along and because of whom he had earlier decided to leave active duty at the first opportunity. When Tiger reported the destruction of an estimated forty T-55s, Ben Gal, who was in need of some good news, responded, "Tiger, I love you!" Stunned by his commanding officer's ebullient response, Zamir answered, "I love you, too, sir."

Colonel Uri Orr, commanding 679th Reserve Armored Brigade, had just arrived in the area with a jeepborne reconnaissance company, so Ben Gal ordered Tiger's company to return to 7th Brigade headquarters to resume its standby status. Tiger asked to be allowed to go after the Syrian supply column he had just attacked, but Ben Gal was adamant that it was silly to risk the loss of even one Israeli tank on such a venture. Tiger left the Bunker 111 area to Colonel Orr and rejoined Ben Gal.

The main body of the Syrian 51st Independent Tank Brigade resumed its advance at first light on October 7 along both roads leading to Naffach. While the column initially enjoyed a favorable ratio in strength, approaching five to one, it was not free of problems. Chiefly, the tanks' ammunition racks had been stocked with high-explosive rounds in anticipation of fighting infantry. Only a limited number of antitank rounds was available to each gunner.

In a sense, 9th Infantry Division was a victim of its own success. It was the weakest of the Syrian divisions not only in numbers of tanks but also in supporting arms and supply units. The Syrian planners had assumed that it would be able to draw supplies from stocks of the neighboring 5th and 7th Infantry divisions. This surmise was unworkable until road routes to the other sectors could be secured. Thus Colonel Tourkmani was stretching his resources in men, equipment, and supplies in the hope of achieving a successful penetration of the Israeli rear while there was a chance of doing so, and clearly before the expected penetrations to the north and south could be achieved.

Major Baruch Lenschner differed from most Reserve officers in that, by special arrangement, he served on active duty about a hundred days a year rather than the usual thirty. When he had first indicated that he wanted to leave the standing army, several senior officers pressed him to stay. Some voiced the opinion that he had the makings of a "future chief of staff."

It was a classic dilemma. A youth perceived by his superiors as highly promising seems to turn away from their values. There was no way to compel Lenschner to remain on active duty, so they offered a compromise in the hope civilian life might prove unappealing. Thus Lenschner served about a third of the year on active duty and the remainder pursuing civilian goals.

Lenschner's choice of the wadi as his defensive line vindicates all the troubles to which his superiors had gone in his behalf and clearly illustrates what they had seen in him. The wadi provided his force with a classic hull-down position, minimizing exposure to enemy fire. Syrian tanks perched three meters higher would have a hard time seeing his Centurions and an even harder time depressing their guns far enough to do much damage.

When Captain Moshe Waks's understrength company was confronted by an estimated seventy Syrian tanks, Waks decided that his crews needed a bit of settling. This he accomplished by singing to them over the tactical net between fire missions.

When one of Waks's tanks was hit, its turret blown far into the air, he muttered into the radio, "Boys, remember that we are fighting for our homes. If we move, they race on to Haifa." Moshe Waks's own tank was hit a short time later, and he died.

Lenschner yielded ground as necessary. The wadi was eventually abandoned so the Centurions could deploy among the numerous rock walls and farmhouses in the area. As at the wadi, the deployment minimized exposure to Syrian fire.

The Syrians also sought to minimize losses. Whereas most Syrian tank forces had approached the Israeli lines on October 6 in column formation, 51st Independent Tank Brigade shook itself out across a broad front and advanced in fits and starts as dictated by events and the lay of the land.

Checked by Baruch Force, which eventually was reduced to just five tanks, the Syrians moved to outflank the Israeli blocking force at Sindiana. Major Lenschner reported at 0930 hours that he could see Syrian forces deploying on hills to his east.

The eight Centurions placed under Zvika Greengold's command during the night were certainly welcome, but they were also something of a mixed blessing to the young kibbutznik. While the arrival of seven Centurions manned by fresh, veteran crews ended Zvika's solitary role on the vital Petroleum Road, he was frankly uncertain that he was qualified to command so many tanks. After all, he had been on leave in anticipation of *beginning* a company commander's course. There is much to be said for on-job-training, but young Zvika was not particularly thrilled to be trading the loneliness of the night for the loneliness of command. More to the point, he had been badly burned on the hands and face during his latest fight on the Petroleum Road and was in considerable pain, and dizzy from lack of sleep and his prodigious physical and mental efforts.

It certainly never dawned on Colonel Yitzhak Ben Shoham nor his deputy, Lieutenant Colonel David Yisraeli, that their miracle man would doubt his ability to command, but doubtful he was. Unable to reach Ben Shoham by radio, the plucky lieutenant asked Yisraeli to send "somebody more serious." Yisraeli went straight to General Hofi to explain Zvika's dilemma. Hofi agreed to Yisraeli's offer to take charge along the Petroleum Road.

In the end, Yisraeli did pretty much what Zvika had been doing: He kept the Syrians at arm's length. According to Zvika, "A little battle began at a range of fifteen hundred meters. They had a great many tanks, but they didn't know how to fight."

The 51st Tank Brigade crews did all that was asked of them, stolidly regrouping time and again to attack despite mounting casualties and the increasing probability of death.

Major Baruch Lenschner recognized the danger implicit in Tourkmani's repeated attacks. Lenschner had yielded Sindiana when his force was whittled to four operational Centurions. Now he recognized that the enemy—51st Separate Tank Brigade—was sacrificing itself just as his force was being asked to sacrifice itself to win the day.

The crisis was nearly at hand.

· 15 ·

Colonel Hassan Tourkmani had reported the arrival of his 9th Infantry Division at the Hushniya–Petroleum crossroads at about 2200 hours on October 6—just about the time the 7th Infantry Division commander, Brigadier General Omar Abrash, reported that his 78th Independent Tank Brigade was set to commence its planned assault north of Kuneitra. This was the moment for Syrian General Headquarters to settle the matter of sending either 1st or 3rd Tank divisions into offensive action, and where. However, confronted with the choice of immediately committing 1st Tank Division on Tourkmani's front along a secondary roadway near Hushniya or using 3rd Tank Division in the event Abrash's 78th Independent Tank Brigade achieved a breakthrough near Kuneitra, the Syrian commanders hesitated.

The indecision provided the hard-pressed defenders with a double bonus. The Syrians took five crucial hours to make a decision. And their choice—committing 1st Tank Division over the secondary roads—took three more hours to implement.

It was nearly 0300 hours on October 7 before Colonel Tewfiq Jehani's 1st Tank Division was ordered out of Kiswe Military Base to exploit the growing breakthrough in the Israeli line near Hushniya.

In concert with Jehani's move, 3rd Tank Division's 15th Mechanized Brigade was ordered to Tel Hara. In all, 194 Syrian main battle tanks were ordered to the front.

Jehani's fresh division was fully prepared to achieve its objectives. Its 91st Tank Brigade fielded ninety-five modern T-62s, each mounting a 115mm smoothbore gun, the most powerful tank armament on the Golan. Jehani's 4th Tank Brigade fielded ninety-five T-55s, and a divisional reconnaissance battalion deploying sixteen brand-new PT-76 light amphibian reconnaissance tanks plus a battalion of eighteen of the new self-propelled 122mm howitzers were accompanying the leading elements. It is not difficult to imagine that a timely night assault by this formidable force might have imposed its will upon the hard-pressed Israeli defenders. However, the division vanguard units required six hours from the order to move to reach Hushniya. Together with the five-hour wait imposed by the indecision of the General Staff, 9th Infantry Division's Colonel Tourkmani was denied the means for exploiting his breakthrough until midmorning, a total of eleven hours.

The leading T-62s of Colonel Shafiq Fiyad's 91st Tank Brigade reached Hushniya shortly after 0900 hours on October 7, despite a rising tempo of Israeli fighter-bomber sorties. Upon reviewing the situation, Fiyad turned his T-62s northward, toward Naffach. His aim was to aid 51st Independent Tank Brigade's bid to attack along the Sindiana and Petroleum roads.

Fiyad's initial sally northward from Hushniya was accompanied by a rising crescendo of reports from tank commanders whose T-62s were getting hung up on rocks.

The problem arose out of a seemingly minor difference between the T-54/T-55 family of tanks and the T-62, whose transmission housing projected farther downward, giving it a few inches less road clearance. The T-62 drivers, who had to wrestle upslope and downslope, were not familiar with their vehicles, so they initially misjudged the clearance required to breast the outcroppings dotting the landscape. The solution was increased care—at decreased speed. It would be longer still until the crucial reinforcing units would be able to add their weight to the remaining tanks of 51st Independent Tank Brigade.

* * *

Colonel Yitzhak Ben Shoham had spotted the columns of dust accompanying the advance of Syrian T-55s to the edge of the escarpment at sunrise. At that time, Ben Shoham had only his brigade command tank and communications half-track available at Gamla Rise, and he knew there was no sense in sacrificing himself or his forward command group on an impossible stand. Instead, he pulled out ahead of the Syrians and raced downslope toward the Jordan River. The Syrians sent a few rounds after him, and he returned the fire in the hope of deterring them, however briefly. He soon outdistanced the T-55s.

As Ben Shoham led his communications half-track across the Buteiha Valley, he ran into Major Dan Pesach, deputy commander of 82nd Tank Battalion, who had managed to drive offroad down the escarpment in a Centurion damaged at Tel Saki. They left the tank at a repair depot, ran northward on a secondary road along the east bank of the Jordan past the Arik Bridge, and turned up the escarpment toward Naffach on the B'not Yaacov Bridge Road.

When the two sleepless officers arrived at the sector command center at 0930 hours, Ben Shoham reviewed the state of affairs. It appeared that all the command decisions had been made and that everyone knew what to do: Simply block and then overpower the Syrians. There was absolutely nothing for Ben Shoham to do at Naffach, so the stately brigade commander rounded up several tanks and sent Major Pesach down the Sindiana Road with a few of them while he prepared to move off down the Petroleum Road with the rest.

As the Barak Brigade command tank was getting ready to go, Major Benny Katzin, the brigade operations officer, ran from the command bunker and demanded to go along. He had been cooped up all night and wanted in on the fighting. He won his place aboard the command tank after a friendly argument with the brigade Intelligence officer, who had been with Ben Shoham all night.

Before leaving, Ben Shoham ordered his staff to intercept any of Colonel Uri Orr's 679th Reserve Armored Brigade tanks, which were imminently expected, and send them to reinforce him on the Petroleum Road. This mission was accomplished with alacrity. The Barak Brigade Intelligence officer positioned the communications half-track beside the road running through Naffach and intercepted

679th Brigade tanks as they arrived. Each three tanks were organized into a scratch platoon under the senior tank commander, tied
into the Barak Brigade tactical net, and alternately sent off down the
Petroleum Road in the traces of the brigade commander or along
the parallel track after Major Dan Pesach. Two makeshift companies
were thus organized and committed.

Ben Shoham's first report to his command center was, "I must
have knocked out eight tanks so far. It looks good."

It might have looked good to Ben Shoham, but Brigadier General
Rafoul Eitan was sufficiently concerned to take time out from running the entire Golan battle to call in Lieutenant Colonel
Menachem Cooperman and order him to scratch together all the
infantry he could find to secure the southern perimeter of the Naffach camp.

Pinie Cooperman was deputy commander of District Brigade, a
purely administrative unit charged with providing services to the
numerous units that rotated through the Golan sector in peacetime.
He had had a busy October 6, overseeing the pickup and evacuation
of civilian stragglers. And he had done much to ease the burden on
limited medical facilities by arranging for the evacuation of
wounded soldiers through the night. Withal, Cooperman relished
the opportunity handed him by Eitan to take an active part in the
fight. Cooperman had stolidly worked his way through the ranks,
spending nearly his entire career with Golani Infantry Brigade,
where he had been a battalion commander before being transferred
to District Brigade. But for all his know-how, Pinie Cooperman
faced a task easier described than accomplished. He immediately
scoured the bustling camp for bazookas and other heavy infantry
weapons—and the cooks and bakers who would have to man them
in the event the Syrian tanks reached the camp.

The first T-62s of 91st Tank Brigade arrived on the battlefield at
about 1100, fully twelve hours after Colonel Hassan Tourkmani first
announced 51st Independent Tank Brigade's breakthrough near
Hushniya.

Colonel Yitzhak Ben Shoham first heard about the new threat
from Major Baruch Lenschner, who saw them arrive along his left
flank as he deftly sought to outmaneuver 51st Tank Brigade T-55s

that had been dogging him since before sunrise. By then, Lenschner was down to just two Centurions. He told Ben Shoham that he could not hold his sector much longer, but Ben Shoham ordered him to "hold at all costs."

At this point, two makeshift platoons from 679th Armored Brigade arrived under Major Dan Pesach by way of the secondary road from Naffach to cover Ben Shoham's left flank.

The 91st Tank Brigade crews were shocked by the ferocity of the defense put up by the Israelis. What they had initially understood to be a move to exploit a *fait accompli* was turning before their eyes into a desperate, bitter breakthrough battle, contested at every ditch and rock.

Major Lenschner reported over the tactical net just before noon: "The Syrians are getting stronger."

Several Armor School tanks, now under the control of Orr's 679th Armored Brigade, responded by sweeping into the exposed Syrian flank and accounting for ten Syrian tanks. But it was too little and too late for "future chief of staff" Baruch Lenschner, who perished when the warhead of a Sagger missile punched through his Centurion's turret armor.

Syrian tank companies soon slopped over the edges of the Sindiana cauldron in the direction of the Kuneitra Road. An Israeli infantry section at Tel Abu Hanzir reported the arrival of Syrian tanks at 1230.

In the meantime, Ben Shoham maintained a single-minded pressure upon the Syrian formations along the Petroleum Road. The brigade commander pushed on up the road despite the presence of Syrian tanks to his rear. He called Naffach to tell Eitan that his dwindling force was surrounded, and he warned Pesach that he, too, had Syrian tank formations running across his rear.

Pesach was unable to contain the Syrian drive in his sector. He contacted Eitan at 1330 and made what would be his final report: "They are on the fence. They sit on the fence." Naffach was directly threatened.

As soon as Eitan heard that Naffach was about to be attacked, he shot off a message to Ben Shoham, ordering him to break off his holding action around Sindiana and the Petroleum Road and immediately return to save the headquarters base, with its vital stores and workshops.

The message must have come as a great disappointment to the Barak Brigade commander, for he had been battling with all his heart and soul for seventeen hours to retake the Hushniya crossroads, which he perceived as being the tactical key to repulsing the Syrians in his sector. Reluctantly but with instant obedience, he passed the word along to his subordinates.

Zvika Greengold was stunned by the order. Things seemed to be going well for the first time he could recall. The little force he had assembled under the command of Lieutenant Colonel David Yisraeli had just destroyed ten Syrian tanks and armored personnel carriers and had regained one hundred meters along the Petroleum Road—away from Naffach. Now, just as Zvika allowed himself the luxury of thinking he might be on the winning side, his earphones crackled with the deputy brigade commander's voice, ordering a withdrawal.

The Israeli tanks formed up as best they could in an extended column and raced off up the road toward the besieged base camp. Colonel Ben Shoham was in the lead, and Lieutenant Colonel David Yisraeli took charge of the rear guard.

Sergeant Yoav Barkili, a 679th Brigade tank commander bringing up the rear of the column, spotted an abandoned Israeli ammunition truck and radioed Lieutenant Colonel Yisraeli to suggest that they take on fresh stocks of antitank ammunition because the Reserve brigade tanks had been so rushed that they had not taken on a full load at their depot. Yisraeli vetoed the suggestion, pointing out that time was of the essence. Moments later, the rear guard was taken under fire by at least a company of T-62s. Yisraeli coolly ordered his gunner to train on the nearest Syrian tank and open fire. "Sir," the gunner responded, "no ammunition." Yisraeli instinctively ordered his driver to charge the Syrians. This the man did while the gunner fired his coaxial machine gun at the advancing T-62s. The bewildered Syrians stopped where they were for a moment to see what this was all about. Then the lead tank fired once. Smoke poured from David Yisraeli's turret, a funeral pyre.

Colonel Ben Shoham, at the head of the column, had no inkling as to Yisraeli's fate. He continued to relay orders and a running commentary of the Naffach fighting from Eitan's headquarters to his crews; his mind was very much on what lay ahead rather than on what was transpiring behind.

The pressure Ben Shoham's force was able to exert on the Syrians was telling. Concerned with breaching the Naffach defenses, they were apparently startled by the arrival of unfriendly tanks in their rear, and several withdrew altogether from the battlefield. Ben Shoham switched frequencies and called in an air strike, which further dissipated the power of the T-62s bearing down on Naffach. Then, standing tall in his turret hatchway, the brigade commander cut loose with his free heavy machine gun, bowling over Syrian infantrymen who were preparing to follow their tanks into the nearby camp.

Ben Shoham's command Centurion was just three hundred meters from the camp fence when it came upon a disabled Syrian tank by the roadside. Smoke was drifting from the turret, so neither the brigadier nor his operations officer, Major Benny Katzin, who was standing in the other turret hatchway, paid it the slightest heed. The command Centurion was passing abreast the Syrian hulk when the Syrian driver swiveled his bow machine gun and fired a long burst. Katzin and Ben Shoham slowly slumped to the deck, dead before they knew what hit them. The command Centurion lurched forward a while longer and then overturned into a ditch.

The loss of both Yisraeli and Ben Shoham, and their vital command radios, broke the cohesion of the tiny relief force. Yoav Barkili's Centurion strayed from the main force and was hit by Syrian gunfire, as was another 679th Brigade Centurion. Barkili's tank was out of the fight, but the other limped on toward Naffach. Zvika left the roadway as soon as he lost radio contact with his commanders and approached Naffach cross-country from the southeast without encountering any Syrians.

Lieutenant Colonel Pinie Cooperman had just guided the first of his "cooks-and-bakers" squads to the southern perimeter fence when he looked up and saw the first vehicles of an estimated two Syrian tank companies.

As Cooperman looked out at the oncoming Syrian tanks, there arrived at Naffach the first elements of Golani Infantry Brigade's fresh 72nd Infantry Battalion, which had been released from the

General Headquarters reserve to Northern Command by Lieutenant General Dado Elazar late on the night of October 6.

Lieutenant Ephraim Fein's 72nd Battalion infantry platoon had just arrived at Naffach and was setting up in antitank positions when someone shouted the news. A whirlwind of activity left Fein with just his platoon sergeant; everyone else had run. Undaunted, Fein and the sergeant opened fire and knocked out a tank.

Mark Shimon's infantry squad got off two bazooka rounds and stopped a T-55 before being forced to run for cover through a mist of machine-gun bullets.

Meanwhile, Lieutenant Colonel Cooperman relegated himself to the status of a fire-team leader. His team comprised the District Brigade operations officer, the brigade assistant Intelligence officer, and two young infantrymen armed with a bazooka. The five lay prone behind a tiny hummock near the main gate until the leading Syrian tank had closed to within two hundred meters. All Cooperman could think about during those agonizing minutes was how there was nothing left for the defense of Israel between Naffach and the Jordan River and from the Jordan to the sea. Somehow, Cooperman thought, the fate of the nation rested upon his personal will to resist.

The operations officer, who had never before seen combat, rose to his knees and shouldered the bazooka. Lieutenant Colonel Cooperman crouched behind, just to the left rear. The operations officer fired. And missed. Pinie Cooperman rammed home and charged the next antitank round, and tapped the operations officer to let him know he could fire again. When the second round missed, Cooperman screamed into the ear of the rattled virgin, "If you don't hit the bastard with the next round, you lose your job as number one on the bazooka!" Everyone sucked in a deep breath as the operations officer aligned his sights on the oncoming tank and let go. The rocket streaked directly into the driver's viewing aperture. There was a sharp explosion and, in an instant, the Syrian crewmen boiled out of their hatches through columns of thick black smoke.

Even Rafoul Eitan joined in the bazooka-versus-tank battle. At 1350, exactly twenty-four hours into the war, he declared to everyone in his command center who could hear, "Okay, we are leaving," and he led the way into the open. As Eitan emerged into the camp compound he saw a T-62 heading across his line of sight. The commanding general grabbed a bazooka from its operator, who was standing next to him, and fired. The behemoth stopped in a thick cloud of black smoke.

Feeling very much like the junior lieutenant who lurks in every general who has been blooded in combat, Eitan was momentarily torn between retesting his mettle as a combat infantryman and resuming responsibility for all his soldiers. The general won over the lieutenant, and as Eitan pivoted to search for transportation, he was again confronted by a T-62, this one only twenty meters away. Eitan sprinted toward a jeep, which he hit on the fly as another officer pulled it away.

After destroying the T-55 at the camp gate, Pinie Cooperman's fire team had picked up and run for their lives through sheets of machine-gun fire. They got only a short distance before two more T-55s loomed before them. "This is it," Cooperman muttered. He prepared to die.

There was a tremendous roar. Both Syrian tanks blew up. The cavalry had arrived in the form of several 679th Brigade Centurions. The sense of relief that swept over Cooperman was short-lived, for one of the Israeli tanks was immediately hit. Cooperman ran to a nearby half-track and ordered its driver and a medic to help him evacuate the crew. That done, he rejoined his fire team and searched for a new target.

The bazooka was now in the hands of District Brigade's assistant Intelligence officer, who also managed to hurl a round right at the driver's aperture. There was an explosion but no smoke, so Cooperman ordered his ad hoc gunner to try again. This, too, seemed like a perfect shot, but nothing happened except an ineffectual explosion. The last round was mounted in the rear of the bazooka tube, and the assistant Intelligence officer took careful aim. There was a flash and an explosion, and the Syrian crewmen bailed out. (Cooperman later figured out that the assistant Intelligence officer had fired antipersonnel rounds, which were too weak to hurt the tank. The tank crew obviously succumbed to an understandably bad case of nerves.)

Even as the battle within the Naffach camp's fence raged uncertainly, Colonel Tewfiq Jehani, commander of Syria's 1st Tank Division, determined that Naffach was nothing more than a temporary trap in time and space that had to be defused and left behind. Jehani was convinced that once his columns uncovered the B'not Yaacov Bridge–Kuneitra axis, it made little difference whose flag flew over Naffach. Jehani's leading brigades were in firm control of the two roads running from Naffach to Hushniya; he had a fresh tank battalion in reserve; and his fresh, complete 2nd Mechanized Brigade was approaching the battlefield from the northeast.

Once relieved across a significant portion of its area of responsibility by Jehani's fresh armored formations, Colonel Hassan Tourkmani's 9th Infantry Division reopened its drive northward along the Rafid–Kuneitra Road. This move by Tourkmani's mechanized infantry fell upon Israel's last best hope of resecuring the area. From the Israelis' perspective, Tourkmani's new drive came at the worst possible moment.

Colonel Uri Orr's 679th Reserve Armored Brigade was a brand-new formation in the IDF when it was called to convene during the last hours of peace on Yom Kippur. It had received a full complement of early-model Centurion tanks, a mixed blessing in that the brigade tinkerers had not had time to convert from gasoline to more reliable diesel power plants.

The brigade responded well. New unit that it was, it was manned by armored officers and troops who knew their business.

Colonel Orr himself arrived at Ein Zevan, on 7th Brigade's right flank, shortly after sunrise, at about the time Captain Tiger Zamir was overrunning the last remnants of 43rd Mechanized Brigade's tank battalion. The Armor School Tank Battalion companies of Captains Moshe Harel and Yosef Sarig (one of Colonel Ran Sarig's younger brothers) were immediately attached to Orr's command as was, a short time later, the bulk of Captain Eli Geva's company of 82nd Tank Battalion. In all, Orr had direct operational control over twenty Centurions and his brigade's jeepborne reconnaissance company.

Colonel Hassan Tourkmani took note of the Israeli buildup on his northern flank and maintained sufficient pressure to prevent Orr from moving unhindered through his sector. As Tourkmani sparred with the tanks to his north, he quickly worked to concentrate his own tank force, with which he mounted a northward sweep just as Colonel Yitzhak Ben Shoham's situation along the roads leading to Naffach entered a critical phase.

During this sweep, an Israeli lieutenant colonel was separated from his command, wounded, and driven to ground inside an inoperable tank. Other Israelis were similarly trapped in destroyed or disabled tanks at the same time. Colonel Orr thus was obliged to mount a time-consuming rescue operation.

The necessary piecemeal commitment of 679th Brigade prevented Colonel Orr from building anything resembling a formidable response to Tourkmani's unremitting, if not intense, pressure. Orr had no idea that Barak Brigade officers were requisitioning and diverting single 679th Brigade tanks and platoons bound through Naffach, first to Ben Shoham's fight and then to the fight to save Naffach itself. All he knew was that his Centurions were not arriving. The brigade commander directed Lieutenant Shimon Ryan to drive his stolen reconnaissance jeep down the Kuneitra Road to find 679th Brigade elements and hurry them along. As there were no 679th Brigade tanks passing beyond Naffach, Ryan drifted toward the camp at the height of the battle there, the first "official" 679th Brigade element to do so.

When Brigadier General Eitan informed Major General Hofi that he was obliged to abandon the Naffach camp, the morale at Hofi's regional command center plummeted. The entire Northern Command staff became pessimistic about its options. This was a crisis implemented by months of intense Syrian planning, the fruition of Hafez al-Assad's exercise of will upon the future of the Middle East. The Syrians were within a hairsbreadth of achieving their goals. At a given moment, Israel literally ran out of forces in the southern Golan to throw in the path of the advancing Syrian formations. Mass had overcome technical superiority.

General Hofi had much earlier tried to divert a large component of the Armor School Tank Battalion directly to the fighting in the southern Golan, but he had been turned down by Dado Elazar, as the threat then was more perceived than real. When Hofi relayed news of Eitan's desperate situation at Naffach, Elazar softened a bit, asking if Hofi could withhold the Armor School tanks until after dark. Hofi said he could not, and he firmly repeated his request.

With that, Elazar gave Hofi, the man on the spot, complete operational discretion.

Colonel Uri Orr had planned to concentrate his entire 679th Brigade at Ein Zevan, but Eitan's urgent appeal for tanks resulted in the official diversion of one of Orr's battalions to Naffach. Within minutes, all the diffused elements of 679th Brigade and Orr's command group were ordered to fight through to save Eitan's command center.

Orr left a three-tank platoon to cover the critical Kuneitra sector and rushed toward Naffach with fifteen Centurions drawn from 82nd Tank Battalion and the Armor School Tank Battalion. Almost immediately, a T-62 battalion from 1st Tank Division's 91st Tank Brigade was sighted. This was no doubt the same unit that had earlier destroyed Lieutenant Colonel David Yisraeli's rear guard. The Syrians were to the north of the Petroleum Road on a route paralleling Orr's. As they were of no immediate threat, Orr left them in peace. Oddly, they ignored his passage.

General Hofi came up on the command net to tell Orr that the fate of the area around Naffach lay in his hands. It was a well-intentioned appeal, but it undid a little of the steeling of nerves Orr had by then accomplished. His challenge was finding a way to convey the desperate situation to Reserve crewmen who had not yet fully adjusted to the concept of total war.

Orr's counterattack was launched just as the Syrian sweep into the Naffach camp was losing momentum. The tenacity of the Israeli defense had taken a large toll in Syrian tanks. Minefields—and *suspected* minefields—outside the wire had contributed to many Syrian units losing their way or being whittled down before reaching the fence.

Orr's tiny relief force was on the final approaches to Naffach at about 1600 hours. A massive artillery bombardment throughout the area made it impossible for Orr fully to assess the battle in and around the camp, but it was clear that all he really had to do was pitch in and allow Fate to resolve the doubtful issue.

A tiny lull in the madcap battle gave Lieutenant Colonel Pinie Cooperman time to enter the command bunker and roust men hiding there, to make them part of the effort to save their own lives. Exiting the bunker directly in the face of a T-62 forced Cooperman and his reluctant charges to reconsider the wisdom of their aggressive stance. There was no weapon in the hands of the vulnerable bunch of headquarters warriors capable of bringing a tank to grief. Pinie Cooperman once again prepared to die.

The Syrian tank was hit by a single round from an Israeli tank that was crossing the camp's southeastern fence in the vicinity of the tank workshops. Standing in the Centurion's turret was none other than Lieutenant Zvika Greengold.

Only three of the Centurions that had started back with Colonel Yitzhak Ben Shoham actually reached Naffach. The three tank commanders' "adherence to mission"—a standard Israeli doctrinal principle—was remarkable. The three tank commanders could not have known what was going on beyond their immediate lines of sight because the deaths of Ben Shoham and Yisraeli and the destruction of sundry command vehicles had taken the expected stream of information and orders right off the air; the radio net had fallen into silence. None of the tank commanders actually *knew* anything beyond the assigned objective—Naffach—and that is where each of them went. One of the three even ambushed and destroyed four T-55s before joining Zvika on his run around the Syrians, and the third joined them in the camp compound.

At this juncture Zvika, who had left Naffach wholly untried twenty hours earlier, faced a dilemma that would never have been covered in his suspended company commander's course. His faithful driver's will snapped. The youngster stood up in his open hatchway and bolted from the tank to steal an APC, which he drove at top speed from the compound. One of the other Centurions drove off to fight the Syrians, but the other stayed close to Zvika, who continued to fight from his immobile tank by sniping at passing Syrian vehicles.

When the first of Colonel Orr's platoons smashed their way into the camp compound, Zvika dropped to the ground and strolled over to speak with the platoon leader. The other lieutenant was either stunned by the raging battle or the appearance of the grimy, injured redhead, for he immediately acquiesced to Zvika's order to trade places. Mobile once again, Zvika waded back into the fight.

Naffach was a whirlpool of death.

Fresh Golani Brigade infantrymen and 679th Brigade tank crewmen suddenly were thrown into an ongoing action virtually without guidance. Each individual arriving soldier had to cross a line between the peace he had known and the battle he was facing, from a world of order to a world of chaos. New soldiers arrived and were immediately swept away by the shifting eddies and undertow of the battle.

Sorial Birnbaum, a particularly religious member of 679th Brigade, had prayed throughout the long hours of waiting for his call-up orders the day before, Yom Kippur. On this day, at this hour, some of his prayers might literally have been answered, for he died as he entered the swirling cauldron of Naffach.

Captain Haim Hosef, a 679th Brigade tank company commander, succeeded in organizing a makeshift Centurion company and led it to Naffach. He engaged and destroyed two Syrian tanks, transferred to another tank when his own Centurion was disabled, and fought on until he was killed.

As Orr's small force swept in from the east, four Centurions commanded by Captain Amos Ben David arrived on their own from the west, just in time to chase the last operable Syrian tanks from the Naffach compound. Ben David informed Eitan at 1700, "Naffach camp is clean."

When the sole surviving Centurion from the tiny force left to guard the route from Kuneitra announced that it was facing impossible odds, Colonel Orr sent several of his tanks to counter the Syrian force. Eight of the Syrians were destroyed and the others withdrew, thus abandoning the camp's western approaches to the Israelis.

When the battle around Zvika ceased, he found himself standing in the turret of his fifth or sixth Centurion, suddenly unable to make a decision as to what to do next. The Barak Brigade Intelligence officer—now the nominal brigade commander—rushed up to greet the lieutenant. As he fought an overwhelming lethargy, Zvika painfully climbed from the turret and carefully dropped to the ground, where he leveled his eyes on the Intelligence officer and apologetically murmured, "I can't anymore." The Intelligence officer said not a word; he hugged Zvika close and led him to the medical evacuation center.

There is no way to calculate the damage that that iron-willed redheaded youth inflicted upon the best plan with which Syria has ever entered a conflict.

· 4 ·

CONTAINMENT

Prior to the outbreak of this new war and following his retirement from active service after nearly thirty years in uniform, Major General Dan Laner had found Lieutenant General Dado Elazar's request that he organize a new Reserve combat division to be an easygoing pastime. The summer and early fall of 1973 had been spent piecing together a headquarters staff. The division itself, however, remained a paper organization. It had no specific units earmarked to come under Laner's control. Staff meetings during the formative stage were essentially forums for exploring new ideas. The Reserve officers who attended such meetings usually arrived in their own private vehicles.

Laner's deputy division commander was Brigadier General Moshe Bar Kochba, who, as a company commander, had conducted the IDF's first major armored operation during the Sinai Campaign seventeen years earlier. Bar Kochba's classic Battle of the Ruafa Dam in 1956 still was studied for many hours by every Armor School cadet. In 1967, Bar Kochba had commanded a Reserve brigade that, after overcoming Jordan's crack 40th Armored Brigade on the West Bank, had fought in the Golan. And in January 1973, at a conference of senior commanders assessing the then-new Syrian battle-days strategy, Bar Kochba had declared, "If they begin to move, it will be difficult to stop them, and they are likely to cause many casualties. . . . In the Golan Heights, the stopping will be difficult because of the absence of strategic depth and, therefore, they will likely be able to reach the B'not Yaacov Bridge within hours."

General Bar Kochba demonstrated his resourcefulness within an hour of the outbreak of the war. Since vehicles had not yet been allocated to Laner's 240th Armored Division, Bar Kochba went out and "organized" seven half-tracks to form the basis of a divisional mobile headquarters. The division's communications officer was able to tie into the command nets of 7th and Barak brigades, and the division staff was able to follow events on the battleground. However, there was nothing Laner, Bar Kochba, or their staff could actually do, for they had no role in the mobilization of Northern Command.

Dan Laner journeyed to Major General Hofi's Northern Command headquarters in the early hours of October 7 and arrived in time to witness the trauma created by frank reports from Brigadier General Eitan, Colonel Sarig, and Lieutenant Colonel Eres.

On hearing all the bad news, Laner had exclaimed, "The war in the south[ern Golan] is over, and we have lost. We don't have enough with which to stop them."

By that time, Laner had become impatient with standing around awaiting the opportunity to add the meat of newly arriving combat units to his paper division. He suggested that Eitan's responsibilities be narrowed to the northern Golan while he, Laner, assumed command of all the forces in the southern sector. The suggestion made perfect sense and perfect use of Laner's considerable talents, so General Hofi agreed.

It was like a man naming his own poison, for Hofi was rather more generous in assigning the mission than he was in assigning the assets for undertaking the mission. Laner was ordered to assume command of all the ground beginning a half mile south of the B'not Yaacov Bridge–Kuneitra Road axis. The combat units in the sector included the remnant of Lieutenant Colonel Eres's 53rd Tank Battalion trapped in the Rafid–Tel Faris area; 71st Armored Infantry Battalion, still en route from its depot; 9th Reserve Armored Infantry Brigade, also en route from its depot; and Sarig Force, a tiny hodgepodge of tanks en route up the Hushniya Road.

UNITED NATIONS

An Israeli column in the Syrian Bulge

**Abandoned Syrian tanks near the Israeli position
Rafid in the Golan Heights**

UNITED NATIONS

**The Israeli flag being raised over the very eastern
IDF position on Mt. Hermon**

■

**An IDF Centurion tank blocks the entrance to the
village of Hader in the Golan Heights.**

UNITED NATIONS/Y. NAGATA

■

**The devastated town of Qnaitra shortly after
IDF forces withdrew**

**Israeli Centurian tanks withdraw from
Qnaitra in the Golan.**

UNITED NATIONS/ Y. NAGATA

■

**IDF forces lower the flag as they prepare to
withdraw from Tel El Shams.**

**Israeli M-113 APCs withdraw
from Tel El Shams.**

Laner was not given a command so much as he was given an opportunity.

After destroying fifteen of 51st Tank Brigade's T-55s at the Kuzabia crossroads at about 0530, Colonel Ran Sarig's Centurions moved to link up with IDF forces around Tel Zohar, including Berkowitz Force of 53rd Tank Battalion, a platoon of Captain Eli Geva's company of 82nd Tank Battalion, and Major Gideon Weiler's platoon of the Armor School Tank Battalion. As these small units were encountered, they were incorporated into Sarig Force.

Sarig next swept eastward in the hope of retaking the Petroleum–Hushniya crossroads. However, he was forced to reconsider as soon as his tankers reported sighting a tank battalion of 5th Infantry Division's 47th Independent Tank Brigade. Amid cautious maneuvering, the two forces essentially stood off and traded rounds until midafternoon on October 7. Three Centurions were disabled, and Colonel Sarig was wounded and evacuated. The remnants of the Syrian battalion withdrew following the loss of what the Israeli crews estimated to be thirty-five Soviet-built tanks.

When Dan Laner heard of the battle and Sarig's evacuation, he ordered the force deputy commander to regroup and continue to strike along the Kuzabia–Hushniya Road west of the Petroleum Road. The Israeli attack recommenced at about 1700 hours.

As soon as Laner had been given control of the southern Golan, he had moved his purloined mobile headquarters to Almagor, beside the Arik Bridge. Laner arrived well in advance of the headquarters convoy and came upon Major Gideon Weiler, deputy commander of the Armor School Tank Battalion. Weiler, who earlier had turned a platoon of Armor School Centurions over to Sarig Force, was now usefully engaged in placing used tires on the asphalt roadway to protect the crucial bridge from the wear and tear of grinding tank treads. When Laner arrived, Weiler was working right alongside his enlisted charges, carrying out a menial if well-intentioned task. "Gideon," Laner called, "this is war! What are you worried about a road for?"

Within an hour, the first Reserve units began staging into the divisional area. Still lacking his staff, Laner stood on the bridge and personally interviewed the arriving tank commanders, sifting through the units and parts of units arriving at the Arik Bridge, sending them piecemeal into the fight as needed.

The rush to battle had obviated every pretense of organizational stability, and at no time did Laner find more than three tanks traveling together. Section by section, platoon by platoon, he calmly repeated the outlines of his plans to the eager, worrying crews before sending them forward.

Lieutenant Colonel Yoav Vaspe, the tank commander of 71st Armored Infantry Battalion—a Reserve unit normally assigned to bolster Barak Brigade—was the first field-grade Reserve officer to arrive on the scene. Thus Laner entrusted Vaspe with an extraordinary mission, that of ascending the escarpment to the Gamla Rise over the so-called Waterfall Route to establish a toehold near Ein Hamud. Vaspe's route was the only access to the Golan that the Israelis had not improved and asphalted. Vaspe left as soon as his force of two Reserve tank companies could be put on the road.

In a relatively short time, Lieutenant Colonel Vaspe reported that he was in contact with Syrian infantry. Laner's instinct forced him to order Vaspe to withhold fire. It was a good guess, for the "enemy" turned out to be Israeli infantrymen fleeing before the Syrian advances on the heights.

Vaspe next spotted movement as he was approaching the lip of the plateau about five miles from the Arik Bridge. This time he withheld fire on his own—and his lead tanks were fired on. Three were hit in quick succession, including Vaspe's own. The force commander bailed out of his damaged vehicle and sprinted for another tank, from which he was able to reestablish contact over his tactical net and impose order upon his panicky crews.

As Vaspe was casting about for a solution to the tactical inequities going against him, he chanced to see that the Syrians—advance elements of 1st Tank Division—had neglected to secure a knob that dominated the entire sector. He roared off toward the dominant feature and, in so doing, alerted the Syrians to his intentions. There was no choice, and it was going to be a tight race. Vaspe's Centurion and a few others beat the T-55s by little more than one hundred meters. In fact, three of the surging T-55s were destroyed as soon as Vaspe's and the other gunners could bring their guns to bear. As Vaspe's companies continued to climb to the high ground, eight more T-55s were blown from the fight. More important, however, was the fact that Vaspe was firmly established upon a blocking position between the Arik Bridge and the El Al Road, just what Laner had had in mind when he sent the Reservists up along the Waterfall Route.

Vaspe's arrival on the escarpment restored Israeli options. Vaspe Force was virtually the instrument by which Laner hoped to reverse his earlier assessment that "the war in the south[ern Golan] is over."

By 1300 on October 7, Dan Laner had fulfilled Chief of Staff Elazar's basic directive by establishing barriers against further Syrian penetrations from the heights. By that time, blocking battles were winding down along three key axes—the Arik Bridge–Hushniya Road, the Waterfall Route, and the El Al Road. At about the same time, Colonel Mordechai Ben Porat's 9th Reserve Armored Infantry Brigade was approaching the foot of the El Al Ridge. When Laner heard this news, he ordered Ben Porat to mount an immediate counterattack against what turned out to be elements of 5th Infantry Division's 132nd Mechanized Brigade.

Ben Porat's striking arm was Lieutenant Colonel Benzion Paden's 595th Tank Battalion, the first unit to arrive on the Golan equipped with World War II–vintage Sherman tanks (which had been outfitted with modern French-built turrets mounting British-made 105mm guns identical to those aboard the IDF Centurions). Paden rushed his battalion into battle without even pausing to regroup after climbing the escarpment. So quickly did the transition occur from route march to armored assault that one participant later commented, "We went into El Al amid a hellish noise of exploding fire. Only when I saw our guns beginning to shoot did I grasp what was happening."

Until this moment, the extraordinarily level terrain in this sector had worked to Israel's defensive advantage, for Syrian tankers attempting to cross the open ground had been exposed to Israeli fire for three long miles. The Syrians had largely held back here because the risk of exposure was not commensurate with the small strategic value of the plain.

Colonel Ben Porat likewise shied away from mounting an assault across the open ground; he opted to initiate a deliberate long-range duel. The destruction of each Syrian tank by his coolly efficient gunners meant he could more or less safely advance his fighting force a few yards. In five hours his Reserve gunners bagged eight Syrian tanks and his Super Shermans advanced eastward a bit over two miles.

As darkness approached, Ben Porat chose a night laager, though the terrain confined his options. Super Sherman crews arriving at the night defensive position were able to discern that a similar Syrian force had selected virtually the same spot for their night laager. Ben Porat mounted an instantaneous attack, and his crews forced the Syrians to vacate with the loss of nine Soviet-supplied tanks. Ninth Brigade lost three dead, four wounded, and four Super Shermans disabled or destroyed through the afternoon.

Colonel Ben Porat's success was witnessed, in the curious fashion of the Middle East, by a knowledgeable nonparticipant, Jordanian Brigadier Said Ali El-Edroos, who was manning a Jordanian border post where the Yarmuk River meets the Ruqqad Stream, only a few thousand meters from the El Al battlefields. El-Edroos, who was escorting Jordanian Crown Prince Hassan Bin Talal, later drily commented, "The fact that the Syrian forces had remained stationary in the vicinity of Ramat Magshimim for an unduly long period in a situation in which every minute counted was subject of comment and discussion at the Jordanian divisional headquarters in the northern sector."

Shortly after the Syrians had been driven from the environs of Naffach, Lieutenant Colonel Pinie Cooperman was ordered to lead a convoy of specialists down the escarpment to join the District Brigade commander in mining the Jordan bridges and establishing a defensive line on the ancient river's west bank.

The trip was a nightmare. Cooperman had been born in Europe before World War II and could still recall the rabble of European armies fleeing before the Nazi onslaught. The trip down the escarpment in the midst of fleeing Israelis eventually got to him. He ordered his driver to block the roadway and confronted the first officer he saw with news that cowardice in the face of the enemy was handled in the IDF much as it had been in those European armies of memory.

The Barak Brigade Intelligence officer also was shocked by what he saw on the B'not Yaacov Bridge Road in the vicinity of Aleika. He smelled panic among the withdrawing troops, which was bad enough, but he became downright infuriated when he spied operable tanks and self-propelled artillery pieces in the roadbound column. The Intelligence officer ordered the driver of the brigade communications half-track to swing diagonally across the roadway.

"Now," he commanded, "this is where we stop running!" Each unit or group that approached the checkpoint was stopped on the roadway and ordered to turn back for the heights. When the Barak Brigade Intelligence officer had restored a modicum of order, he built an ad hoc force to man a defensive block on both sides of the roadway.

The Intelligence officer soon was joined by Brigadier General Menachem Avirem, deputy commander of Rafoul Eitan's 36th Division, who had been manning the divisional rear base when news of the Syrian breakthrough at Naffach arrived. Avirem had automatically cobbled together a force of five barely usable tanks drawn from the repair shops and had set out across the B'not Yaacov Bridge. His arrival added considerable force to the Intelligence officer's sentiments and authority. Under Avirem's scrutiny, the Intelligence officer managed to gather and deploy twenty damaged tanks through his defense locality.

When there was time, the Intelligence officer called together the officers and senior sergeants he had assembled and presented a stirring, brutally clear description of the fighting he had seen almost from the onset of the war. He stated in unequivocal terms that nothing stood between this barely organized motley group and the depots and villages of the Jordan Valley and Galilee. If the Syrians breached the roadblock, the Intelligence officer averred, they would be able to penetrate unhindered as far as they desired.

Next, the Intelligence officer radioed the Barak Brigade rear depot and ordered up specified technical units to repair the tanks he had gathered. They were to bring forward as much fuel and ammunition as they could carry on short notice. Platoons and companies were created from the coalescing rabble and tied into a tactical radio net created from out of the ether by the Barak Brigade communications officer.

Later, on a shopping foray to the nearby Aleika camp, the Intelligence and communications officers found a working telephone. The Intelligence officer dialed the Naffach camp's operations officer and briefed him on his accomplishments. Then the Intelligence officer placed a call home to tell his tearfully thankful wife that he was alive and unharmed.

Later that evening, the Barak Brigade Intelligence officer passed control of his force to 679th Armored Brigade and climbed aboard his communications half-track to complete his interrupted journey to Barak Brigade rear headquarters. The next day, Monday, he led volunteers back up the escarpment to recover the bodies of Yitzhak Ben Shoham, David Yisraeli, Benny Katzin, and the crews of their tanks.

While Israeli attention was riveted on Naffach, Colonel Tewfiq Jehani focused on the area to the west. He had held back a T-62 battalion from his 1st Tank Division's 91st Tank Brigade and was further bolstered in midafternoon by the arrival of forty T-55s from the 2nd Mechanized Brigade tank battalion. The Israelis were retreating on the Petroleum Road and, at that moment, fleeing from Naffach, so Jehani reached westward.

Three companies of the 2nd Mechanized Brigade tank battalion were moving cross-country in route column along the northern side of the Arik Bridge–Hushniya Road, and one company was in column south of the roadway when an Israeli tank column suddenly appeared on the roadway itself—right up the middle between the Syrian formations and heading in the opposite direction.

The Syrians reacted first by stopping in place all at once to create a fishhook-shaped ambush. At least four Israeli tanks were disabled before the bulk of the Israeli column could get closer. As the Syrian tank battalion commander emerged from the fight with less than an hour's daylight remaining, he ordered his unit into a night defensive laager.

Farther north, a 91st Tank Brigade T-62 battalion moved downslope unopposed and overran a four-gun battery of 155mm guns mounted on old Sherman tank chassis. The T-62 battalion suffered only minor damage, but the brush with the self-propelled battery—one of the first Reserve artillery units to reach the Golan—unnerved the battalion commander. Next the battalion vanguard crossed north of the B'not Yaacov Bridge Road at 1700 hours and ran into desultory fire from a small group of newly arrived Golani Brigade infantrymen. This ineffectual gunfire confirmed the battalion commander's worst fears, and he ordered his tanks into a night defensive laager near Snobar, a major Israeli supply point just over seven kilometers from the Jordan River, a mere ten minutes from the strategically vital B'not Yaacov Bridge. This was the Syrian high-water mark. The only Israeli force standing to the west of the T-62s consisted of parts of two Golani Brigade infantry battalions centered on Mahanayim.

Colonel Jehani had moved his 1st Tank Division forty miles from Kiswe Military Base by nightfall. His battalions had established a strong blocking position on the Hushniya Road, denied Israel full use of the logistical base and command center at Naffach, and stood poised only four miles above the absolutely vital B'not Yaacov Bridge. Five of Jehani's seven powerful tank battalions remained virtually unscathed.

The most successful of the Israeli efforts to stabilize the southern Golan involved yielding territory. The Ein Hamud toehold carved out by Lieutenant Colonel Yoav Vaspe's Reserve tank force provided a back door for the forces cut off at Tel Saki and Tel Faris.

Sometime after Vaspe's armored force had secured the toehold, Major Uri Goldfarb passed through the position on a perilous mission. Goldfarb was the first fruit of Lieutenant General Dado Elazar's decision to release 205th Reserve Armored Brigade from his General Headquarters reserve to the control of Northern Command. When the brigade arrived, it would wield nearly seventy first-line Centurions. However, the unit was on the march through the West Bank, a show of force to residents of the occupied areas. For the moment, it was represented in its entirety on the Golan by just one jeep and Major Uri Goldfarb.

After leaving Vaspe's position, Goldfarb succeeded in reaching Lieutenant Colonel Oded Eres and the small mixed force trapped with him at Tel Faris. On the way in, he had reconnoitered a possible evacuation route. As soon as Eres was briefed, Goldfarb went to work supervising the tank crews, assessing damage and wear-and-tear, providing solutions to the hundred and one problems that might be encountered during a fighting withdrawal, and personally lending a hand at cannibalizing damaged tanks to get other damaged tanks into running order. In all, he remained in constant motion in Eres's enclave for three full hours.

Eres and Goldfarb were considerably helped by the inattention of the Syrian battle forces streaming westward just beyond sight. The tiny enclave was subjected to just one probing attack, which was promptly repulsed. In the late afternoon, however, it became clear that the Syrians had the Israelis pinpointed.

At about 1600, following a quick artillery preparation, eight MI-4 helicopters were reported on the way at three to four hundred feet and rapidly closing. Lieutenant Oded Bachman's loader was on an errand, so Bachman grabbed his Centurion's free turret .50-caliber machine gun and cut loose. One of the Soviet-built helicopters seemed to jump backward, then drop heavily to earth. Lieutenant Boaz Tamir saw Syrian commandos jumping from a second helicopter drop in the face of heavy machine-gun fire, and Lieutenant Bachman saw another MI-4 plummet from the sky. The six surviving helicopters flew away to the southeast.

Several of the Centurions rushed after the helicopters and arrived at a landing zone east of Tel Faris in time to help Israeli infantrymen turn back the commando assault. Two of the MI-4s were destroyed on the ground.

On reflection, it was clear that the Syrian commandos had been interested in neutralizing the still-active Israeli electronic Intelligence complex atop the tel. Israeli operators had been able to monitor and report the activities of 1st Tank Division continuously since its arrival on the battlefield.

Lieutenant Colonel Eres began forming his force at 1820 hours, just after sunset. All vehicles except fourteen tanks and one half-track were disabled and left behind, as was the electronic Intelligence station. Nearly 180 infantrymen, dispossessed tankers, and technicians climbed atop the armored vehicles, each infantryman armed with an Uzi submachine gun or better, extra ammunition, and hand grenades.

After hours of harrowing progress through the dark and broken countryside, the column safely penetrated to the Petroleum Road, where it unavoidably passed within two meters of a line of Syrian vehicles. The first two Centurions were past the Syrian night encampment when a Syrian soldier fired his weapon and hit the right fender of the third IDF tank. Over a hundred hand grenades, uncounted 9mm bullets, and fourteen 105mm cannon rounds were instantly sent in reply. At least one Syrian tank was left burning, all the Israelis could confirm before their column roared from sight. The recovering Syrians fired illumination rounds after Eres's column, but the Israelis were long gone.

According to one participant, "We didn't travel on the roads, but by secondary tracks, passing through a lot of their units. . . . At this stage, my responsibility was over. The company commander took charge of my force. I could close my eyes. Somebody bandaged me and poked around my face, which was full of shrapnel. The boys in the turret said they saw abnormal-size Syrian forces along the way. I knew it already because I had seen them coming in. I wondered why all this Syrian force had suddenly halted at Hushniya."

The column was nearing Ein Hamud near dawn when still another Syrian encampment was sighted. Eres figured that he would have to fight through to friendly forces. He ordered all the riders off the tanks and sent them on foot down a canyon. Nothing happened, however, and the last organized remnant of Barak Brigade's 53rd Tank Battalion linked up with Vaspe Force. Though Eres lost no men or tanks, Lieutenant Oded Bachman, who had fought bravely in the face of insurmountable Syrian frontal assaults, thought of the trip to safety as a "lane of fear."

· 17 ·

Even as the battle surged back and forth in the Kuneitra Gap, the Syrian Army completed its deployments to defend its conquests of the Hermon and the southern Golan. As with the initial assault upon the Israeli lines, the defensive strategy had been planned in detail. Syrian General Headquarters based everything on the assumption that its forces would roll over the IDF units in place on the Golan long before meaningful, large Reserve forces could intervene in the fighting. Thus the Syrian strategic goal was to erect a defensive array that would discourage Israeli leaders from initiating an effort to retake the Golan.

The roundup of Israeli infantrymen and technicians in the warren of Hermon bunker continued through the night. After many hours of indecision, a large party of Israelis, including Reserve technician Sergeant Gideon Ehrenhalt, tried to sneak out of the position. After hours in the dark bunker, the open air filled Ehrenhalt with boundless hope. Soon, however, Syrian gunfire raked the group, and four Israelis were killed. The survivors laid low for about ten minutes, all the time drawing Syrian fire and a shower of hand grenades. A

Golani Brigade sergeant raised his head to look around and was drilled in the forehead. The survivors decided to surrender.

Lieutenant Ahmed Jojo spent the morning of October 7 cleaning up the site of his ambush of Israelis retreating from the electronic-warfare complex on the Hermon during the night. He supervised the burial of Israelis killed in the withdrawal and undertook to transport prisoners out of the area. In the afternoon, Jojo's company of 82nd Parachute Regiment was ordered to establish a blocking position downslope of the former IDF bunkers.

There was only a single road climbing the barren basaltic desert above the Hermon tree line. The defensive position chosen maximized the use of terrain in cheaply defending the Syrian Army's cheapest trophy. The narrow roadway was mined along the length of a curve that would prevent attackers from bringing adequate firepower to bear. The commandos were deployed well away from the roadway itself, in individual fighting positions from which they could cover a very narrow front with RPGs, machine guns, hand grenades, and their personal weapons. Any attacker attempting to outflank the Syrian defensive block would have to operate while silhouetted against the skyline. The only drawback to the defensive arrangement was the exposure of the Syrian fighting positions to the raw autumnal elements at elevation. Since the defensive deployment precluded use of the ample Israeli bunkers, Lieutenant Jojo and his subordinates were resigned to spending the second of no one knew how many cold nights in the open.

The Israelis, of course, were ignorant of Lieutenant Jojo's defensive arrangements. Colonel Amir Drori, the Golani Infantry Brigade commander, thus advanced the bulk of Lieutenant Colonel Yankeleh Shahar's half-track-mounted 72nd Infantry Battalion from the Jordan Valley to Majdal Shams, a Druse village, under the cover of darkness and prepared these forces to launch an immediate assault to retake the strategically vital Hermon bunkers.

Almost without pause, the troop-filled half-tracks moved out on the road to the Hermon, a line of tanks in its wake. Drori planned to employ the roadbound column as his main striking force, though he took the necessary precaution of sending a footborne column along a route to the west.

The very speed of Drori's response to the loss of the Hermon complex provided the column with its greatest success and the Syrians with their best opportunity, for that very alacrity had prevented Drori from placing his tanks at the head of the half-track column, where they should have been. The unhindered movement of 72nd Infantry Battalion from the Jordan Valley at a time when it should have been under direct observation and fire from the heights was a major triumph of planning and discipline. Placing the tanks in the rear of the column was simply dumb.

The morning mist clung to the peaks at precisely the point where Lieutenant Jojo's company had set its ambush. The Israelis could see nothing, had no idea the Syrians were in place until the battalion commander's half-track set off a mine and thus triggered the fire fight.

Within minutes, of course, the Syrians had halted the column by disabling several half-tracks. The tanks were trapped at the rear of the column, out of range and useless behind the curve in the roadway. The only troops who could bring weapons to bear were manning the lead half-tracks, and there were not enough of them. Colonel Drori placed a priority call for air and artillery support, but the mist precluded any sort of response. What had started as a triumph of positive thinking had become a rescue mission of the men in the lead vehicles.

A bitter battle raged on for three hours, its ultimate outcome never in serious doubt, its only purpose the rescue of the injured and recovery of the dead. Naturally, still more Israelis were killed or injured in the course of the rescue efforts. In the end, twenty-two Israeli soldiers died and fifty were wounded in the no-win, no-gain situation.

Thus ended the second battle for the Hermon, another stinging Israeli defeat.

· 18 ·

Nowhere in the northern Golan did the Syrians enjoy the successes the southern divisions were able to achieve.

Simultaneous attacks around both sides of the Hermonit by units of 7th Infantry Division were met at about 0800 on October 7 by forces under Major Yosef Nissem, in the North, and Lieutenant Colonel Yosef Aldar, in the South.

Major Nissem, deputy commander of 74th Tank Battalion, actually had to defend against two separate assaults in the Dan Road sector. The first attack, by a mechanized infantry force, lashed out against Bunker 104. Nissem ordered Captain Eyal Shacham's Centurion company to the defense while he concentrated on a developing tank assault farther to the south.

Shacham's unit was perfectly situated to observe Syrian movements. It took several hours for Shacham to achieve victory, and he did so largely through the expedient of directing fire from a friendly 160mm self-propelled mortar battery, which broke up the attacking force. Another assault developing under Shacham's observation was also broken up by the mortars and the Centurions' guns.

When the defenders became concerned about the cumulative

impact of the serial Syrian attacks, Shacham used his radio to calm and encourage his crews. When his own tank was sufficiently damaged to require repairs, he relieved the crew of another Centurion with his trusted driver, loader, and gunner. When Bunker 104's communications went down, Shacham assumed responsibility for relaying messages to and from its commander.

It was just coming up to 1300 hours on Sunday, October 7, the twenty-fourth hour of the war. Lieutenant Yonatan Midvonick, the Bunker 104 commander, was speaking with Eyal Shacham by radio when the tank commander's voice suddenly faded. A direct hit on Captain Shacham's borrowed Centurion ended the lives of the newly promoted company commander and his gunner and loader. The driver pulled the damaged tank off the line.

The Syrians, who lost most of their armored personnel carriers to Shacham's and Nissem's Centurions and the 160mm mortars, withdrew shortly after Shacham died.

The Syrian southern pincer attack was mounted by strong components of 7th Infantry Division's 78th Independent Tank Brigade, which moved along a four-kilometer-wide front between the Hermonit and the Booster positions. The Syrian objective was a wadi running in the direction of Vasit along the base of the Hermonit.

Lieutenant Colonel Yosef Aldar, the commander of 7th Armored Brigade's 75th Armored Infantry Battalion, had been wounded by a Syrian thrust during the first afternoon of the war, and he was wounded again in attempting to parry the new threat. The battle raged on as the Syrian armored force fought the Israelis at distances of from twenty-three hundred to just ten meters.

As pressure mounted, Colonel Avigdor Ben Gal fed in part of his tiny brigade reserve. Captain Moshe Rosenwig, of the Armor School Tank Battalion, led a force to evacuate Aldar and the other wounded. Rosenwig took charge of the Israeli defensive effort despite a painful shoulder wound acquired during the evacuation.

Later in the morning, after standing off the main Syrian assault in his sector, Rosenwig was shifting the components of his ragtag command to better advantage when he saw a platoon commander moving into the wrong position. Unable to reach the strays by radio, Captain Rosenwig ordered his driver to intercept them. The force commander's tank was hit and disabled, and Rosenwig was severely wounded. He died en route to a hospital. The Syrian attacks, however, petered out at about 1300 hours.

The town of Kuneitra had become a no-man's-land, defended by some Israeli infantry, several APCs, and a few Centurions. The Syrians mounted constant pressure in the form of infantry attacks supported by BRDM armored fighting vehicles armed with Sagger antitank missiles. When a Centurion from Lieutenant Colonel Avigdor Kahalani's 77th Tank Battalion was damaged in the town, Captain Yair Sweet moved forward to assist the crew and see if the tank could be saved. Sweet was rolling through the center of town when he was hit in the head and killed. Lieutenant Avinoam Shemesh dismounted from his own Centurion and dashed through the fire to instruct Sweet's crewmen on how best to reduce their exposure in the killing ground. When a Syrian tank force attempted to enter Kuneitra from the south, Lieutenant Shemesh formed up the last remaining Israeli tanks and contained the Syrian drive a half mile short of the town line.

The effects of the sustained combat in 7th Brigade's sector were becoming apparent. Colonel Ben Gal had lost three company commanders in the morning fighting, and not one of over a dozen Centurions damaged or destroyed was replaced.

Late in the day, Ben Gal arranged a meeting with Lieutenant Colonel Avigdor Kahalani, of 77th Tank Battalion, and Lieutenant Colonel Yosef Aldar, of 75th Armored Infantry Battalion; the latter had been treated and released after sustaining his second set of wounds in the war. The three met on the southern slope of the Booster and reviewed events. Ben Gal explained what he thought the Syrians would do next, and he discussed with the battalion commanders how the tide should be stemmed. Kahalani pointedly inquired about reinforcements.

While the commanders conferred, Major Eitan Kauli, Kahalani's deputy battalion commander, turned his attention and considerable talents to supporting the combat forces in the sector. Working mainly with troops from Aldar's 75th Armored Infantry Battalion, Kauli went to work rearming, refueling, and salvaging tanks and APCs. Three Centurions at a time were withdrawn from front-line positions and worked over by large crews of armored infantrymen, armorers, and ordnancemen as soon as they arrived at the makeshift center at Vasit. The armored infantry did it all, giving the murderously fatigued tank crewmen the opportunity to eat, drink, talk with friends, relax in the latrines, and generally unwind. Seventh Armored Brigade's morale and combat efficiency rose to new heights in the wake of Kauli's efforts, which continued unabated until the last organized tank unit was returned to the front at about 2200 hours on October 7.

Brigadier General Omar Abrash, commanding Syria's 7th Infantry Division, was a rarity among high-ranking Syrian officers in that he was a graduate of the U.S. Army's Command and General Staff College. The Syrian General Staff placed the means for destroying Colonel Ben Gal's premier 7th Armored Brigade in Abrash's hands.

As the bulk of Abrash's division fought on through October 7 against burgeoning Israeli strength, 81st Independent Tank Brigade and 64th and 66th Field Artillery regiments were turned over from the General Headquarters reserve so Abrash could mount a fresh offensive in the vicinity of the Petroleum–Vasit crossroads, in the north-central Golan.

The fresh tank brigade was far more than a mere augmentation for 7th Division, for 81st Tank Brigade represented half the armored strength of the Assad Guard and was, by all accounts, one of the Syrian Army's finest combat units. The brigade was outfitted with new T-62 tanks equipped with 115mm smoothbore guns. The crews were totally confident in their equipment and their ability to use that equipment. Many of the crewmen were combat veterans, part of the Syrian force that had invaded Jordan three years earlier in the wake of King Hussein's brutal crackdown against PLO forces that threatened his regime and his life. No one who was party to the plan against Ben Gal's brigade doubted but that 81st Tank Brigade was the instrument for delivering the *coup de grâce*.

Unlike 1st Tank Division's 91st Brigade, which had required twelve wearing hours to reach the southern Golan from Kiswe Military Base, 81st Tank Brigade arrived only five hours after being ordered out of the same encampment. This, however, is less a reflection of the comparative abilities of the two brigades than a measure of the significance of the Israeli holding action upon Syrian time and movement plans during the first twenty-four hours of the war. The hordes of Syrian tanks that had been committed across the Golan front through the first half of October 7 were by then in action, leaving the roads clear for whatever else the Syrians chose to commit—or had left.

General Abrash was determined to mount a massive blow. Backed by nearly four hundred artillery pieces, 85th Infantry Brigade would commit a company each of tanks and infantry in its divisional northern sector; 78th and 81st Independent Tank brigades would commit over a hundred infantry-supported tanks in the divisional central sector; and 121st Mechanized Brigade would press home its assault against Kuneitra with the aid of BRDM-mounted Sagger antitank missiles. All the infantry units would be equipped with numerous antitank weapons, chiefly tank-killing RPGs. In all, about five hundred Syrian tanks were attacking about forty operable Centurions manned by 7th Brigade or attached crews.

The first attacks began at about 2200 hours on October 7.

Lieutenant Colonel Yair Nofshe's force of five 74th Tank Battalion Centurions, hunkered down near Bunker 107, was the first to report the new Syrian assault in the 7th Brigade sector.

Nofshe's immediate disadvantages were numerous. The position he occupied was vulnerable to a massive assault such as the Syrians were throwing in. Nofshe's own tank had been damaged—the turret traverse mechanism was inoperable; to bear on a target, the entire Centurion had to be turned, a tedious and time-consuming process in a war that had consistently given victory to the swifter gunnery. Fighting at night without night-fighting equipment against tanks with such equipment is suicidal, and most of the Israeli crews were keenly aware of this form of vulnerability.

Rather than engage the fresh Syrian tanks at long range, Nofshe decided to allow the T-62s to close on his positions—in hope of somewhat ameliorating the Syrians' twin advantages of numbers and night-fighting capabilities. Nofshe had long ago earned a reputation as an iron-willed disciplinarian and a hard taskmaster in training. The crews he commanded this night had no doubt suffered from his perfectionist's bent, but the best the battalion commander could hope was that they would hold steady until he gave the word.

It was coming up to 2200 hours, and the Syrians had approached to within 450 meters of Bunker 107. It was time. Nofshe's 105mm gun barked once. A hit. As the battalion commander whispered instructions through his microphone, the damaged Centurion tracked a second target. A second 105mm round was fired. A second T-62 was halted in its tracks.

It ended in just four minutes. Nofshe could plainly see that "all that was left was thirty bonfires. This was exactly what our training was aimed at."

In fact, Nofshe's five Centurions accounted for only twenty-five of the thirty T-62s claimed, a quibble, for the entire Syrian T-62 battalion was stopped, its assault disrupted. The Israelis suffered no casualties.

General Abrash's main blow, conducted with the support of a vicious, unremitting artillery barrage and preceded by fast-moving infantry antitank forces equipped with RPGs, fell upon IDF units farther to the north.

Following the loss of several of his precious 77th Battalion tanks, Lieutenant Colonel Avigdor Kahalani warned everyone to keep a particularly sharp lookout for the roving antitank squads. This was just what Abrash had in mind. Israeli crews preoccupied with searching for men on foot could not be as keen at finding tanks moving across their fields of fire.

The pressure grew most intense just south of the Hermonit, where Lieutenant Ofer Tavori was directing both the fighting and the evacuation of the crews of two damaged Centurions. Heeding a frantic call for help on the battalion tactical net, Kahalani moved to assist Tavori. It began raining as the battalion commander took to the dark road and, despite the intense combat, he could not help thinking with relief about the new roof he had completed just before being called back to the Golan.

The confusion was total as gunfire was exchanged at distances of as little as thirty meters. The crew of one Israeli Centurion was drawn from its vigil by the shouted warning of its tank commander: "Reverse, you fool! Reverse, or we'll run him down!" Immediately there was a grinding collision. Then the tank jerked backward, right into another tank, the impact reverberating through the steel chassis and the men riding it like a blow from a sledgehammer. No one had a clue as to whether either or both collisions involved Israeli or Syrian tanks; there simply was no time to look.

One of the T-62s penetrated to within fifty meters of the medical aid station at Vasit but bore off in another direction, no doubt in search of a predetermined objective. It is doubtful the Syrian crew even knew the aid station had been in its path and at its mercy.

The mounting pressure had fully occupied Kahalani's attention when his earphones crackled with news from "Yona Force." Surprised, an elated Kahalani had visions of an adequate reinforcement by an ample and fresh unit of Reserve tanks. The elation quickly passed, for it was soon made clear that "Yona" was Major Yona Teren, and he had arrived on the Golan alone. An armor officer without official assignment, Teren had made his own way to the Golan with the intention of joining Kahalani's tank battalion. Yona Force was born when Teren came across a tank that had been abandoned in the field when its commander had been killed. Hopefully, the brief radio traffic announcing the arrival of Yona Force confused Syrian eavesdroppers more than it confused Kahalani.

As Kahalani's Centurions overcame uncountable T-62s (really about a hundred), a twenty-man Golani Brigade infantry platoon was struck on the Hermonit itself by the full strength of two infantry battalions from 85th Infantry Brigade seeking to dominate the high ground cheaply. Dozens of Syrian infantrymen died in the close but ultimately vain attempt.

The wild night battles came to an abrupt halt after three hours, at 0100 on October 8. The Syrians had sustained serious losses at Ben Gal's hands, and they opted to withdraw and regroup. Ben Gal continued to order artillery-fire missions to disrupt Syrian salvage operations and to cover the rotation of his own tanks and crews from the immediate front for revictualing and repairs.

The Syrians began harassing 7th Brigade at 0400 hours, mainly with artillery fire, but did not renew any meaningful tank assaults. Israeli crews continued to rotate off the front lines despite the pressure.

At first light, Ben Gal drove forward to tour the battlefield beside Kahalani. The two, and their entourage, counted 130 Syrian tanks and numerous armored personnel carriers destroyed or disabled all across the battlefield, both in front of and behind Israeli fighting positions. Seventh Brigade would evermore know this ground as the Valley of Tears.

As Ben Gal left, he issued standing orders that any moving target out to three thousand meters was to be engaged and destroyed.

Only in 7th Armored Brigade's southern sector did Israeli resistance seem slack. At least, 7th Syrian Infantry Division's 121st Mechanized Brigade was able to hold its own.

Following his failure in the Valley of Tears, Brigadier General Abrash regrouped his fighting units against the southern portion of Colonel Ben Gal's thin line. As Ben Gal and Kahalani counted Syrian wrecks, Abrash moved against Bunker 109.

The Syrian attack looked initially promising. One tank broke into the bunker compound, and elements of other units appeared to be gaining room to maneuver. It was clear to observers and participants on both sides that the Israeli tank line had been seriously depleted.

When Kahalani was informed of the mounting threat, he pulled a platoon from the Booster sector and ran to the sound of the guns. On the way, he grabbed a platoon of Captain Tiger Zamir's intact 82nd Tank Battalion company.

It took Kahalani's cobbled-together and badly outnumbered force three hours of unremitting combat to seal off the battlefield and slowly drive the Syrians from their initial gains. When General Abrash realized that he stood to lose more than he could hope to win around Bunker 109, the stymied attackers were ordered to withdraw.

To the north, in Nofshe's sector, Bunker 107's reluctant bazookaman, Private Yosef Zadak, continued to amaze his fellow defenders. When Nofshe's five tanks were called elsewhere, a company of Syrian tanks moved against the exposed bunker complex. Israeli artillery accounted for one of the Syrian tanks, and the minefields damaged several others. Private Zadak personally left four of them smoking ruins before the bunker.

The stunning repulses of the 81st Tank Brigade and 7th Infantry Division attacks were a major jolt to officers manning desks at Syrian General Headquarters. In just forty-two hours, five tank, infantry, and mechanized brigades fielding nearly four hundred first-line tanks and supported by over four hundred large-caliber artillery tubes, air strikes, and commando raids had failed to dislodge the single Israeli armored brigade from the Kuneitra Gap. The Syrian leadership had been so confident of victory that 4th Tank Brigade—comprising ninety-five T-55s—remained at Kiswe Military Base, uncommitted, useless.

On orders from General Headquarters, Abrash continued to press home attack after attack with his dwindling resources. He was defeated at every turn. At length, 78th Independent Tank Brigade had to be withdrawn. (It had been so badly hurt that it would require three days to reorganize itself into a battalion-strength unit.) According to one Syrian officer, "Everyone was exhausted." At one point during the day, it has been reported, Abrash had just seven operable tanks left at his disposal.

On the plus side of the ledger, Abrash's waning attacks nevertheless obliged the Israelis to maintain complete vigilance, tying down forces and resources that might have been useful in other sectors. Without massive reinforcement, however, Abrash's augmented 7th Infantry Division could not hope to orchestrate a breakthrough leading to the return of the Golan to Syrian hands.

19

Syrian Colonels Tewfiq Jehani and Hassan Tourkmani, respectively commanding 1st Tank and 9th Infantry divisions, did what they could to bolster Brigadier General Omar Abrash's failing effort. Like Abrash, however, they lacked sufficient strength by then to mount a decisive blow.

Tourkmani managed to scrape together a force of some thirty tanks supported by two mechanized infantry companies, a stunning accomplishment for the weakest of the divisions on the field. This force was sent in along the Rafid–Kuneitra Road.

At the same time, Jehani pressed on along the Sindiana and Petroleum roads with elements of 91st Tank Brigade, now down to about half strength, little more than fifty T-62s. Simultaneously, Jehani's 2nd Mechanized Brigade was ordered to continue westward along the F !Hushniya–Arik Bridge Road. In this case, however, the Israelis were diverting and distracting the Syrians from a potentially useful concentration of forces. At very little expense, the IDF was tying up 2nd Mechanized Brigade's forty T-55s in little fights in the center at a time when those T-55s could have been put to splendid use to the north.

* * *

The bulk of the fighting continued to fall upon 7th Brigade throughout Monday, October 8. Despite the pressure, however, Ben Gal was able to send two of his precious Centurion companies to bolster 679th Armored Brigade units holding the mid-Golan line.

Captain Tiger Zamir's 82nd Tank Battalion company—down to seven Centurions following Kahalani's detachment of a platoon to save Bunker 109—moved to stop the 9th Infantry Division advance by thirty tanks along the Rafid–Kuneitra Road, at the southern edge of the 7th Brigade sector. Tiger fought at long distance for the entire day, relying upon nerveless gunnery to destroy or disable an estimated thirty Syrian tanks and two companies of ten armored personnel carriers each.

Ninety-first Tank Brigade's relentless advance along the Sindiana and Petroleum roads made good progress on Monday morning. An attached antitank unit even managed to ambush Captain Yosef Sarig's company of the Armor School Tank Battalion near Kuneitra. Sarig was able to get his own tank to a firing position requiring minimum exposure to the Sagger antitank missiles fired by the Syrian BRDM missile carriers. In the bitter contest, however, most of Sarig's company was destroyed.

When several of the Syrian T-62s again reached Naffach, Colonel Uri Orr, the 679th Armored Brigade commander, ordered Captain Amos Ben David's company to repel the threat. Ben David soon reported that he had pushed the attackers far from the camp fence.

This rebuff at the Naffach camp gates forced Colonel Shafiq Fiyad, the 91st Tank Brigade commander, to reconsider his options. As soon as Orr's countermoves became clear, Fiyad ordered the bulk of his battalion-strength force to stream along westward, cross-country, and avoid key crossroads and other points the Israelis were bound to have defended.

Meantime, Orr needed to concentrate a company to meet a threat east of the Sindiana Road. Sarig's and Ben David's companies were then heavily engaged; 679th Brigade had nothing to commit. Colonel Orr placed a priority call to Brigadier General Eitan, who arranged the temporary transfer of six Centurions from Ben Gal's hard-pressed 7th Brigade.

Captain Amnon Sharon, whose Reserve company had been ambushed in the night south of Naffach, had one of the better views of the widening battle in Orr's sector. After seeing to the evacuation of crews from knocked-out tanks, Sharon had blacked out as a result of his own injuries. He eventually awoke to the noise of armor on the move. "At first, the Syrians passed from Hushniya toward Naffach [grouped], in three tight rows, just like a parade. I waited for about an hour. When they returned, they shelled us again, then opened the battle. I tried to discover who they were fighting. They were not in travel formation this time, but spread out over the entire area."

A Syrian infantry sergeant accompanying the tanks was climbing over a large boulder when he spotted the Israeli company commander alone on the battlefield. Immediately the Syrian tried to surrender to Sharon, who was trying to surrender to the Syrian before some other Syrian shot him down. Shortly after 0800, Sharon "won" the bizarre standoff; he became a prisoner.

Unable to commit more tanks, the Syrians moved to break the impasse near Naffach by mounting a helicopter assault against the Israeli camp itself. Israeli tank crews south of Naffach were startled by the sudden appearance of low-flying, troop-carrying helicopters, but nevertheless recovered in time to down three of the aircraft. Israeli fighter-bombers hit the assault formation, claiming three helicopters downed. In fact, one of six helicopters in the formation actually reached Naffach, where its crew and passengers were killed by small-arms fire before they could disembark.

It was not all going Orr's way, however. Two of his tank companies had been ambushed, the commander of another company had been wounded by a Sagger missile, and an acting company commander was killed in action.

The stalemate fighting ground on. The brigade's jeepborne reconnaissance company, under Lieutenant Shimon Ryan, served a pivotal role in the Israeli stand. According to Ryan, "There was a need to help the injured, and to look at the area all the time in order to give directions and warn of flank attacks and surprise attacks. I saw Syrian tanks trying to flank us and attack our tanks without them being aware of what was happening. I would immediately organize another force of tanks to help those being flanked."

Slowly Orr's 679th Brigade tankers, and helpers from other units, gathered momentum. By late afternoon, the initiative had passed to Israeli hands simply because the IDF crews were able to outlast the

Syrians in what had long since become a battle of attrition. Assisted by precious tactical air support, Orr's tankers were able to reoccupy Sindiana and surrounding heights by sunset. The Syrians suffered major personnel losses in the final 679th Brigade attacks. When it was over, Orr's tanks were oriented southward along the Hushniya–Ramatnia–Sindiana Road and along the east–west road just north of Sindiana.

The southernmost Syrian thrust in the central Golan, that against the Hushniya–Arik Bridge Road, fell upon the sector covered by the remnant of Sarig Force, whose commander, Colonel Ran Sarig, had been wounded and evacuated on Sunday morning. On Monday morning, Sarig Force was fighting on with makeshift platoons drawn from all the armored brigades deployed in its sector. By midmorning, under relentless pressure from the Syrian 2nd Mechanized Brigade, a crisis was developing. The urgent need for strong leadership became critical when the officer who had carried on in Colonel Sarig's place was killed on Monday afternoon.

On hearing of the force commander's death, Major General Dan Laner ordered his deputy, Brigadier General Moshe Bar Kochba, to assume control. Bar Kochba immediately took leave of the 240th Armored Division command post and drove forward with a tiny advance headquarters.

The deputy division commander's half-track was fired on by Syrian tanks well short of Sarig Force's mobile headquarters. At one point, Bar Kochba and his companions counted fourteen Syrian tanks firing at them as the driver frantically maneuvered across open terrain. Miraculously, the command half-track reached the Sarig Force rear collection area unscathed.

Bar Kochba's first impressions were negative: No one was in charge; crews of damaged tanks were sitting among abandoned equipment. The general stalked through the disorganized encampment until he found an officer who seemed to be at least in control of himself. The man was promoted on the spot to command Sarig Force, at which point Bar Kochba began spewing forth specific recommendations for improving the unit's position and fighting capabilities.

The young officer soon had men and machines in motion toward threatened portions of the sector. Damaged tanks were pulled into stationary positions from which they could cover the camp's outer perimeter until ordnance crews had an opportunity to repair and refit them. Gradually the position took on the look and feel of an organized collection point.

Bar Kochba next turned his attention to the forward combat elements. Even as the general spoke aloud of his plan, the young brigade commander he had so recently appointed was severely wounded by incoming fire.

The next commander of Sarig Force was Major Giora Bierman, a Reserve staff officer who had checked himself out of the hospital when he heard about the start of the war. As the force's advance ran headlong into a Syrian ambush, Bierman immediately evolved into an effective combat commander by leading ten revitalized Centurion crews in a wide flanking maneuver against thirteen Syrian tanks. Bierman's force hit the Syrian rear and won the decision by destroying all thirteen Syrian tanks.

Never one merely to direct a fight, Brigadier General Bar Kochba moved to the forwardmost combat elements and personally directed the action, which he strove to conduct with minimum force and maximum technical expertise—preferring steady if minimal gains to costly leaps into Syrian-held sectors. Bar Kochba's steady, intelligently applied pressure stabilized the Sarig Force sector and returned ground to Israeli hands.

The final attack of the day was mounted by 7th Infantry Division's 121st Mechanized Brigade. Brigadier General Omar Abrash had concluded that the Booster position was the Israeli defensive key point, and he was so determined to secure it that he personally joined in preparation for the assault.

Early Monday evening, the combined tank-mechanized infantry force made excellent initial contact against weakened Israeli armored formations and minuscule Israeli infantry elements near the boundary between Laner's and Eitan's divisions.

While the Israeli center held, Colonel Ben Gal ordered his southernmost unit—Captain Tiger Zamir's six-tank Centurion company from 82nd Battalion—to pitch in a surprise flank attack and proceed across the divisional boundary into the Syrian rear. Ever faithful, Tiger moved out on cue. As the company advanced, it came face-to-face with at least seven Syrians tanks. Tiger joined battle and eventually evicted the Syrians. From that point, the battle went entirely against the Syrians. Three hours after jumping off in quest of the Booster position, 121st Mechanized Brigade was forced from the field.

Brigadier General Abrash did not share in the early elation nor in the ultimate sorrow. The leonine American-trained commander of 7th Infantry Division was killed by Israeli tank fire even as his assault was getting under way.

Ben Gal's brigade had held in the center, Orr's 679th Armored Brigade was poised for a southward thrust along the cease-fire line at Sindiana, and Bierman's revitalized Sarig Force was holding the line in front of Hushniya.

· 5 ·
COUNTERATTACK

20

The only place on the battle-field where the Syrians came close to attaining their strategic goals was the southern Golan, where Brigadier General Ali Aslan's powerful 5th Infantry Division had penetrated some twenty miles along the El Al Road. In this sector Aslan supervised the creation of a defense in depth, positioning 132nd Mechanized Brigade and a battalion of 47th Independent Tank Brigade—some sixty T-55s—along a front based upon the constricted El Al Ridge.

Five miles to the rear, while Israelis on Tel Saki stubbornly clung to a tiny enclave of bunkers, 5th Infantry Division's organic antitank battalion set up a defensive locality heavily sown with 106mm recoilless rifles and BRDM-mounted Sagger antitank missiles. The entire battalion dug into carefully sited positions for several miles around the tel and had itself well situated before dawn on Monday, October 8. Supporting the Syrian defense of the Tel Saki sector was a strong, otherwise uncommitted tank concentration.

An additional five miles to the north, at Tel Juhadar, Aslan emplaced a commando unit that could be supported by nearby elements of 112th Infantry Brigade.

Between Tel Juhadar and the Rafid crossroads, spread across four miles of ground, was an array of eighteen 106mm antitank guns and the division's organic SU-100 self-propelled gun battalion. Adjoining this force, on the north side of the El Al Road, were elements of 9th Infantry Division's 43rd Mechanized Brigade, deployed in support of the commando unit holding Tel Faris. And four miles to the northeast, at Tel Kudna, in Syria, was the main body of 43rd Brigade. Also in the north, around Hushniya, were further elements of 43rd Brigade, two antitank battalions, and a 122mm howitzer battalion. In strategic reserve, at Tel Hara, northeast of Tel Kudna, was 3rd Tank Division's 15th Mechanized Brigade, which had not yet seen combat and which fielded forty T-55s. In addition, the entire roadway was within range of 50th Artillery Brigade, which had displaced forward in the night to positions nine and a half kilometers east of Tel Saki. The brigade's fifty-four large-caliber guns could be brought to bear against virtually any point on the Golan.

To General Aslan's way of thinking, the key to the southern Golan lay at the eastern end of the El Al Ridge, before Ramat Magshimim. As long as the line held there, Aslan believed, the Israelis would be restricted to the ridge and thus would be obliged to funnel their efforts into a single approach.

Ein Hamud, the Waterfall Route north of the ridge, was not perceived as being a major access. Even so, the Syrians had dispatched a reinforced tank company to the area and, unbeknownst to the Israelis, had begun laying minefields to close off potential outlets.

As envisioned by Syrian General Headquarters, the Army would have reconquered the entire Golan before the IDF was ready to launch a counterattack. The Israeli Reserve formations rushed to the Golan thus would face a victorious army operating beneath a dense air-defense umbrella, supported by artillery, stiffened with commando forces occupying strategic positions, enjoying superiority in firepower and in numbers of men and machines already occupying the best positions. By Tuesday morning, 5th Infantry Division, at any rate, was confident of repulsing any possible Israeli counterattack.

Though Brigadier General Mussa Peled was called back to duty on Saturday morning and had been brutally working himself ever since, his war really began Sunday evening, at a meeting with Major

General Yitzhak Hofi and Lieutenant General Haim Bar Lev at Northern Command headquarters.

Bar Lev, a former IDF chief of staff and the incumbent minister of trade and industry, had gotten back in uniform in response to an urgent request by Prime Minister Golda Meir to act as her direct representative at Northern Command headquarters. By the time Peled met with Bar Lev and Hofi, the two senior generals had succeeded in outlining a general plan aimed at first containing the Syrians, then driving them back to the Purple Line. Hofi and his staff, with Bar Lev's concurrence, had reasoned that Peled's fresh brigades should assume responsibility for sweeping the southern Golan.

At length, Peled received orders from General Hofi to mount a counterattack in the southern sector of the Golan early on October 8. Hofi was convinced that the best way to eject the Syrian Army to the prewar border was to implement a southward thrust through Laner's division along the Rafid–Kuneitra Road. This meant that Peled's Reserve brigades—205th Armored Brigade and 9th Armored Infantry Brigade—would have to assemble upon the Golan by way of the Arik and B'not Yaacov bridges, both congested and quite far from the division's depots, which were south of the Kinneret.

It all added up to a formidable task for a division that had not been among the very first Reserve organizations called up. Already Peled's uncommitted tank formations were reporting difficulties arising out of the shortage of tank transporters and the necessity of moving long distances on their own tracks; breakdowns were being reported all along the division's several lines of march. Thus Peled requested that he be allowed to take 205th Armored Brigade along a more direct route, which would bring him to the far southern end of the Golan by shorter roads. Once on the Golan, Peled's brigades would mount immediate attacks along the first roadway they encountered: the El Al Road. The trade-off was clear: Peled would enjoy less artillery support in the far southern Golan than he would farther north, and his tanks would have a greater distance to maneuver in combat. On the other hand, his divisional attack could be mounted three hours earlier. Hofi acceded to Peled's suggestion, and the decision soon was confirmed by General Bar Lev.

Generally speaking, the agreement meant that Peled would have to form his 146th Reserve Armored Division—and absorb assorted units already in combat along the southern Golan—on the narrow strip of ground overlooking the Kinneret, then drive by all available access roads in a northeasterly direction along the dominant El Al Ridge, sweeping the border areas from south to north, from the frontier with Jordan to Rafid.

By the time Peled met with his senior staff and commanders at 2200 hours on Sunday evening in Tzemach, at the southern end of the Kinneret, the divisional plan had been refined and processed. Essentially the division would fight its way along two roughly parallel routes. The main effort would be made by Colonel Mordechai Ben Porat's 9th Reserve Armored Infantry Brigade along the El Al–Rafid Road. In support would be Colonel Yossi Peled's 205th Reserve Armored Brigade, which would initially follow Ben Porat, then branch off or advance through 9th Brigade, as required. Even farther behind—actually as a backup—would be the independent and third-rate 70th Reserve Armored Infantry Brigade, which would both mop up and screen the divisional right flank above the Ruqqad Stream. Screening the divisional left as it advanced from the Gamla Rise to Hushniya by way of Mazrat Kuneitra and Nahal Geshur would be Colonel Zvi Bar's reconstituted District Brigade, essentially an ad hoc unit created from Bar's administrative headquarters and from battalions originally earmarked for Barak and 205th Armored brigades.

By dawn on October 8, the assembling elements of General Peled's 146th Armored Division had fielded 109 Centurion and Super Sherman tanks on the southern Golan. This was a larger force than could be accommodated by the restricted terrain, so Peled endlessly juggled with the concentration of firepower and the dispersion of subordinate units. At no other time in the conflict were so many IDF tanks concentrated upon a single roadway. Amazingly, neither Syrian missiles nor warplanes disturbed the coalescing force.

Arrayed on the plateau itself were the forces Peled had taken over from Major General Dan Laner's control: Lieutenant Colonel Oded Eres's fourteen Barak Brigade Centurions, newly arrived from Tel Faris, and Lieutenant Colonel Yoav Vaspe's two diminished tank companies of 71st Reserve Armored Infantry Battalion, also technically a Barak Brigade formation. These units, which were concentrated around or supported through Ein Hamud, were operating under the command of Colonel Bar. To round out Bar's force, Peled turned over most of 205th Brigade's 61st Tank Battalion. Thus, in addition to Eres's fourteen Centurions, which would be held in reserve until the crews had been rested and the vehicles resupplied and repaired, Bar would control twenty-seven tanks on the divisional left flank.

On the El Al Ridge itself, Colonel Ben Porat's 9th Reserve Armored Infantry Brigade fielded eighteen Super Shermans from Lieutenant Colonel Benzion Paden's 595th Tank Battalion, a Peled unit first attached to Laner but now returned to Peled. General Peled added a tank battalion and a reconnaissance company when they arrived from the Jordan Valley depots, but he had to withhold Ben Porat's armored infantry battalion simply because there was no place to deploy it.

Unlike other Reserve units ultimately bound for the Golan, Colonel Yossi Peled's 205th Armored Brigade, a unit with a long history and an unblemished combat record, was called up rather late, a result of the sheer congestion on Israel's communications and road networks.

Typical of 205th Brigade's Reservists were Asaf Kotef and Hillel Bernstein. Kotef was a resident of the Golan, and the war had begun for him early Saturday morning, when the women and children of his village were hurriedly sent down the escarpment. Later Kotef's village was one of the very first civilian targets struck by Syrian artillery. However, it was late afternoon before Kotef could leave the village; he was obliged to wait at home until his call-up notice arrived, in midafternoon.

Hillel Bernstein was a resident of a Jordan Valley village just below the Golan escarpment, so he was not affected by the evacuation above. The village phones were busy throughout Saturday as individuals were called to join their units. When a truck picked up a group of tankers, Bernstein took note. The war had not yet begun, but he felt his time was at hand. He was still at home when news of war arrived, and he had to wait three more hours before he was summoned.

Bernstein did not reach his reconnaissance company's depot in central Israel until 0300 hours on Sunday, thirteen hours after the war started. He and his comrades, including Asaf Kotef, found that by then another unit had cleared out their vehicles and supplies. In the best tradition of the IDF, the reconnaissance company "organized" itself anew with "borrowed" jeeps.

The leading elements of 205th Brigade were on the move by 0930 hours on Sunday, heading north through West Bank Arab villages. The jeep company was short by over one fifth of its strength in vehicles, and the jeeps it did have on hand were not properly outfitted for light reconnaissance. During a stopover in one village, the troops welded makeshift mounts for their machine guns. Then, guessing rather than knowing they were bound for the Golan, the company commander dispatched a jeep to nearby villages to collect maps.

Sometime later, Bernstein's and another jeep were detached and ordered to Ramot, near the Waterfall Route. Bernstein was shocked by the appearance of some of the troops he encountered. These were soldiers in retreat from the Syrian onslaught. Their uniforms were ragged, and many had no weapons.

At dawn on Monday, Hillel Bernstein was ready to move on the Waterfall Route, and Asaf Kotef was deployed on the El Al Ridge. They and their portions of the reconnaissance company were ready to join the battle, though their unit and most others were understrength. The reconnaissance troops were expected to perform their duties from makeshift vehicles, with borrowed maps, and without the binoculars their work normally required.

When Bernstein's section climbed to the top of the Waterfall Route, Bernstein happened to recognize Colonel Zvi Bar, under whom he had previously served. Bernstein was struck by the number of things the District Brigade commander was doing at one time. Though Bernstein was eager to join the battle, he nevertheless spent a frustrating day guiding damaged tanks down the Waterfall Route to repair depots in the Jordan Valley.

Constrained by the terrain as much as anything, Brigadier General Peled felt that it was impossible to mount an assault up the long axis of the El Al Ridge with anything larger than Lieutenant Colonel Paden's 595th Tank Battalion of Colonel Ben Porat's 9th Brigade. Thus Paden's Super Shermans moved off their line of departure at

0830 hours on October 8, while trailing 205th Brigade elements provided a base of fire. Syrian opposition on the exposed ridge was initially fierce.

The Syrians of 47th Independent Tank Brigade were quite surprised to see the Israelis leading off with the Shermans. In fact, they took it as a sign of weakness. They certainly did not read the attack as posing any danger, nor certainly as a harbinger of a major threat to their conquest. Initially their feelings were justified. In the first hour, Paden lost seven Super Shermans destroyed or disabled, but his battalion also advanced into terrain that could support a broader attack.

General Peled next ordered 205th Brigade to take over the assault. The brigade commander, Colonel Yossi Peled, committed Lieutenant Colonel Guy Jacobsen's battalion, which moved out at 1015 hours. Shortly, the fresh Israeli Reserve crews felt they were slowly gaining the upper hand in the tank-versus-tank combat. Companies led by Captain David Livney and Captain Uri Efri claimed eleven T-55s destroyed in just thirty minutes. Just before 1100 hours, Jacobsen reported that his tanks had secured the first objective. In the meantime, Syrian crews on 47th Tank Brigade's left flank were deeply rattled by the advance of Asaf Kotef's reconnaissance unit—so unsettled, in fact, that 47th Brigade simply crumbled under light pressure. By 1125 hours, the advance reconnaissance element—three jeeps—reported that they had entered Ramat Magshimim. Thus the bottleneck on the El Al Ridge was behind them, and the way to the east lay open.

The collapse of 47th Tank Brigade was catastrophic, and it has never been adequately explained. Many Syrian crews abandoned their undamaged T-55s and escaped on foot. As many tanks as were destroyed or disabled by Israeli gunfire were abandoned without a fight. Maintenance problems might have contributed to the rout, but the rigid Syrian command system seems to have played a major role; a tank commander retiring in the face of the enemy was automatically in violation of orders. In that sense, a usable tank placed its crew in jeopardy; a crew that arrived in the rear on foot could at least say that its vehicle had been destroyed or disabled by enemy fire or as a result of equipment failure or the expenditure of all its ammunition. Who could prove otherwise?

* * *

General Peled did not question his luck; he simply exploited it. He ordered Lieutenant Colonel Moshe Meler's 61st Tank Battalion of 205th Reserve Armored Brigade to mount an assault against the Syrian right flank, but Meler erred in navigation, and the battalion ran off in the wrong direction. When the division commander realized what had occurred, he ordered 205th and 9th brigades to attack the Syrians head-on. While 205th Brigade peeled northward, 9th Brigade slowed to take on fuel and ammunition as well as seal the division's left flank. Shortly, Peled ordered the 9th Brigade commander, Colonel Mordechai Ben Porat, to swing off onto the lateral roadway running northward from Ramat Magshimim. This move would considerably broaden the divisional front. Thus Peled could commit a far greater proportion of his strength and bring on fresh formations.

Lieutenant Colonel Jacobsen's battalion, bound for Tel Juhadar, streaked forward but did not reach the place unscathed. The Syrian 5th Infantry Division's antitank battalion, deployed around Tel Saki since before sunrise, had been unable to assist 47th Tank Brigade because of distance, but the gun crews had been able to observe 205th Brigade's advance since about 1000 hours. Well dug in and concealed, the Syrians stayed put without disclosing their presence. In time, Jacobsen's battalion drove abreast of Tel Saki.

According to one Israeli tanker, "We had been attacking for some hours along the main road, and it seemed we had succeeded in pushing back the enemy. Suddenly the Syrians opened fire with antitank guns and missiles, firing from well-concealed positions in the rocky ground on both sides of the road. Several of our tanks brewed up. A shell cracked off our front plate and went screaming away, shaking us badly."

This Israeli tank commander spotted an antitank gun but was prevented from firing on it when another Israeli tank blocked his main gun. Then the intervening tank blew up. Moments later "we found ourselves right in front of a Syrian crew manning a missile launcher. We simply ran over them."

By 1245 hours, 146th Reserve Armored Division's vanguard battalion was approaching the foot of Tel Juhadar, marking a sixteen-kilometer advance in just two and a half hours. Miraculously, despite the loss of several tanks, Jacobsen's tank battalion had yet to suffer a single fatality.

The Israeli breakthrough—sudden and unexpected—prompted Brigadier General Ali Aslan to make direct contact with Major General Yousef Chakour, the Syrian chief of staff. Aslan reported that the destruction of 47th Tank Brigade and the loss of over fifty of its T-55s left him without a mobile reserve. He further pointed out that the loss of Ramat Magshimim provided the Israelis with plenty of room to maneuver. Aslan considered the Israeli breakthrough to be major news. On the other hand, Chakour erred in his assessment of the report, and acted as though it were a purely local tactical event and thus of little strategic importance. Chakour simply ordered Aslan to concentrate sufficient forces to finish off Bunker 116, which was tying down units that could be used elsewhere. Then he directed Aslan to concentrate his remaining tanks and hold the strategic tels. The Syrian chief of staff reiterated his view that Israeli forces denied access to the Petroleum and El Al roads could not provide a strategic threat in the southern Golan. He acceded to Aslan's request to stretch a battalion of 1st Tank Division's 4th Tank Brigade southward to defend the Petroleum Road, but he refused to release 15th Mechanized Brigade's tank battalion, at Tel Hara.

It was by then about 1300 hours, and Colonel Yossi Peled's 205th Brigade was running at full stride. Asaf Kotef's reconnaissance element was screening the brigade and division right, sweeping northward along the prewar cease-fire line. On its left was Jacobsen's tank battalion, and farther on was Lieutenant Colonel Tuvia Teren's tank battalion.

The advance elements of 9th Brigade reaching Nahal Geshur were greeted by a lone Israeli infantryman armed with his service rifle and one hand grenade. Asked what he was doing there alone, the soldier replied that his last order on Saturday had been to hold the village. He had lost contact with his officer in the rush of events since but had clung to his directive. Fortunately for him, the Syrians had bypassed the place.

Numerous Syrians had themselves been bypassed in the headlong Israeli rush to replace the collapsed 47th Tank Brigade, so throughout the day, Israeli follow-up units had the opportunity to fire on trucks, armored personnel carriers, and groups of soldiers fleeing on foot—the effluvia of an army in retreat. Many Syrian units remained fully organized and in possession of their weapons and defensive sectors, but even these eventually succumbed to the inflexibility of the directives they had last received from any central or unifying authority.

Though its purpose had been obviated, the 5th Infantry Division antitank battalion arrayed around Tel Saki had no authority to withdraw or even to regroup or redeploy within the defense locality it was charged with holding. Jacobsen's tank battalion of 205th Brigade, the first Israeli unit to encounter this defensive key point, underestimated its strength and depth and thus was badly mauled by a storm of missiles and RPGs. The battalion commander quickly realized that he had bitten off more than he could chew, so he called up assistance. When it arrived, the somewhat chastened battalion continued on toward its objective, Tel Juhadar.

The Syrians fought ferociously when directly threatened. By the early evening, this single defensive locality had drawn off elements of 205th, District, and, 9th brigades, fighting head-on and to the left and right flanks, respectively. Units of 9th Brigade finally stove in the right flank simply by attacking straight ahead, all guns blazing. The force of the attack drove through to an undefended sector, from which the Israelis could exploit the breakthrough. In time the balance of the Syrian antitank battalion was destroyed in detail.

The relief by 205th Brigade of the Israelis trapped by the Syrian onslaught at Tel Saki was a shock. Once trapped, the survivors had turned their bunkers into a casualty collection point, segregating the dead from the badly wounded. In fact, only one man was unscathed, though any of the wounded capable of bearing arms did so. The driver of the jeep routinely sent to check on the tel position was unprepared for the scenes of horror he encountered. He placed an immediate call for doctors, medics, and transportation.

The first doctor on the scene was Jacobsen's battalion surgeon, who was followed in quick succession by Teren's battalion surgeon, 205th Brigade's chief surgeon, and ten medics—nearly the entire brigade medical component. Within minutes, the doctors decided to evacuate everyone by air, and three separate helicopter lifts were completed by 1600 hours.

It was evident that Aslan's 5th Infantry Division was stunned beyond hope by the power and swiftness of Mussa Peled's attack. Some Syrian units were able to maintain discipline and motivation and even maneuver effectively into the rear of the Israeli assault brigades, but even those lost heart in the course of confrontations they should have won.

Two half-tracks in the care of Major David Caspi, deputy commander of Teren's Reserve tank battalion, were making their way across rolling terrain in the wake of their unit's swift advance when, on emerging from a fold in the ground, they were confronted by a pair of T-55s escorting three armored personnel carriers. Caspi, who was headmaster of a school in civilian life, instinctively ordered the two utterly outclassed 1943-vintage half-tracks to charge the Syrian armored vehicles. The only weapons the Israelis possessed were several .50- and .30-caliber machine guns and 9mm Uzi submachine guns. The bewildered Syrian crews leaped out of their vehicles and responded to the Israeli fire with their own infantry weapons and hand grenades. Without ever making a move to fire the T55s' 100mm guns, the Syrians were all shot to death by Caspi's incredulous headquarters warriors.

Elsewhere, and just a little later, the crews of two Israeli self-propelled artillery pieces that had set up west of Tel Saki were shocked to find several T-55s heading right at them. Lacking anti-tank weapons or even armor-piercing shells, the artillerymen lowered the barrels of their guns and prepared to confront the Syrian armor in what must certainly be a last act of defiance. Given the agility of the tanks, their relatively quick-firing main guns, and their ability to traverse their turrets through 360 degrees, the Israelis were certain of dying. To their utter relief, the Syrian tanks withdrew.

Following its battle at Tel Saki before 1300 hours, Jacobsen's tank battalion had continued its advance toward Tel Juhadar, first passing beyond the fires of the Syrian antitank defensive locality at Tel Saki but eventually coming within range of antitank formations bolstering 5th Infantry Division's 132nd Mechanized Brigade, which was charged with holding Jacobsen's objective. The Syrian mechanized brigade pulled back in the face of the Israeli armored advances, but the dug-in SU-100 gun carriers, BRDM antitank missile carriers, and 106mm antitank guns, all bolstered with infantry wielding numerous RPGs, did not. Thus a formidable—immovable—defensive locality very much like the one around Tel Saki stood between Jacobsen's tank crews and their objective.

Captain Boaz Gilboa's vanguard company was permitted to advance to within three hundred meters of the tel before Syrian commandos backed by numerous antitank weapons cut loose. The sudden onset of the ambush thoroughly nonplussed the Israeli tankers, and the company's cohesion disappeared in the face of massed fire. Several tanks were lost, and Jacobsen's battalion suffered its first fatality of the day.

On hearing from Jacobsen, Colonel Yossi Peled informed division headquarters that Tel Juhadar was strongly held. Next, Colonel Peled personally led Captain Yair Zur's tank company off the vulnerable roadway and threw in a quick assault to the south. Five T-55s were overcome and destroyed, but it became clear that Israeli tanks alone could not reduce the defenses. Then Syrian jet fighter-bombers attacked Jacobsen's battalion, and that really drove the lesson home.

At 1330 hours, Colonel Peled requested that infantry he brought forward to the tel, but the request was denied initially because there simply was no infantry available. However, a reconnaissance officer who overheard the exchange took it upon himself to round up stray bodies, including an 81mm mortar platoon, which he loaded aboard four APCs and two half-tracks.

The attack was delayed for a few moments while the Israelis argued among themselves as to whether the makeshift armored infantry force should be sent up the tel aboard the fighting vehicles or on foot. It was finally decided that the troops would go in aboard the APCs and half-tracks. A radio frequency was assigned, and the little force assaulted the bristling heights.

The better part of an hour was consumed in fighting the armored infantry to the summit. Even then, it was found that the area was far from secure. Fortunately, several tanks from Teren's battalion arrived in time to reduce the odds further, in this case two more Syrian tanks and several BRDM missile carriers. By nightfall, after hours of mopping up, the main strength of 205th Armored Brigade was concentrated around the quiescent height.

An Israeli armored infantry column spent most of the afternoon picking its way along the patrol road overlooking the Ruqqad Stream, at the former cease-fire line. Its immediate objective was Bunker 116, which had been under intense pressure since Syrian Chief of Staff Chakour had ordered 5th Infantry Division's Brigadier General Aslan to break in and destroy the complex. The deliberate advance was slowed by the incessant need to chase down Syrian rear guards either abandoned and forgotten by their superiors, or left in place specifically to slow the Israeli advance.

The Syrian assault force at Bunker 116 had broken into the compound and would not withdraw. Lieutenant Yosef Gur led the spectacular action for four long hours, holding the Syrians to their initial gains where possible, pushing them back where and when possible. At length, the battle boiled over into the trenches, where the sheer weight of armored machines gave way to hand-to-hand fighting. The Israeli armored infantry finally came within sight of the beleaguered bunker complex at about 1600 hours, and the Syrians immediately pulled back, leaving a dozen wrecked tanks and armored personnel carriers. Yosef Gur and his tiny garrison had held out against monstrous odds for over fifty-one hours. Word of the relief of Bunker 116 provided Colonel Yossi Peled's tired crews with a needed uplift in morale.

On the far left of Brigadier General Mussa Peled's divisional sector, Colonel Zvi Bar's upgraded District Brigade had spent the better part of the day screening the flank and supporting thrusts by sister brigades. By 1330 hours, 71st Armored Infantry Battalion Centurions under Lieutenant Colonel Yoav Vaspe had reached the Petroleum Road north of Tel Juhadar. At that point, Colonel Bar ordered Lieutenant Colonel Moshe Meler's 61st Tank Battalion to attack eastward to the Rafid–Kuneitra Road.

No sooner had Meler jumped off than a reinforced Syrian tank company fielding fourteen T-55s counterattacked. The battle briefly raged, and ten of the T-55s were destroyed. However, the Syrians' sacrifice was not in vain. It was late enough for Colonel Bar to have to reconsider his planned thrust. In the end he decided to order Meler's battalion to withdraw to a seemingly safe night laager.

Meler's final report of the day claimed the destruction by his battalion of twenty-seven Syrian tanks without the loss of one Israeli life.

In the wake of the morning breakout battles along the El Al Ridge, Colonel Ben Porat's 9th Armored Infantry Brigade had reorganized and replenished fuel and ammunition at Ramat Magshimim, following which it set off to the north, bound for Hushniya. Elements of 9th Brigade became embroiled in the bitter reduction of the Syrian defensive locality around Tel Saki, but the bulk of the formation contributed to the assault along the brigade's main axis.

After advancing eight miles, the brigade's vanguard company spotted a Syrian force deployed at Um a Danger. The lead company spread out into battle formation without halting, and it smoothly opened fire on the Syrians at ranges of about one kilometer—a textbook assault. The next company in the column swung to the right and mounted an immediate flank assault. The nonstop pincers reduced forty antitank positions within minutes. Only two of the Israeli tanks were hit, and both remained operational.

By nightfall of October 8, Brigadier General Peled's 146th Armored Division had succeeded in retaking most of the southern Golan and had relieved several small but emotionally vital garrisons. The cease-fire line had not been quite secured, nor had all the division's objectives for the day been reached. However, the Syrians had lost the use of a long stretch of the Petroleum Road and had lost access to most of the southern road net. Most important among the Reserve division's formidable achievements was the essentially strategic jeopardy in which its advances had placed numerous Syrian battle formations facing Israeli units to the north. In the southern Golan, at least, the Israelis had won strategic depth on the battlefield, a crucial victory from which bountiful fruits stood to be harvested in the hours and days to come.

21

None of Israel's reactions—Colonel Amir Drori's infantry attack in the far North, Brigadier General Mussa Peled's penetration in the far South, or Major General Dan Laner's give-and-take in the center—was significant enough to divert Syrian attention from the one reaction that prevented the fulfillment of their grand design. The Israelis simply refused to be budged from the ridge between the Booster position and the Hermonit.

The failure of 81st Tank Brigade to dislodge the Israelis was a shock to the senior officers manning Syrian General Headquarters. They were not unlike scientists who know that if object A is struck by object B, result C is predictable. The formula had worked on October 6 at Hushniya, along the El Al Ridge, and on the Hermon. Inexplicably, it had not worked when tried in the north-central sector by Brigadier General Omar Abrash's 7th Infantry Division. Syrian General Headquarters thus repeated the formula by committing 78th Tank Brigade, and the result was even more startling: It was rendered ineffective. So Syrian General Headquarters had tried again to find a more perfect object B: T-62 tanks and additional artillery. The results had been perplexing. Eighty-first Tank Brigade, one of the jewels of the Syrian Army, had perished upon the slopes of the ridge the Syrians designated "Red."

The Syrians faced a compound problem. On the one hand, they had expended their budget for the war. To regain the Golan fully, they would have to dip into their strategic reserves. If not, they had to abandon their goals, entirely or in part.

Serious doubt existed as to the efficacy of tactics employed thus far in the north-center.

After some debate, Syrian General Headquarters resolved to try again. The budget was increased at the expense of the strategic reserves, and the battlefield tactics were altered.

Of the three tank brigades set aside to guard Damascus, Colonel Rifat Assad's 70th "Republican Guard" Tank Brigade was released to continue the assault. This was the first time any army had committed the new BMP armored personnel carrier, with its turreted 73mm gun and Sagger missile capability. The Republican Guard's combination of BMPs and T-62s comprised a mobile force unique in the Middle East at the time, a force on par with the best-equipped American or Soviet forces.

Three specific tactical changes were made. In contrast with the attacks of 78th and 81st brigades, the Republican Guard would mount its assault in broad daylight. Thus a MiG-17 squadron could be directly allocated to the brigade for close air support. Finally, commandos would be helicoptered to the battlefield to seal the breakthrough sector against reinforcement.

On Tuesday, October 9, the morning mist that clung to the front in the area held by the IDF's 7th Armored Brigade gave no hint of the impending Syrian assault. Uppermost in the mind of Colonel Avigdor Ben Gal was the sheer exhaustion of all his troops. Some had not rested since the last night of peace, now fully three days and two long nights in the past. The combat crews had been under incessant fire since the war began, and the men of the support units had worked around the clock to ease the burden on the tank crews, to keep the tanks running. Their achievements had been remarkable. Ad hoc ordnance crews had returned fourteen Centurions to combat just in the first twenty-four-hour period. Word got around fast: A tanker coming in to refuel or rearm knew that everything that could be done would be done to ease the burden of his concerns.

However, some crews missed even this solace. Captain Tiger Zamir's dwindling company of 82nd Tank Battalion was refurbished in the field following an all-night, fire-and-move battle. Tiger had kept his crews buttoned up in their Centurions since the shellings began on Saturday. Even the calls of nature had been answered into empty shell casings.

Physical, mental, and emotional depletion was becoming as big an enemy as the enemy. Many tricks were adopted to remain alert, but Captain Avraham Palnet, an acting company commander, came up with the most effective: He roused his crews by firing a machine gun at the armored hulls of his company's tanks.

The continuous shelling by the Syrians seemed ominous to Colonel Ben Gal as he tried to balance the need to remain at a high state of readiness with the physical needs of his crewmen. As the brigade commander acted, the Syrian fire picked up, and Katyusha rockets were added to the artillery crescendo. Between 0615 and 0625 hours, the Syrian MiG-17 squadron assigned to support the Republican Guard Brigade flew nearly a dozen combat sorties around Kuneitra.

Ben Gal's 7th Armored Brigade was by then divided into five combat groups. None of these groups, even when designated as a battalion, approached company strength. In all, between forty and forty-five Centurions comprised the ragtag brigade. To create a new reserve—for Ben Gal remained compulsive in such matters—Kahalani's 77th Tank Battalion, now only seven Centurions strong, was ordered to the rear. As Ben Gal was seeing to Kahalani's relief, he called Brigadier General Rafoul Eitan's divisional headquarters to impress the staff further with his need for relief.

The easternmost Israeli force in the 7th Brigade sector was a small band of survivors of Barak Brigade's 74th Tank Battalion—eight tanks and crews under Lieutenant Colonel Yair Nofshe spread out in ones and twos around Bunker 107. This small force had been in combat longer than any other IDF tank formation.

After spending the night in a copse barely large enough to hide his Centurion's chassis, Yair Nofshe saw a T-55 and three armored personnel carriers in the early dawn light. All were within three hundred meters of his position, their crews sitting atop the vehicles, preparing their breakfasts. Nofshe's own tank was still incapable of traversing its turret. To bear on a target, the gunner and driver had to work in close harmony to turn the entire tank. There was no way Nofshe was going to be able to destroy all four Syrian vehicles in the little time necessary, so he placed a hurried call to his nearest platoon leader. Both Centurions—Nofshe's and the young lieutenant's —started out amid Nofshe's reminder that moving at battle speed would raise telltale dust.

The platoon leader's first shot was a kill: The T-55 erupted in flame. As the Syrian crewmen scattered, the lieutenant's gunner quickly destroyed the three armored personnel carriers.

The platoon leader's tank was just returning to its fighting position when it was struck by a Sagger antitank missile. Sergeant Yosef Nidos, whose Centurion was nearest to the stricken tank, rushed to help. He thus drew all the fire, and his Centurion was likewise hit by a Syrian missile. A third tank commander contacted Nofshe for permission to assist the crews of the two damaged Centurions. Nofshe denied the request. His tiny force was down to six tanks, and he could not risk the probability of losing another on the killing ground.

Nofshe then added to Colonel Ben Gal's deepening gloom by reporting all that had occurred and adding that all his remaining tanks were about out of 105mm ammunition. In its turn, Ben Gal's frank report, passed through Eitan's divisional headquarters, jolted Major General Hofi's Northern Command headquarters, which had been monitoring the efforts by 7th Brigade to regain lost ground.

The reduction of Nofshe's force occurred at dawn, before the Syrians mounted their assault in the sector covered by Eitan's 36th Armored Infantry Division. Eitan then was headquartered several kilometers north of Naffach, on the Petroleum Road. He had been there since narrowly escaping the Syrian tanks that had first broken into the Naffach camp. Conditions and facilities at the new headquarters were primitive.

At first light, following MiG sorties across the divisional sector, Eitan was physically cut off from his front-line elements by the quick assault of seven Syrian helicopters, which landed between the division command post and Naffach. Artillery rounds and rockets were impacting all across the battlefield when the helicopters were sighted. Everyone who was watching knew that the airborne attack precursed a major ground effort.

The Syrian helicopters flew through heavy fire toward Bukata, where three or four of them flared out low and headed for the ground. Major Yoni Netanyahu, the American-born deputy commander of the crack 18th Parachute Battalion, had arrived in the vicinity with a company of troopers during the night, and he was busily setting up when the helicopters flew low overhead, ducking and weaving through intense fire. Netanyahu ran through the company defensive sector, among half-tracks, trucks, and APCs, shouting the names of men he wanted to lead into action against the Syrian commandos. He briefed his troopers by radio as they drove northward toward the suspected landing site.

An IDF APC that had driven in from the North was just engaging the Syrians when Netanyahu's troopers arrived. Return fire immediately took one Israeli life as Netanyahu led a charge through the grass. Without the time to dig in or even assemble, the Syrians were thrown off balance as the paratroop squads combed the landing site. At length, the surviving commandos of the main body tried to move eastward, toward friendly lines, but they ran into an IDF Centurion, which broke up the group and killed many.

The Syrians retaliated by disabling the Israeli tank with an RPG; then the survivors dug in.

The first violent clash claimed four Israeli paratroopers killed and one wounded, while forty Syrians died and two were taken prisoner. The Syrian mission had failed, but the fighting around Bukata was far from over.

General Eitan had ordered Golani Brigade to mount a counterattack just as the Syrians were landing, and a force of half-tracks bearing the infantrymen arrived to take on the Syrians.

The Israeli vehicles left the roadway and entered the field, which seemed flat because of the high grass that grew there but which actually was split by gulleys and hummocks that both concealed the surviving Syrians and threw the half-tracks topsy-turvy as they streamed off the roadway. Several of the half-tracks were struck by RPGs, and casualties had to be hauled out of the flaming wrecks by their comrades or by volunteers from other vehicles. Soon eleven APCs from the 7th Armored Brigade reconnaissance company joined the hunt. These moved from the roadway—where they were amply silhouetted against the sky—into adjacent fields east of Bukata. The deadly game of hide-and-seek persisted and spread.

Two of the reconnaissance APCs established a base of fire while three more worked their way into one of the fields. One of the three was immediately hit by an RPG and set afire, and a second RPG struck it seconds later.

The APC commanded by Ephraim Bader pulled in between the burning vehicle and the Syrian grenadiers as the crewmen bailed out and took cover. When the survivors had reached safety, the two remaining APCs ground on through the high growth. Suddenly a Syrian grenadier popped out of the grass and aimed his RPG at Bader's APC. The commando was killed by machine-gun fire, but Bader and his crew were transfixed for a moment while the RPG scraped down the length of their vehicle's hull. Moments later, Bader's .50-caliber machine gunner was wounded as he searched for targets from the exposed hatchway.

In time the reconnaissance troops, convinced that they had finished off the Syrians, loaded their wounded and those of the Golani unit and roared off down the road. They were ambushed by a second, hitherto unperceived group of Syrian commandos who had gone to ground upon landing just south of Bukata. Two APCs fell out of the column to engage the Syrians while the balance of the column passed. By the time the main body reached the aid station, the two APCs that had been left behind had been destroyed. A relief force had to be sent to rescue the surviving crewmen.

The Syrians would not be silenced until the late afternoon, when Captain Amos Ben David's company of 679th Armored Brigade was sent to Bukata from Laner's divisional sector. By that time 7th Brigade's reconnaissance company had lost twenty-five killed or wounded. By nightfall, the Israelis had picked up over a hundred Syrian corpses. No one doubted that other Syrians had survived and were laying in wait of targets.

Elsewhere, what was left of the main body of 7th Armored Brigade was again fighting for its life.

22

There simply were not any tank forces available to relieve, or even reinforce, Colonel Avigdor Ben Gal's 7th Armored Brigade.

Northern Command had just begun assembling a potential command reserve the evening before—and this pitiful assemblage was merely the battle-weary survivors of Lieutenant Colonel Oded Eres's 53rd Tank Battalion.

Barak Brigade had all but ceased to exist, but it remained "operational" as an administrative convenience. Its commander and key staff officers were dead, and nearly all its surviving troops and equipment had been absorbed into other brigades on the line. Scattered individuals and equipment, however, were slowly finding their way to the brigade depots in the Jordan Valley.

The survivors were undefeated. A team of physicians, psychiatrists, psychologists, and social workers dispatched to assist the Barak Brigade survivors had first to fight its own shock. According to one, "The full realization of how close the Syrians were to coming right into Rosh Pina hit me only when I saw the burned-out Syrian tanks already on the slope down the Golan Heights. They had overrun most of the bases and were on the way down."

A psychiatrist monitoring the Barak Brigade troops as they silently and industriously repaired their tanks remarked, "If they are going into battle again, I had better forget everything I ever learned."

Lieutenant Colonel Yossi Ben Hanan had arrived the night before to take command of what was left of the brigade. Commander of 53rd Tank Battalion until two weeks earlier, Ben Hanan had been honeymooning in Nepal when the war erupted. Following an adventure-laden journey to Israel, he had reported on Monday to IDF General Headquarters and had spoken directly with Major General Yitzhak Hofi by phone from there. Hofi's attitude about many things was capsulized in his first question: "What are you doing there? They don't know anything." Ben Hanan saw his opening and pushed the Northern Front commander for a promise of a command of his own. But Hofi was not committing: "Come on up. We don't know anything, either." On arrival at Northern Front headquarters, Ben Hanan was sent to reorganize Barak Brigade.

The new brigade commander was just approaching the battle zone when he recognized several men in tankers' jump suits along the road. These turned out to be a Centurion crew from his former command, 53rd Tank Battalion. They told Ben Hanan that they had walked down the escarpment following the destruction of their tank, that they were looking for someone to tell them what they could do. Ben Hanan ordered them to the nearest police station to round up any other Barak Brigade personnel they could find.

When Ben Hanan arrived at the Barak Brigade depot late on Monday, he found the repairwork going full steam ahead. The job had been started by the brigade Intelligence officer, who had rallied the crews and support personnel he could find following the death of Colonel Yitzhak Ben Shoham on Sunday. Following his escape from Tel Faris on Monday morning, Lieutenant Colonel Oded Eres had arrived with numerous 53rd Tank Battalion personnel; he now had the repairwork firmly in hand. Major Shmuel Askarov, the 53rd Battalion deputy commander who had been severely wounded early in the war, had taken leave of his hospital bed at Safed and also was hard at work among the tank-repair crews.

Yossi Ben Hanan called everyone together and explained what

General Hofi wanted done. Since these men had intimate knowl-edge of the battlefield, they would be going into the Northern Command reserve. The chances were excellent for returning to combat the next day, Tuesday. When Ben Hanan finished speaking, he asked for volunteers to man the repaired tanks. There was no shortage of willing crewmen.

As Syrian pressure mounted in the central sector early on Tues-day morning, Hofi ordered Ben Hanan to the northern Golan to bolster Brigadier General Eitan's 36th Armored Infantry Division, of which the Barak Brigade had been a part at the outbreak of the war. Ben Hanan contacted Eitan at 0800 hours to report that he was ready to bring forward the thirteen Centurions thus far repaired at the brigade depots. Eitan ordered the reinforced company to head for Naffach.

As Ben Hanan's tiny force made all speed toward the Golan, the Israeli Air Force was confirming Colonel Avigdor Ben Gal's worst premonitions. Behind the morning mist and clouds of dust raised by the increasing artillery preparation was a force estimated at a hun-dred tanks. Most of the new force, it was reported, seemed to be heading directly toward 7th Armored Brigade's sector. One particu-larly clear aerial photograph depicted a complete Syrian battalion of thirty-eight T-62s and four BMPs.

The seventeen Israeli infantrymen manning Bunker 107 had been isolated from the moment the war began. Lieutenant Colonel Yair Nofshe had run supplies to the compound on October 6 and 7, but the tenuous link had been severed through October 8. Exposed, at times completely on their own, and always under Syrian artillery fire, the garrison had adopted various psychological defenses against the pressure and fear each man felt. Each simply refused to acknowledge his fear to the others. The fall of the Hermon bunker, which was many times stronger than Bunker 107, was a taboo sub-ject. Thus, more than any single factor, false bravado sustained the tiny garrison through three long days and nights of incessant battle.

The approach of the fresh Syrian armor threatened the garrison's emotional security. When one of the Israeli soldiers observed the approach of the T-62s, he reported, "Commander, fifty Syrian tanks approaching to the south." There was something new in the voice:

Panic. Lieutenant Avraham Elimelech restored order when he laconically responded, "So what? There are fifty more to the north."

The Syrian armor could be seen from the 7th Brigade line shortly before 0900 hours. Fortunately, the advances by the two Republican Guard T-62 battalions were not fully coordinated, which came as an immense relief to the outnumbered Israelis. Still, while the dilution of mass had an important positive psychological effect upon the IDF crews, everyone on the battlefield knew that the numbers were heavily weighted in Syria's favor.

The Syrians were first engaged by Israeli artillery units—virtually every gun in Eitan's divisional sector, and many that would otherwise have supported an attack by Laner's division in the sector just to the south. In fact, Northern Command postponed a major assault in Laner's sector until the issue could be settled in Eitan's.

Major Mohamed Rawbadawi, commander of one of the Syrian T-62 battalions, later wrote:

> We spread out and began advancing. The enemy covered us with fire while we crossed the antitank ditch. After we crossed the ditch, we regrouped.
>
> We resumed advancing and were told to expect a counterattack. I ordered units to each flank and we moved west firing. I saw seven tanks in the center, and we destroyed those seven tanks. From the south, we saw a brigade of enemy tanks. I saw MiG-17s attacking them. And then our tanks were hit.

Major Rawbadawi and his crew bailed out of their tank and took cover behind a low barrier while the battle raged around them. Later, one of the major's crewmen was nearly run over by a passing Centurion.

The Israeli Centurion gunners opened fire at maximum range. The Syrian formations were in tight battle order, but the individual tanks were quite spread out. So, sighting through billows of dust and right into the sun, the Israeli gunners had to work doubly hard for each hit. Despite the incoming fire, Israeli tank commanders naturally stood up in their turret hatchways to follow the action and track targets better. As a result, the heavy incoming fire resulted in injuries and fatalities 7th Brigade could ill afford.

When it became obvious that his brigade could not fight from the center of the maelstrom, Ben Gal reluctantly decided to give some ground. He could concentrate only the slim resources at his disposal, and these he ordered back to an adequate line about four hundred meters behind the prepared tank ramparts along the front. Lieutenant Colonel Nofshe's combat group from 74th Tank Battalion—six Centurions—was reluctantly pulled back from Bunker 107, which Nofshe's tanks had been defending from the outset of the war. Captain Tiger Zamir's six Centurions of 82nd Tank Battalion were moved to the center of a ridge near Tel Git.

Yair Nofshe narrowly escaped death as his turret-damaged Centurion was shot from beneath him on the rear slope of the hill he was defending. Though bleeding from new wounds, the tough blond ran across the fire-swept ground and resumed command of his force from yet another tank, his third of the war. Nofshe's Centurion force, now numbering five, continued to withdraw in accordance with Ben Gal's plan. As Nofshe pulled into a new position, he ordered everyone to take adequate cover, then called down Israeli artillery to stave off a Syrian thrust right through his sector. When the danger had subsided, Nofshe's Centurions resumed firing from the high ground overlooking the Valley of Tears, picking off T-62s one after another.

One of Major Rawbadawi's tank commanders, Saleem al-Hamsi, later recalled: "I advanced until I reached the beginning of the plain, when I was taken under heavy fire. We were hit, but damage was minimal. [After some time] we were hit again, this time seriously, but could still move."

Tiger Zamir manned his new position near Tel Git—on the approaches to the Damascus Highway north of the Booster—with six battle-worn Centurions and but fifteen rounds of 105mm ammunition among them. He placed a hurried call to Ben Gal, asking that he be allowed to withdraw only long enough to replenish his ammunition racks. Ben Gal told Tiger to use his machine guns, for, "Maybe the *sight* of Jewish tanks will frighten them off."

The situation on the front became yet more desperate, so Ben Gal ordered his reserve—the seven 77th Battalion tanks remaining under Lieutenant Colonel Avigdor Kahalani—to counterattack and to restore the line just south of the Hermonit.

As Kahalani's crews waded eastward through fire and smoke,

which reduced visibility to nil, they managed to down a Syrian helicopter as they approached the front.

Next, the battalion commander spotted a T-62 through the smoky gloom as he led his small force up the ridge toward his assigned sector. A barked command was followed by the flat *crack* of the command Centurion's main gun.

Immediately three T-62s loomed out of the haze, all drawn by the flaming wreck of Kahalani's most recent victim. "Rapid fire," the battalion commander spat into his mike. The lead T-62 traversed its gun to bear on the Israeli command tank. "Fire! Fire!" The gunner had not yet seen the target, but it came into his sights, as if by Kahalani's urging. The big gun fired, then the gunner turned the turret on the next T-62. *Crack!* The turret continued to swing through its smooth arc, and the last T-62 was caught as it erupted out of the gloomy surroundings. Kahalani's gunner had accounted for four T-62s in about ninety seconds.

Most of the Syrian force of which the four destroyed T-62s were a part withdrew, and Kahalani did manage to stabilize the front. However, there was nothing he could hope to do about actually stemming the headlong advance of the Republican Guard's 2nd Battalion, which was moving westward through the dead ground along the dry wadi at the southern edge of the Hermonit.

Ben Gal ordered Lieutenant Colonel Memshalom Carmel, commander of the largely disbanded Armor School Tank Battalion, to leave a platoon near the Hermonit and drive north to El Rom to bolster the brigade's northern flank against mounting pressure. The Armor School force swept into the fight.

Syrian tank commander Sharif Abu Essau later told an interviewer, "After we crossed the antitank ditch we took battle positions. We were under heavy fire. I told the driver to speed up. We were told of a counterattack from the left, so I took the hull-down position. I saw the left side of the counterattack that was four tanks. I destroyed them all. A fifth tank showed up, which was carrying three antennas, a commander's vehicle. I fired and destroyed it."

Abu Essau might well have killed Lieutenant Colonel Carmel, who died in his Centurion within ten minutes of joining the close, intense tank combat.

Ben Gal ordered Kahalani to absorb the remnant of Carmel's force into 77th Battalion.

The brigade commander found some needed relief in the chain of bad news during one hurried exchange with Kahalani. As the 7th Brigade line teetered on the brink of collapse, Kahalani told Ben Gal, "Don't worry, sir. . . . They won't get by me!"

Kahalani rammed his minuscule combined force between the two T-62 battalions and their objectives in the brigade's rear. The Syrian formations quickly became unglued. Truckborne infantry units following the T-62s were stalled, and soon the wadi was filled with running men, many of them T-62 crewmen, scrambling toward the rear.

Kahalani maneuvered his force forward to the high ground and ramparts that Ben Gal had sacrificed during the pre-assault artillery barrages. From there, Kahalani's fifteen Centurions all but destroyed the cohesion of the Syrian battalions.

However, sheer weight of numbers soon achieved for the Syrians what tactics had thus far failed to resolve. Fifteen Israeli tanks could not hope to hold back the numerous survivors of a hundred T-62s attacking across a relatively broad front. Soon individual T-62s and small groups of them were slipping past the Israeli firing line. Many of these turned to fire at Kahalani's force from the rear, and they took their toll. The two forces became inextricably intermingled on the swirling battleground. Artillery fired by both sides added to the mayhem.

Ben Gal was swept by the conviction that he would die this day, on this bit of embattled hillside. He and his valiant tank crews were being beaten by numbers, by time, by the limits of their bodies and mental agility. It never occurred to Ben Gal, nor to any of them, to withdraw. The 7th Brigade operations officer crumpled to the floor of the command APC, asleep on his feet, even as Ben Gal yelled instructions into his ear. Some tanks were reporting that they were down to three or four antitank rounds, or completely out. Ben Gal called Rafoul Eitan to describe the condition of his force, and Eitan shouted back over the ether, "For God's sake, Avigdor, hold on! Give me another half hour! You will soon be receiving reinforcements! Try, please! Hold on!"

But the news continued to grow worse, and the situation became more desperate.

Tiger Zamir reported that his tiny force at Tel Git was down to just three or four rounds. Ben Gal pleaded with Tiger to hold for just ten more minutes. Tiger said he would, then began passing hand grenades among his desperate crewmen. A short time later, when Tiger reported that his Centurions had completely used up their ammunition, Ben Gal finally allowed him to pull back. Thus 7th Brigade counted but seven operational tanks covering the entire sector. There was nothing left.

When Major Yoni Netanyahu was informed that the collapse of 7th Brigade's front was imminent, he passed the news to his parachute company. "In a few minutes, our last tanks will be pulling out, and it will be up to us." One of the troopers, perhaps among many, groused, "Why do we have to stay and get killed?" Netanyahu referred to the dawn fight against the helicopterborne Syrian commandos: "Just fight as you did this morning and we haven't anything to worry about."

Each side had fought the other to a standstill. Ben Gal informed Eitan that he had no hope of holding the Syrians, that 7th Brigade was about to collapse. The division commander had not yet absorbed this nugget when Lieutenant Avraham Elimelech reported from besieged Bunker 107 that he could see the truckborne Syrian infantry and supply columns heading east—back across the old cease-fire line.

At this heart-stopping juncture, Lieutenant Colonel Yossi Ben Hanan and Major Shmuel Askarov led thirteen refurbished Barak Brigade Centurions into the fight just north of the Booster position, where they joined Lieutenant Colonel Yair Nofshe's four surviving 74th Battalion tanks—also Barak Brigade Centurions. Together with Kahalani's three surviving Centurions still operating south of the Hermonit, 7th Brigade then fielded just twenty operational tanks.

Ben Hanan and Askarov carried onward to the Vasit crossroads, split their group in two, and pitched in their counterattack with Askarov on the north and Ben Hanan on the south.

It was extremely slow going. When Ben Hanan was wounded and evacuated, Askarov consolidated the survivors and led them yet farther eastward. Soon Ben Hanan returned; he had paused at the aid station only long enough to have his wound dressed.

Shortly after noon, Major Askarov targeted and destroyed a Syrian tank at a range of only forty meters. As Askarov, who was standing tall in his Centurion's turret, turned his head, one of the Syrian crewmen abandoning his own disabled tank paused to fire. Ben Hanan saw it happening and opened his mouth to warn Askarov by radio. He was an instant late. The Syrian fired a single round, which entered the left side of Askarov's head and exited from the right side. Askarov slumped in the turret hatchway. He was carried wounded but alive to the rear.

Yossi Ben Hanan led the survivors onward toward the Booster position.

Reserves of strength and will beyond known reserves were applied in the pursuit of the receding Syrian tide. Reflexively, the battered Centurions gave chase to the withdrawing T-62s and their numerous wheeled and tracked consorts. Only the utter depletion of ammunition took Centurions from the fight. And the fight ended only when the last 7th Brigade tanks stood upon the rampart overlooking the antitank ditch that was the Israeli side of what had been the cease-fire line.

One of the infantrymen manning Bunker 107 noticed a Syrian soldier walking toward the Israeli compound. The intruder made it clear that he wanted to surrender, so he was allowed to enter the complex before and throughout which scores of his countrymen had died. Upon questioning, the Syrian said, "My name is Shaul. I'm a new [Jewish] immigrant from Russia and got lost on the way." There was simply nothing the amused Israelis could think to ask the Syrian soldier after hearing that.

The first resupply of Bunker 107 was dispatched late in the afternoon aboard three APCs protected by the guns of Lieutenant Colonel Yair Nofshe's last two operational 74th Battalion Centurions. The five Israeli armored fighting vehicles were still well short of the compound when two Syrian RPGs streaked after them from the nearby outskirts of Kuneitra. Both antitank grenades hit the battalion commander's tank and prompted an excited radio report by the commander of the accompanying Centurion that Nofshe was dead.

Miraculously, however, the husky blond emerged from the smoking ruin and boarded the other tank, from which he led the tiny column to its objective. Lieutenant Avraham Elimelech's tiny garrison, which had ample cause to consider Nofshe its personal guardian, grieved openly until the plucky battalion commander's arrival gave them renewed cause for celebration.

In the words of Chaim Herzog, in *The War of Atonement:*

[Ben Gal] stood in a daze looking down on the Valley of Tears. Some 260 Syrian tanks and hundreds of armoured personnel carriers and vehicles lay scattered and abandoned across the narrow battlefield between the Hermonit and the Booster. In the distance he could see the Syrians withdrawing in a haze of smoke and dust, the Israeli artillery following them. [Eitan's] quiet voice came through on the earphones as he addressed them on the network of the 7th Brigade: "You have saved the people of Israel."

· 23 ·

The hilly terrain that was so crucial to Brigadier General Rafoul Eitan's ability to hold the Purple Line in his sector was a significant barrier to Major General Dan Laner and Brigadier General Mussa Peled in their bids to eject the Syrian Army from their sectors of what had been the Israeli-occupied Golan. Eitan's command enjoyed all the advantages conferred by the heights, but Peled's and Laner's soldiers fought literally yard-by-yard upslope against the prepared Syrian defenses.

It is a measure of Peled's initial successes that 1st Tank Division's 4th Tank Brigade, which arrived to replace 5th Infantry Division's 132nd Mechanized Brigade on the battlefield during the evening of October 8, was dispersed to stiffen the Syrian southern defenses. This decision, while sound on the face of things—and which would have been correct if the Syrians merely wanted to hold what they had won at such high cost—deprived Colonel Tewfiq Jehani, the 1st Tank Division commander, of his best chance to concentrate a major strike force for a renewed assault. The ninety-five fresh T-55s were dispersed along a wide arc from south of Sindiana through the Rafid Gap.

Jehani was further unable to support the Republican Guard assault north of Kuneitra with more than a rather minor thrust northward along the Sindiana Road. The tactics employed by Jehani at this juncture reflected his division's exceptionally high losses. For the first time, he had to employ mechanized infantry to lead the assault. At a point where the roadway shifted westward, the infantry struck out overland toward Tel Yosifon, which would provide excellent observation of the Kuneitra area and would have dominated some of the ground over which the assault upon Sindiana would take place.

Israeli tank gunners enjoying excellent observation from the tel opened fire at long range, thus preventing the Syrian infantry assault from gaining momentum at the outset. In the meantime, the tank force continued on up the road until brought to a stop by Israeli long-range gunnery. In the face of those odds, the best Jehani could hope to do was tie down, or even divert, Israelis who might otherwise have been employed to bolster 7th Brigade's stand in the northern Golan. In this, at least, he was successful.

Laner, in his turn, had to withhold his planned divisional assault until he was certain that Jehani was firmly engaged. So it was after 1000 hours on Tuesday before Laner perceived that the moment was right to order up Colonel Yaacov Pfeiffer's fresh, newly arrived 4th Reserve Armored Infantry Brigade, then on the Arik Bridge Road. In its combat debut of the war, Pfeiffer's brigade was to pitch itself into Jehani's western flank.

Soon after Colonel Pfeiffer's brigade jumped off, the tank battalion that led the assault found itself in a tough fight. The Israelis had to face T-62s and T-55s with Shermans. Of even greater consequence, however, was the skill these Syrians displayed in utilizing the terrain and belts of antitank mines. When the vanguard company was ambushed, Captain Moshe Nir's company was sent to assist. Nir was killed while he was helping to rescue the crew of a disabled Sherman.

However, despite the setbacks and losses, Pfeiffer reported within an hour, by 1100, that his 4th Armored Infantry Brigade had overcome the Syrian screen and was in position to continue on into Hushniya. However, Laner ordered Pfeiffer to halt.

* * *

Even as Jehani concentrated on the attack in his northern sector, elements of Brigadier General Mussa Peled's 146th Armored Division were endangering 1st Tank Division's southern flank with a renewed advance at dawn.

Peled had met with all his subordinate commanders at 0300 hours on Tuesday, for the first time since the division's hurried and rather haphazard commitment to the Golan front. Together they planned a three-pronged assault.

Colonel Yossi Peled's 205th Brigade was to advance up the right (east) side of the Rafid–Tel Faris Road, retake the Rafid crossroads, and secure Tel Faris. On his left, in the divisional center, Colonel Zvi Bar's reconstituted District Brigade was to sweep the Rafid–Kuneitra Road as far north as Bunker 111 and the crossroads to Tel Kudna, in Syria. On Bar's left, Colonel Mordechai Ben Porat's 9th Armored Infantry Brigade was to retake Hushniya. The sum of the attacks was to regain the Purple Line. For the division to count itself successful, the Syrians would have to be overcome, or enticed to withdraw.

For once, the Israeli operations order carried a section dealing with prearranged, coordinated air preparation and support. Unfortunately, the arrival of the Israeli Air Force jets tipped General Peled's hand. A Syrian participant later recalled, "On October ninth, in the morning, before dawn, enemy planes started bombing in the area, and we were under artillery fire. We knew we were going to be attacked." Another late arrival added, "On October eighth, we occupied the line. On October ninth, we got orders to stop the enemy tanks."

The Syrians had substituted masses of armor for the infantry antitank units that had engaged the Israelis the day before.

Lieutenant Colonel Guy Jacobsen's tank battalion of 205th Armored Brigade jumped off at 0500 hours with the companies of Captain David Livney and Captain Yair Zur leading. The Syrians—elements of 4th Tank Brigade—immediately countered with very heavy artillery fire. Livney's tanks advanced through the barrage for nearly a mile without encountering any other form of resistance.

This alarmed General Peled, who warned Colonel Peled, "Don't trust the quiet."

Livney's advance came to a sudden halt when he encountered a minefield along the El Al–Rafid Road, and Syrian tanks were seen moving on his right flank. Zur's company turned south to deal with the tanks, and knocked out five of ten within minutes. The surviving T-55s rushed into prepared positions near Bunker 115, which forced Zur to undertake a difficult and slow fire fight that was not at all to his advantage or liking.

Lieutenant Colonel Jacobsen became convinced that he would be under severe pressure until Syrian artillery forward observers atop Tel Faris could be located and silenced. The dense artillery fires were making it impossible for tank commanders to stand up in their turret hatchways to observe the battlefield. Jacobsen was seen standing tall in his hatchway despite a shell that burst within five yards of his Centurion.

Livney's company breached the minefield and was engaged by PT-76 light amphibian reconnaissance tanks near the Rafid cross-roads. Seven of the PT-76s were destroyed within moments, though they put two of Livney's tanks out of action. No sooner had Livney disposed of the PT-76s than he was faced with overcoming thirty T-55s.

Jacobsen's Reserve tank battalion was under intense pressure at both ends of its sector. Livney's reduced company contested the T-55 counterattack near the Rafid crossroads while Zur's Centurions continued to exchange fire with the five T-55s dug in near Bunker 115. On the other hand, Israeli armored infantry pushed through on Zur's left and reached the cease-fire line near Bunker 113.

Colonel Yossi Peled's other tank battalion, which was commanded by Lieutenant Colonel Tuvia Teren, had meanwhile advanced north of the El Al Road. Captain Gideon Reiss's company was sent to secure Tel Faris while Teren led companies commanded by Captain Uri Kaplan and Captain Rami Givoni around the southern part of the tel. Teren reported to Colonel Peled at 0830 that he had reached the Rafid–Kuneitra Road. At this point, Teren sent Kaplan's company to hold the El Al–Kuneitra crossroads as well as support the armored infantry at Bunker 113 and Livney's company of Jacobsen's battalion, to the south.

Teren next moved forward with Reiss's and Givoni's companies, and was engaged amid bursting artillery fire by Syrians just east of Tel Faris. Reiss's tank and one other were destroyed in a Syrian counterattack. The battle raged on—eventually consuming the balance of the day—with opposing tanks often firing from within one hundred meters of one another. In time, the Israelis accounted for seven SU-100 gun carriers and ten T-55s destroyed.

What the Israelis did not yet realize was that the Syrians were constantly moving in fresh forces from their side of the cease-fire line. Unbeknownst to either General Peled or Colonel Peled was the fact that 205th Brigade's advance had actually crossed 1st Tank Division's three routes of advance to the Golan from Syria. Thus, as 205th Brigade advanced and destroyed Syrian armor, it was in turn being challenged by a constantly replenished supply of fresh tanks arriving across most of its lengthened flank. In time, then, 205th Brigade's situation became increasingly precarious.

The fight for Tel Faris raged on through the morning. Syrian commandos were ejected from the lower slopes by Captain Amos Kellerman's armored infantry company, and a final assault on the summit was organized by Captain Amir Levy, deputy commander of 205th Brigade's reconnaissance company.

Unlike most of the tels with rounded mounds—usually ancient occupation sites built up by generations of town-dwellers—Tel Faris was a sprawling affair with a well-developed volcanic crater. Access was extremely rugged and served only by one Israeli-built road that branched off eastward from the Petroleum Road. The only practical way to advance vehicles up the tel was via the road. Thus Captain Levy placed a pair of the reconnaissance company's tanks (he rode the second one) ahead of four troop-filled APCs.

The tiny column encountered numerous ambush sites on the long climb, but no ambushers. As the lead tank approached the westernmost line of bunkers, elation naturally soared. It seemed as though Tel Faris would fall without a fight.

The commander of the lead tank—the eyes and ears of the column—was hurled by a sudden blast from his turret perch as the tank entered the fortified area. The man, who had been wounded in the neck, lay where he landed on the slope.

Captain Levy attempted to direct the crew of the lead tank from his tank, but the crewmen were shocked and panicked by the sudden and violent ejection of their commander. They did not respond. Levy was not sure he could safely maneuver his tank around the stalled leader, so he called brigade headquarters to request tank reinforcements. Brigade headquarters responded that none was available.

Levy's driver carefully dodged around the stalled lead tank, and his gunner fired five 105mm rounds. Three of them took out a Syrian antitank gun. In the interim, however, a Syrian PT-76 tank fired two rounds at Levy's tank. The first hit the Israeli tank's tracks, and the second struck and damaged the turret. Thus Levy's tank was added to the wreckage blocking the entrance to the fortified sector.

The PT-76 was commanded by an extremely brave man who was willing to take the initiative. Free to move without challenge by the two Israeli tanks, the light Soviet-built tank aggressively attacked the APCs, destroying two.

Several reconnaissance troopers who had been left at the base of the tel rushed up the road to help, but they mainly added to the congestion on the restricted battlefield. The PT-76 was clearly the king of the hill. The Israelis had no antitank weapons, and the battleground was devoid of useful cover. Thus there was no incentive for men to risk their lives trying to fight a formidable target they could not hope to destroy.

Unusual in this vast mechanized war, the duel for the summit of Tel Faris was eventually reduced to a personal war between the Syrian tank commander and two reconnaissance troopers, Asaf Kotef and Dan Baron, who arrived by jeep after learning that Levy's assault had been stopped.

A resident of the Golan, Kotef knew the terrain. The day before, at Tel Juhadar, he had commented that the reconnaissance company was fortunate it did not have to take Tel Faris by foot. This day, he and Baron left their jeeps to do exactly that.

Baron and Kotef carefully worked their way toward the PT-76— close enough, in fact, to be able to chuck hand grenades at the turret every time the Syrian commander opened his hatch. At length it seemed as if the duel was over. Baron managed to get a grenade through the hatchway, but elation was short-lived. The missile was thrown out of the tank and exploded without doing damage or injury.

The Israelis felt a genuine admiration for the Syrian commander and his crew. They were worthy adversaries. Baron found himself thinking during one quick trip downslope to get more grenades, "Why are we doing this?" The Syrian crew was as neutralized as the Israeli attackers. They waited within the steel confines of their tank for forty-five interminable minutes, knowing that flak-jacketed Israeli soldiers were moving in ways they could not see and could only dimly imagine—all to their ultimate detriment. It was, they knew, only a matter of time before they were destroyed along with their tank.

What those Syrians were thinking, or how they suffered, cannot be known. The game ended when the hatches were thrown open and the crewmen boiled out and bolted. Many of the Israelis simply looked on, unwilling to fire on such brave men. After all, without their tank, the Syrians were basically harmless. Then someone opened fire with his Uzi submachine gun, and others joined in. It was over in seconds.

Tel Faris was returned to Israeli hands at 1215 hours on October 9 (though bypassed Syrians fought on), but the fall of the heights did not bring Jacobsen's tank battalion the sought-after relief from Syrian artillery. The battle astride the Rafid–Kuneitra Road raged on.

The Syrian defenses around Bunker 115 were overcome at 1335 hours by Captain David Livney's company, which had meantime been bolstered by the company commanded by Captain Boaz Gilboa. After reporting that the bunker was secure, the two companies swept forward to the Petroleum Road, destroying a Syrian strongpoint on the way. Livney reported at 1425 hours that he and Gilboa had destroyed ten more Syrian tanks and stood upon the Purple Line.

The fall of Tel Faris, the Rafid crossroads, and the area around Bunker 115 effectively placed the Syrian 5th Infantry Division on its October 6 line of departure.

Colonel Mordechai Ben Porat's 9th Armored Infantry Brigade withheld its initial attack until 1100 hours to coordinate its drive with units in the neighboring sector of Dan Laner's division. Ben Porat himself observed masses of Syrian tanks deployed across an area some two miles by one mile, directly in his path. His lead battalion, comprising no more than fifteen tanks, soon was engaged by about fifty Syrian tanks supported by antitank missiles, antitank guns, and other defensive weapons. The assault became futile, and Ben Porat was obliged to withdraw within ten minutes, after a battalion commander was wounded and nearly all the tanks in the assault were disabled or destroyed.

Lieutenant Colonel Tuvia Teren of 205th Armored Brigade responded to Ben Porat's plight by dispatching a platoon of his tank battalion around the north side of Tel Faris, hopefully to ease the pressure on the disorganized and withdrawing 9th Brigade force. All three of Teren's tanks were disabled, and two of the tank commanders were killed.

The palpably increasing pressure upon Mussa Peled's brigades was largely a factor of Israeli successes. Colonel Jehani of 1st Tank Division had concentrated his divisional train around Hushniya in anticipation of a successful drive by his armored brigades into Israel. Peled's successful attack from the south, and Laner's drive from the north and west, had placed both the divisional train and Jehani's fighting units in considerable jeopardy. Jehani had to hold the line, and the best way he found to do that was to order units in the Hushniya area to exert pressure eastward against the very forces of Peled's division that threatened the pocket. The net result was that Peled found himself facing aggressive Syrian forces in two opposing directions; he was in a vise.

For his part, Peled directed Colonel Zvi Bar's District Brigade to mount its attack from the divisional center and penetrate the Syrian-held sector to the greatest possible depth.

In response to Peled's directive, Bar sent in Lieutenant Colonel Moshe Meler's 61st Tank Battalion, numbering just eight tanks. Remarkably, Meler's force overcame the Syrian defenses just above Tel Faris, then reached the Rafid–Kuneitra Road, losing only two tanks on the way. Once at his objective, Meler established his defenses. The three-tank "company" under Captain David Friedman drew an immediate hostile response, and fought off attackers through the rest of the day; the company destroyed fifteen T-55s and several armored personnel carriers.

Even while Friedman's company was fighting to hold its position,

Lieutenant Colonel Yoav Vaspe's tank companies of 71st Armored Infantry Battalion fought through the area and continued northward along the road to Kuneitra. With only six tanks in the vanguard, Vaspe raced through the "Elbow" position, which was held by elements of 1st Tank Division's 2nd Mechanized Brigade. When challenged by a Syrian howitzer battery on his right flank, Vaspe ordered his tanks to continue northward; they shot up the howitzers as they passed but did not stop. Fully exploiting Syrian surprise and disorganization, 61st Tank Battalion hurried on toward Tel Aksa.

Meler's and Vaspe's twin successes for the second time in two days decisively altered the battle. Loss of the Rafid–Kuneitra Road left 1st Tank Division with but a single secondary road as its umbilicus to bases and support in Syria. Colonel Jehani could find no alternative, so he ordered his headquarters and division train to retire from Hushniya to Tel Kudna, back across the cease-fire line.

The battle in the southern Golan was becoming extremely fluid once again, and it was increasingly favoring Mussa Peled's division over Jehani's 1st Tank and Aslan's 5th Infantry divisions.

Once Meler's breakthrough screened 9th Armored Infantry Brigade's right flank in the early afternoon, General Peled ordered Colonel Ben Porat to resume his aborted brigade assault. Artillery and air support were, for once, continuously supplied, and ample. In a bruising headlong rush beginning at 1600 hours, the Super Shermans of Lieutenant Colonel Benzion Paden's 595th Tank Battalion pierced the defenses of 1st Tank Division's 4th Tank Brigade and rolled right over the command post of a Syrian infantry battalion. The loss of the battalion headquarters, along with the attendant seizure of a locally important height, unsettled the Syrians.

Without pausing, Paden's Super Shermans drove around to the rear of Hushniya, formed up in column on the road, and entered the town, firing all guns to the left and right. After passing through and severely shaking the defenders of what had been 1st Tank Division's logistical center, the Super Sherman battalion retraced its steps eastward and drove on toward the height at Tel Fazra, which was stormed and secured at nightfall. Paden's battalion, equipped with modernized and upgunned thirty-year-old fighting vehicles and manned by Reserve crews, had lost one third of its strength but had achieved an astonishing mastery of the battlefield.

Lieutenant Colonel Yoav Vaspe's 71st Armored Infantry Battalion Centurion companies meanwhile had been advancing steadily upon their objective, Tel Aksa. One of the companies, which went up against the tel with only five operational Centurions, lost two tanks in the process of driving the defenders from the heights. Once the tel was secure, Vaspe oversaw the establishment of a defensive locality blocking access from Tel Kudna.

Though very thin in tank assets, Brigadier General Mussa Peled's overall situation was sterling compared to that of 1st Tank Division. The aerial umbrella that for days had protected Jehani's formations had folded, allowing Israeli aircrews—which by then had destroyed the Syrian antiaircraft missile defenses—total access to the battlefield.

All the successes in Peled's sector, combined with the achievement of aerial superiority, provided Colonel Uri Orr's 679th Armored Brigade of Major General Dan Laner's division with an opportunity to sweep southward along the cease-fire line from Sindiana.

Following a heart-stopping morning stand against an artillery- and rocket-supported Syrian counterattack near Sindiana, 679th Brigade was ordered to await an opening and then pounce southward to secure Tel Ramatnia, the height dominating 1st Tank Division's administrative center at Hushniya. If possible, Orr was to link his force physically to Peled's division. It was made clear to Orr that the vast concentration of antitank firepower assembled on the tel but oriented toward the road passing in its shadow made it imperative that the height be stormed and, until it fell, the roads be avoided.

Orr's battalions jumped off in midafternoon. As the brigade advanced, fragmented Israeli forces that had fought for days in isolated places, by platoon and company, were reorganized and absorbed to bolster the rather thin assault elements.

The Israelis had hoped for two long days to achieve the opportunity to attack down the Rafid–Kuneitra Road and seal the Syrian penetration in the central Golan. When the opportunity finally presented itself, however, Orr opted to pass; the Syrian defenses were simply too formidable for his battered and depleted brigade. Rather than administer a questionable knockout blow on one axis, Orr ordered three columns to advance southward.

Captain Amos Ben David's company, which had fought through much of the day against Syrian commandos at Bukata, behind 7th Brigade, was placed on the brigade's right to protect it against Syrians on the Rafid–Kuneitra Road and to engage and neutralize Syrian anti-tank concentrations on the east side of Tel Ramatnia. In the course of their southward advance, Ben David's ten Centurions overcame a Syrian tank unit of equal strength.

Orr posted several scratch platoons along the Petroleum Road to seal the brigade's left, then joined the main assault up the center, along the Sindiana–Hushniya Road. This force drew exceptionally heavy artillery fire, which hampered its ability to advance with cohesion, a difficult task in the best of situations for a force composed of odds and ends and operating in large part under a commander its components did not know.

It is indicative of the cumulative impact of Israeli aerial supremacy and Syrian disorganization that Orr's 679th Brigade accomplished in just one hour what had taken the Syrians six hours to do on October 7.

Here, on the broken slopes crisscrossed by stone walls and deep wadis that Major Baruch Lenschner had defended unto death, the Israelis accomplished in reverse, and with less loss of life, what the Syrians had fought so hard to overcome.

When the commander of the platoons guarding the Petroleum Road was hit, Orr ordered the survivors to join his effort in the center, which was just approaching Tel Ramatnia a half hour before sunset. The added weight, which was little enough, pushed 679th Brigade onto its objective. Literally at sunset, and under heavy air support, 679th Brigade crawled to the summit of Tel Ramatnia, the last strategic height overlooking Hushniya.

The balance had definitely shifted to the Israelis by Tuesday evening. Brigadier General Rafoul Eitan's depleted 36th Division had held in the north, Brigadier General Mussa Peled's depleted 146th Division had swept the southern Golan of the better part of two Syrian divisions, and Major General Dan Laner's depleted 240th Division had closed the northern and western pincers on the main

Syrian concentration at Hushniya. For the most part, the consistently outnumbered and outgunned IDF had regained the Purple Line and had surrounded or forced the retreat of the bulk of the Syrian Army committed to the Golan.

24

The general initiative for the war on the Golan passed from Syrian to Israeli hands at sunset on Tuesday, October 9. From that moment, Syrian decision-making focused less upon regaining the Golan than upon containing possible Israeli initiatives. Highlighting the new Syrian priority was the order to regroup the shattered T-62 brigades, for each of these state-of-the-art tanks was a prime resource required to defend Syria and, indeed, the Assad regime.

Colonel Shafiq Fiyad's 91st Tank Brigade, which had been caught in the Hushniya pocket, was ordered to break through and regroup at Tel Kudna. Fiyad passed the order and the T-62s moved out in the darkness. Most were able to fight their way back across the cease-fire line. The largest action of the evolution took place near Tel Fazra, where Colonel Mordechai Ben Porat's weakened 9th Armored Infantry Brigade drew some blood before being bypassed.

Though the Syrian Army ceded the initiative to the IDF, Syrian commanders were by no means inclined to ignore possible advantages when they were presented. Many units and individuals of 1st Tank Division's 2nd Mechanized Brigade were able to coalesce near Hushniya in the wake of 9th Armored Infantry Brigade's rush to the cease-fire line, and the new concentration in Ben Porat's rear was of considerable concern through the night. Also, 3rd Tank Division's 15th Mechanized Brigade mounted a night counterattack to reinforce 1st Armored Division in the Hushniya pocket and to test the possibility of reconstructing a defensive line along the axis Rafid crossroads–Tel Faris–Hushniya. The Syrians penetrated to the southern slope of Tel Faris, where their momentum was checked by a tank battalion from Colonel Yossi Peled's 205th Armored Brigade. The last of the Syrians did not retire from this area until 0850 hours on Wednesday.

The Syrians gambled upon securing at least one tangible prize from the campaign.

Kuneitra was the largest town on the Golan prior to its capture by Israel in June 1967. The town had not been reoccupied by civilians in the intervening years, merely outposted by the IDF. The Israeli garrison had been swiftly bypassed in the October 6 assault. Confined to their bunkers on Tel Abu Nida, the Israeli soldiers had been harassed ever since and were expected to surrender in due course. The back-pedaling Syrians realized that if they could storm and hold the dominant Israeli-held height, they could probably retain possession of the town beyond any cease-fire. The symbolism of retaining Kuneitra was worth a major confrontation.

Syrian infantry assaulted Tel Abu Nida, but the attack could not be sustained in the face of determined opposition by Israeli soldiers whose backs were to the wall. In time, the Syrians withdrew into the town.

While Major General Yitzhak Hofi painstakingly collected sufficient armor and infantry for the attack, Israeli artillery pummeled the town. At length, the Israeli assault force moved up to the foot of the town's main street, the Damascus Road, behind the rolling barrage, shooting up everything in sight.

The tank crews were extremely nervous about the specter of slow, protracted street fighting. Tank crews are virtually blind unless the tank commander can stand in his turret hatchway to observe events. In city fighting, where the vista is closed in and where even the tall Centurions could be dominated from windows, balconies, and roofs overhead, tank commanders are either unwilling to take the "usual" risks or, too often, shot on sight. The advent of plentiful RPGs in the hands of Syrian infantry and Sagger missiles in the hands of trained antitank troops added considerably to the doubts shared by the tankers. Fortunately, the IDF had developed a standard procedure for dealing with defended towns, and it was employed in Kuneitra.

Two separate tank-APC columns were formed up behind the artillery screen. One of the columns was slightly behind the other, but the point tank of each column was exposed so as to be able to bring its main gun and frontal machine gun to bear frontward. Trailing tanks trained their guns out to either side. When ready, both columns jumped off as one, tearing along the street as quickly as possible and without stopping for anything, all guns firing as fast as gunners and loaders could make them. When the armored column reached the end of the street, it turned and tore back through the town again. The aim was to shock and demoralize the defenders, and this was certainly accomplished.

When the tankers had finished, Lieutenant Colonel Elisha Shelem's battalion of Colonel Chaim Nadel's newly committed 317th Parachute Brigade executed a street-by-street reduction of Syrian strongpoints and outposts. The last Syrian vehicles to evacuate were caught by Israeli fighter-bombers about three kilometers northeast of Kuneitra and destroyed with air-to-ground rockets. Lieutenant Colonel Shelem reported the town as being secured late Wednesday afternoon.

The Tel Abu Nida garrison was relieved at its bunkers after nearly a hundred hours under siege.

Despite the withdrawal of 91st Tank Brigade's remaining T-62s, the Syrians clearly had no intention of yielding ground as long as there was any hope of resupplying the forces left in the Hushniya pocket. Indeed, considerable forces still remained: Elements of 2nd Mechanized Brigade had managed to regroup during the night; elements of 4th and 51st Tank brigades still were able to fight on; and two 9th Infantry Division antitank battalions that had been committed in the area were able to muster combined strength comparable to one full battalion.

Israeli observers and their commanders had misinterpreted the eastward flight of 91st Tank Brigade and the headquarters of 1st Tank Division as part of a general withdrawal by Syrian forces on the Golan. Thus, unaware of Syrian intentions or capabilities, Major

General Dan Laner ordered Major Giora Bierman's Sarig Force to link up with Colonel Uri Orr's 679th Armored Brigade at Tel Ramatnia.

Laner's divisional plan envisioned three columns sweeping the "abandoned" Hushniya pocket: Captain Amos Ben David's company of 679th Brigade would continue to advance southward on the division's left, along the Kuneitra–Rafid Road; the balance of 679th Brigade, with Captain Yosef Sarig's company of the Armor School Tank Battalion (by now filled out with bits and parts of other units) in reserve, would be the center element; Sarig Force drew the divisional right flank, which was the Ramatnia–Hushniya Road. Laner further decided to attack in echelon. Bierman's Sarig Force would move ahead; it would be followed somewhat by the main body of Orr's diminished brigade, which thus would guard Bierman's left flank; and Ben David's company would hang back to guard Orr's left.

Laner anticipated an occupation, not a battle.

Bierman quickly found his way barred. Operating on the assumption that the enemy was a disorganized remnant, Orr threw in Sarig's company, which advanced too quickly and lost five tanks in a headlong rush against a position held by a major Syrian tank force. This brought all three columns down to a respectful and methodical pace. Soon Ben David reported that he could see many Syrians fleeing eastward.

The Israelis had been lucky. Had Bierman attempted to rush westward, leaving the first strongpoint entirely to Orr and Ben David, he would have run right into an even more strongly held sector guarded by wide belts of antitank mines. As it was, Captain Yosef Sarig was killed, as was Sergeant Danny Berkowitz, one of the heroes of the first night of the war.

Laner's second, more considered, effort was decisive. Just after 1000 hours, the Syrians faced up to the reality that they would not be able to seize, much less hold, a suitable roadway into the pocket. Thus all units in the Hushniya pocket were ordered to trek back into Syria by whatever routes they could find. The Syrians left most of their equipment and stores to the Israelis, who occupied Hushniya at about noon.

* * *

Not one of the nearly fourteen hundred Syrian tanks that had crossed the Purple Line since Saturday afternoon remained in fighting condition west of the line. It is estimated that the Syrians left 867 T-54/55, PT-76, and T-62 tanks destroyed or disabled—all eventually good pickings for Israeli ordnance teams. In addition, hundreds of other tracked and wheeled armored fighting vehicles—SU-100 gun carriers, BRDM missile carriers, half-tracks, BMP armored personnel carriers, and numerous other models—littered the battlefield along with hundreds more soft vehicles of every type inventoried by the Syrian Army.

It is certain that the IDF never fielded, in total, as many tanks as it destroyed in those four days of battle.

The achievement has no parallel in modern history.

There remained some mopping up to do. And in the absence of a clear mandate for follow-up by the government of Israel or IDF General Headquarters, some high-ranking Israeli officers seized the initiative to balance some advantages the Syrian Army had enjoyed at or before the outbreak of the war.

One of the advantages had redounded to Syria during the drawing of the Purple Line in the wake of the Six-Day War of 1967. At that time, the Israelis were mainly intent upon a line that could easily be accessed by a good all-weather north–south road in close proximity to the new frontier. This had been the basis of the Purple Line (literally a purple line on Israeli maps), but the hurried situation to mark off a line in 1967 had allowed Tel Kudna to slip back into Syrian hands. The significant oversight resulted in the Syrians holding an enclave in an otherwise natural defensive line following the El Al Ridge.

The matter of Tel Kudna always had been a sore spot among Israeli commanders. It was a natural fortification. Many Israeli commanders agreed with the officer who once had boasted, "Give me a platoon and I'll hold it." It was widely held in the IDF that Tel Kudna had been seized by Israeli paratroopers in 1967. After nearly two days, the squad that had been left to outpost the tel had gone down to the Rafid crossroads for food and supplies. By the time the paratroopers tried to return, however, a United Nations truce team marking the cease-fire line had placed the tel in Syrian hands.

While Eitan's small, thoroughly exhausted division focused upon rearming, refitting, and resting, and as Laner's was mopping up around Hushniya, Brigadier General Peled's brigades were ordered to initiate an attack aimed at bringing Tel Kudna into Israeli hands. The initiating order was issued by Major General Yitzhak Hofi, who wrote it as soon as Peled's battalions had secured Tel Faris.

The seizure of Tel Faris provided Peled with the opportunity to order the bulk of his uncommitted 70th Reserve Armored Infantry Brigade up to the Golan from the Jordan Valley. A tank battalion, an armored infantry battalion, and smaller tactical units staged into the reoccupied southern Golan during Tuesday afternoon and evening. These joined advance elements of the brigade, which had been screening Peled's right along the Ruqqad Stream.

At an orders-group meeting at 0300 hours on Wednesday, Brigadier General Peled directed Colonel Mordechai Ben Porat's 9th Armored Infantry Brigade (numbering about fifteen tanks) to pass through Colonel Zvi Bar's District Brigade to assault north of Tel Kudna and link up with Lieutenant Colonel Tuvia Teren's battalion of Colonel Yossi Peled's 205th Armored Brigade. In the South, Colonel Gideon Gordon's 70th Armored Infantry Brigade's armored infantry battalion was to overcome Syrian defenses at El Hanut. To the southwest, Lieutenant Colonel Guy Jacobsen's Centurion battalion of 205th Brigade would launch its assault south of the Petroleum Road to the west bank of the Ruqqad Stream. Jacobsen was to link up with the fresh 70th Brigade Sherman battalion, which was to put in its assault from the southern end of the line, through El Hanut, northward along the Ruqqad Stream to Buka'a. Once 9th Brigade had cleared its sector, Bar's District Brigade was to mount a supporting action on the Kudna Road.

Peled's complex plan was almost exactly the opposite of a plan used in a 1970 punitive raid over the same ground. At that time, the IDF had pushed three intact and full-strength tank battalions, supported by combat engineers and ample air and artillery, across the frontier in a single mass. Once the assault force had pierced the Syrian forward defenses, its components had fanned out to the right and the left to secure the area until ordered to return to its line of departure. Peled's October 10 plan called for relatively weak and widely dispersed units to break into Syria, at which point they would reconcentrate to hold the captured ground against possible Syrian counterattacks.

It is revealing of the exhaustion of staffers and commanders at Northern Command headquarters that the plan was even approved. Peled's division would be mounting assaults with three weakened tank battalions across a fifteen-mile front. Three times as many Syrian tanks had struck this portion of the front only ninety hours earlier, and they had been backed by an awesome array of artillery and air power.

All of General Peled's assault prongs quickly bogged down in the face of well-sited Syrian anti-armor defenses.

Ben Porat's 9th Brigade passed Tel Fazra and drove into the hilly ground guarding the approaches to Tel Kudna. As Ben Porat was about to signal his tanks to cross the Purple Line, he had a change of heart and radioed Mussa Peled with the opinion that a direct assault upon Tel Kudna from his current position was futile. His views were amply punctuated by real events. Even as the brigade commander spoke, two 9th Brigade tanks were blown up as they breached a Syrian minefield. Ben Porat's attack was canceled, and General Peled immediately began rethinking his planned assault by manifestly inadequate forces.

Lieutenant Colonel Teren's battalion, numbering just eight Centurions, was able to advance around the southern face of neighboring heights to within a half mile of Tel Kudna, but it drew a blistering rebuke when it came within range of the Syrian defenses. Colonel Zvi Bar attempted to add some weight to Teren's faltering assault and, in the process of hours of fighting, oversaw the destruction of a dozen Syrian tanks by District Brigade crews. Teren's weak battalion did nearly as well; it accounted for eight Syrian tanks in the wild melee. However, at 1630 hours, Teren lost Captain Rami Givoni killed and two Centurions destroyed in a volley of Sagger missiles. The Israelis withdrew.

To the south, Lieutenant Colonel Jacobsen's tank battalion of 205th Brigade lost two tanks to mines north of the Petroleum Road while just getting its advance under way. By 1020, four more of Jacobsen's Centurions had been taken out, by mines. Jacobsen sought permission to pull back, but the request was not answered before Captain Boaz Gilboa tried to advance his company to support Jacobsen and lost two of his tanks to artillery fire. Jacobsen eventually withdrew his battalion, by then down to nine operational Centurions.

Seventieth Brigade's assault on El Hanut went as planned. The newly arrived armored infantry battalion, equipped with a full company of Shermans, moved all the way to the Purple Line without drawing any fire. However, the defenses stiffened as the battalion approached El Hanut. At this juncture, the lead Sherman stood aside to provide direct fire support while the second tank led the assault. The thrust came unglued on the rocky ground, which was littered with mines and covered by heavy artillery concentrations.

This was the fresh battalion's first combat as a unit, and confusion took a toll, particularly when the battalion commander was wounded and evacuated. The deputy commander also was wounded, but he refused relief. At one point the battalion's discipline had deteriorated to such an extent that the deputy commander ordered all his gunners to cease firing so they could determine if their targets were, in fact, Syrians. In the end, the tanks and APCs overcame the opposition by spiritedly leapfrogging right into the El Hanut position.

Given all the grief to which Peled's division had come, it was no wonder that he and General Hofi decided to end the matter, at least for the time being, well short of victory.

Hofi's decision was considerably enhanced by a direct order from Lieutenant General Dado Elazar, who had arrived at Northern Command headquarters just as, from his standpoint, Peled's unauthorized assault was grinding into the Syrian anti-armor belts. Northern Command's tactical goals did not meet Israel's strategic needs of the moment, so Elazar ordered all Northern Command units that had crossed into Syria to return to the Purple Line. These included Lieutenant Colonel Yossi Ben Hanan's fragment of Barak Brigade, which had successfully seized a commanding height on the Syrian side near the Damascus Road east of Kuneitra.

Elazar was not the least bit squeamish about his subordinates' tactical initiative. His order was the product of his conviction that the IDF needed to mount a "general offensive" into Syrian-held territory. Indeed, he left Hofi with the impression that Northern Command would be ordered to launch such an attack within the next twenty-four hours.

In an official message prepared for release to the public, Hofi reported to Elazar:

I am happy to report that, after an exceptionally difficult battle lasting four days, the northern army corps, together with the massive support of the Air Force, has succeeded in breaking the Syrian Army. The enemy lost hundreds of its tanks in the battles. The Golan Heights cease-fire line is in our hands. Taking advantage of our success, we are attacking across the cease-fire line.

EPILOGUE

The Israeli seizure of Tel Ramatnia irretrievably changed the nature of the seventy-six-hour-old conflict. "Assad's War" had hinged upon the ability of the Syrian Army to seize land while the Israel Defense Force was plunged into defeat or retreat and while the Israeli Air Force was isolated from the battlefield by an impregnable missile umbrella.

The Syrians achieved not one lasting battlefield goal. As a practical matter, "Assad's War" was lost well before control of the Purple Line was regained by Israeli armored and armored-infantry formations.

The fundamental prewar Israeli strategic plan in the event of war initiated by both its strong Arab neighbors placed the burden upon those forces facing Egypt. However, the actual nature of the war—particularly the shallow strategic depth on the Golan—dictated an early powerful effort on the Golan. The division built up from Golani, Barak, and 7th Armored brigades under Rafoul Eitan held the line while Dan Laner's and Mussa Peled's Reserve divisions were thrust helter-skelter into the battle. Even as IDF units were closing on the Purple Line, additional Reserve brigades were being formed and sent toward the Golan battlefields. Given a temporary stalemate in Sinai and the clear victory on the Golan, the Israelis opted to use the opportunity to build up needed strategic depth at the expense of Syria, and to punish that nation for its temerity.

The Israeli Air Force's initial contributions on the Golan front were minimal. Disproportionate losses resulted both from the initially seamless Syrian missile defenses and the need to commit IAF jet fighter-bombers on a piecemeal basis contingent upon battlefield emergencies. Most of the losses were sustained when Israeli jets were used in emergency "flying artillery" sorties. In time, the IDF's artillery capability was built up, thus freeing the jets for work more consistent with the capabilities of their pilots. As the Syrian missile defenses were whittled down and as senior Israeli officers and officials hammered out a cogent plan for the conduct of the war, the opportunities for achieving superiority above the battlefields evolved toward a plan to undertake strategic raids against Syrian targets far from the arena of the armored war.

The concept of "Syria first" took root from a combination of factors, chiefly the early defensive successes on the Golan and the emerging strategic possibilities seen by IAF pilots and commanders. Once taken, the strategic decision spelled doom for Hafez al-Assad's hopes and, indeed, for the Syrian military establishment.

Even as the close-run battles of October 8 were under way on the Golan, IAF planners were busily drawing up a list of choice military *and economic* targets all across Syria. The objective was less the hammering of nails into Assad's military coffin than a fundamental weakening of Arab resolve and damaging the foundations of Arab society through a clear demonstration of Israel's awesome recuperative powers.

On the morning of October 9, Israeli jets destroyed the El Burak radar facilities—in Lebanon. This was a clear message that Israel was overlooking the old rules, whereby the aiders and abettors of aggression against the State of Israel got off on technicalities arising out of internationally accepted rules that never seemed to be applied in Israel's favor. The strict, long-standing concept of "an eye for an eye" that had governed Israeli retributive operations was at least temporarily lifted.

With the key Syrian-used Lebanese-run radar facility neutralized, Israeli jets next struck Damascus, another quantum departure from the old rules. Among the first targets were Air Force headquarters and the Ministry of Defense compound. The Israeli jets delivered their attacks from treetop height, as much to minimize losses as to impress the Syrian man in the street. A power station, a radio station, and an oil-tank farm also were left in ruins. A noon follow-up raid wiped Radio Damascus off the air as it was delivering a "victory" exhortation to the entire Arab world.

Later in the day, economic targets in Homs were attacked, and a power plant and oil refinery there were destroyed. A second raid in the same area turned the Al Hami Army Base into a vortex of destruction.

Syria, which had minimal strategic air capabilities, asked Egypt to undertake retaliatory raids against civilian targets in Israel. The Egyptians refused, no doubt considering themselves lucky to have thus far avoided serious IAF intervention against economic targets around Cairo or even farther from the Sinai battlefields. The Egyptian refusal nearly shattered the resolve of the Syrian architects of the Golan strategy, and it seriously affected the decision-making powers of the Syrian warlords. A similar request to Iraq brought an early agreement, but this was nullified within hours when the Iraqi warlords decided that all-out strategic warfare against Israel was not in their best interests.

On the afternoon of October 10, Soviet military advisers urged the Syrian High Command to withdraw its forces on the Golan and bring fresh forces forward to man the middle defensive barrier, the Sasa Line. The Syrians did not yet feel obliged to heed this advice, but they were wavering.

Meanwhile, the IAF continued to work its way down its long list of strategic targets within Syria. A second oil refinery near Homs was leveled, as was a major power plant near Katana. Port facilities at the Syrian coastal cities of Latakia, Tartous, and Banias were struck by Israeli jets, and Syria's naval headquarters at Minat al Badya was brutally attacked.

Though Israeli aerial observers missed seeing the forward deployment of FROG surface-to-surface missiles aimed at the Ramat David Air Base and the city and port of Haifa, Israeli pilots did note the arrival of fresh SAM missiles at or near the forward antiair cordons. This resulted in a telling air strike against Damascus International Airport—a clear message to the Soviets that Israel had no intention of losing its hard-won advantage to a massive influx of fresh munitions. It remained to be seen how the Soviets would react to the inherent risk of committing their limited fleet of large cargo aircraft directly to an active war zone, which is precisely what Damascus had become.

That night, October 10, Israeli gunboats closed on the Syrian coast and bombarded Minat al Badya, Latakia, and Banias. When missile-armed Syrian patrol boats tried to intervene, the Israelis fired their domestically produced Gabriel surface-to-surface missiles and vaporized a pair of the Syrian vessels. The battle was observed from the shore, and its outcome—evidenced by continued incoming fire from the Israeli gunboats—caused shaky morale in Latakia to plummet. In addition to wrecking harbor facilities and destroying oil stocks and Syrian naval facilities and vessels, the Israelis sank three foreign-flag commercial vessels. This last had the effect of at least temporarily isolating Syria from maritime trade with the outside world. Combined with the air strikes against Damascus International Airport, the closure of the Syrian ports sent shudders of depression through the Syrian economy.

Once the issue of holding the Golan and preventing Syrian land assaults from reaching Israel-proper had been decided, the Israeli military and civilian leaders were able to consider the reassertion of the power of their military forces in the Sinai, where a sort of stalemate had been achieved at great expense to both Egypt and Israel.

As the situation in Northern Command neared stability, the Israeli leadership was able to stop *reacting* to Arab initiatives and do a little forward planning of its own. This "breathing space" culminated in the consideration of a clearheaded proposal by some military and some civilian leaders to direct more ground and air assets into the Sinai than had been prudent earlier, and to retain forces on the Golan only insofar as they were required to stabilize the front and continue to interdict Syria's war-making capabilities.

The Israeli war leaders met late in the evening of October 10 to discuss their options and make their decisions.

A plan was put forth by the Israeli deputy chief of staff for operations, Major General Israel Tal, to shift one of the three Golan divisions to the Sinai. His reasoning: Only two divisions were needed to defend the Golan against the weakened Syrian Army and the collection of brigades and battalions offered up by Syria's bet-hedging allies.

Dado Elazar disagreed. He theorized that since no strategic plan had yet been put forth for defeating Egypt, the IDF might just as well go ahead and pound Syria into the ground; once that was done, the relatively stable Sinai front could be heated up with an all-out attack to regain the Suez Canal frontage lost in the initial Egyptian assault of October 6.

Defense Minister Moshe Dayan wavered; he personally wanted to defeat Egypt, but he also desired to punish Syria. "The war should cost Syria so dearly," he affirmed, "that they will regret what they did."

Dayan nearly regretted his rhetoric, for the Northern Command representative translated the defense minister's statement to mean that IDF forces deployed on the Golan should push the Syrians far enough back to render Syrian artillery incapable of reaching Israeli villages in and beyond the Jordan River Valley. Such a move would have been tantamount to an all-out invasion of Syria.

Tal said he understood the emotions articulated by Dayan and translated by the Northern Command liaison officer, but he tartly added that he personally preferred to run the war on the basis of intellect. If the Purple Line was to be crossed for any reason, he said, then the only worthwhile objective was Damascus.

Elazar picked up on Tal's affirmation, but not in the way Tal would have desired. First, the chief of staff agreed that no *tactical* goal was worth the potential loss of lives and equipment that a confrontation with Syrians manning fixed defenses would entail. However, in keeping with Israel's strategic requirements, Elazar allowed that a limited offensive to bring Damascus within range of Israeli artillery was well worth some additional losses. If Syrian citizens could feel the repercussions of the war initiated by their leaders, there was reason to believe that some reasonable and re-sponsible considerations might be given by the incumbent or a future ruling clique when it next was confronted with its cyclical urge to destroy the Jewish state.

As far as Tal was concerned, Syria was out of the war, and there was no sense in frittering away lives and resources as long as Egypt had not also been brought to her knees. The IAF had neutralized

Lebanon and Syria and, by terror alone, Jordan. The only possible target for Israel's might was, in Tal's formidable mind, Egypt.

Dayan flip-flopped again, stating in Tal's behalf that an advance toward Damascus could bring on an undesirable Soviet reaction, up to and including direct Soviet intervention, which clearly was not in Israel's best interests.

The opposing views could not be reconciled on their intrinsic merits; all had validity. However, they could be *resolved* by one hitherto silent player. Prime Minister Golda Meir listened to the arguments and counterarguments and countercounterarguments as they rolled from the minds of old comrades and trusted advisers. She asked questions but otherwise kept her counsel. Anything she said, when the time came, would have the force of law. For the time being, Mrs. Meir preferred to let her counselors achieve their own sort of consensus.

Slowly the forces supporting the crossing into Syria coalesced: Elazar stated that the risk of becoming bogged down on the road to Damascus was worth the implicit message to the Arab peoples that Israel had recovered so swiftly from the despair and shock of October 6; the Air Force commander, Brigadier General Benny Peled, reported that for days his pilots had been observing the continuous weakening of the Syrian air defenses, but he also pointed out that massive Soviet materiel outlays could reverse the trend in a matter of days, that the time to strike might never again be better; Major General Eli Zeira declaimed that his sources in Syria reported that only 350 to 400 first-line tanks remained operable and that there had occurred blatant acts of disobedience or outright mutiny at or near the front, that morale within the Syrian military establishment was minimal.

Dayan was swayed by these arguments and, while he offered no support, he dropped his objections to the proposed thrust toward Damascus.

On one thing all agreed: The worst possible action was inaction; standing pat would send all the wrong messages.

Just before dawn on October 11, Golda Meir agreed to a limited offensive in the direction of Damascus. If things went well, the mandate could be expanded; if not, it could be canceled.

* * *

Things went well. Within days, Israeli long-range artillery was able to bombard Damascus International Airport and other targets with pinpoint accuracy. The repercussions were staggering. The Syrian Army was virtually destroyed in the field, as were contingents from other Arab states, chiefly Iraq and Jordan. By the end of six days of fighting, Arab allied contingents constituted virtually the only first-line forces standing between the IDF and the Syrian capital, so soundly had the Syrian Army been beaten.

Israeli losses were large but by no means crippling. Sadly, the roll of dead and wounded Israelis included the names of many of the brave young men who had stood up to the Syrian onslaughts and turned the tide on the Golan: Avner Landau, severely wounded; Yossi Ben Hanan, severely wounded; Yoav Vaspe, killed; Moshe Meler, wounded. . . .

In time, battle-hardened first-line IDF units were shifted from Northern Command to the Sinai, where the Israelis fought back to the Suez Canal, invaded and occupied Africa, and forced the surrender of the cream of the Egyptian Army.

The Egyptian-Syrian alliance came unraveled in the face of separate and mutual defeats. Presidents Assad and Sadat exchanged telegrams and less direct messages for days, and these culminated in an October 21 decision by Sadat to throw in the towel. Assad wavered on into the next day, hopeful that he might retain just one trophy of his abortive and ill-starred war. However, the decision over the ultimate ownership of that single trophy had to be decided far beyond Assad's ability to control events.

The trophy was the Hermon.

On October 20, 1973, with the war clearly drawing to a close on the Egyptian front and on the approaches to Damascus, Major General Yitzhak Hofi turned his attention to the only unreclaimed prize in his Northern Command.

The Hermon had been secured by quick-striking Syrian commandos on October 6, and the one Israeli counterthrust had been bloodily repulsed on October 8. Since then, the Syrians had built up the force holding the former Israeli Hermon bunkers with but a minimum of harassment.

So, on the night of October 20, General Hofi ordered Colonel

Amir Drori's Golani Infantry Brigade and Colonel Chaim Nadel's 317th Parachute Brigade to plan and undertake the recapture of the Israeli Hermon and, if possible, the destruction or capture of structures on the higher Syrian Hermon.

The plan that evolved called for the isolation of the Hermon positions during the night of October 21 and the final reduction of the Syrian defenses on the morning of October 22. Given this timetable and the universal Israeli desire to deny Syria *any* of the early fruits of its war, it was decided by the Israeli Cabinet to stonewall all efforts by either Egypt or Syria to achieve a cease-fire under any sponsorship—Soviet, American, or United Nations—until the Hermon had been returned to Israeli hands. The fact that a U.N. resolution to end the fighting was even then being considered in New York had no impact on the Israeli decision to proceed with the operation.

Existing Golani Brigade deployments provided a base for one arm of the assault, on the west side of the objective. Similarly, the village of Hadar, which was accessible to the Israeli attack forces to the east of the Hermon, was occupied by a company of 18th Parachute Battalion paratroops commanded by Major Yoni Netanyahu; the village would be used as an anchor for the company's projected long climb to positions from which it could block an eastward retreat by Syrian commandos once the main blow fell.

The key to the Hermon compound lay farther up the mountain. This was the original Syrian position itself, for it was serviced by the best of the mountain roads and it dominated the best access route to the former Israeli positions. The only way to get at the Syrian Hermon was the way the Syrians had gotten to the Israeli Hermon on October 6: by helicopter.

The danger to the heliborne force was extreme. The approach would require an hour's flight time, mainly through Lebanese airspace, during which the helicopters would be vulnerable to Syrian aircraft and all forms of ground fire, including missiles. The danger of loss from accidents in the uncertain updrafts was very high. However, if the helilift was successful, the Syrian battalion manning the former Israeli compound would be totally isolated from resupply and reinforcement.

The risk was considered so extreme that General Hofi visited the assault elements as they were preparing to lift off. "Now, my veteran foxes," the seasoned paratroop general began, "will you do it?"

The paratroopers, who had felt underutilized in the predominantly armored war on the Golan, were more than willing to face the risks. These were Israel's premier soldiers, formed into what they believed was Israel's premier fighting brigade; doing the job was all they asked in return for their years of grueling training and the high risk each had run of perishing in a training accident.

"We'll do it," one of their officers bellowed, "perhaps without losses!"

This was not what Hofi wanted to hear; he was in no mood for casual braggadocio. "I don't ask you to say that. If you cross enemy territory, over Fatahland [PLO-occupied southern Lebanon], and reach a landing, you'll have done the main job."

Golani Brigade, which was holding positions to the north of the objective, was to mount an attack similar to its abortive October 8 thrust—but for three new wrinkles. The supporting fires that had been lacking on October 8 would be available from five artillery batteries and at least one fighter-bomber squadron, on call; many more tanks and armored fighting vehicles would comprise the attack force; and the approach would be made in the dark rather than in full daylight. Most important, this Golani Brigade attack was a thoroughly planned, minutely coordinated set-piece assault, not the improvised abortion that had resulted in the needless loss of valuable lives on October 8.

Israeli artillery raised the curtain when several batteries opened fire at noon on October 21 against all the Syrian positions. As the suppressive salvoes sought their targets, the helicopters lifted off to begin the long, roundabout approach.

In the end, the helicopters bearing the lead assault element feathered into the objective area, along a ridge twenty-five hundred meters above the Jordan Valley, without incident. The Syrians brought the landing zone under immediate artillery fire.

The commander of the parachute battalion, Lieutenant Colonel "Hezi," ordered his troops to the west side of the steep ridgeline to minimize losses. Syrian "overs" would plunge hundreds of feet out of range before exploding, and the rest would impact on or in front of the rock wall. Only one Israeli was injured by the Syrian rounds.

Additional increments of paratroopers were set down by helicopter every fifteen minutes. As "Hezi" Battalion was built up, Israeli and Syrian jets vied for control of the air over the tiny landing zone. Some of the dogfighting took place below the level of the waiting parachutists. The Israelis, by far the better pilots, were in no way threatened by Syrian SAM missiles, so they could devote their full attention to swatting the Syrian jets, whose prime mission was downing troop-carrying Israeli helicopters. In this, the Syrians failed. Seven Syrian jets were destroyed in the first two hours.

About an hour after "Hezi" landed with the first wave, the Israelis spotted five Syrian troop-carrying helicopters trying to lift reinforcements to the soon-to-be-embattled Syrian bunkers. These were intercepted by Israeli jets at 1730 hours, and three were destroyed in the air while the two survivors fled back to Syria.

In the meantime, the IAF was mounting two related operations. In one, a helicopter lifted an artillery forward observer team to a lonely vantage point about 2,600 meters up the Hermon. And a flight of Israeli fighter-bombers sprang a trap on a Syrian tank company confined to the winding road leading up from the Syrian village of Arna. The burning tanks left in the wake of the IAF strike effectively blocked the key road link to further significant motorized or mechanized movement.

Between 1600 and 1700 hours, half-naked Israeli paratroopers rocked on their backs and buttocks along the broken summit of the landing zone ridge as they pulled on the long woolen underwear they had carried to the heights in their packs. Everyone knew it was going to be a long, cold night up there.

Captain Uri Zur ordered his company to its feet at 1700 hours and led it toward the first Syrian-held objective. The long wait was over.

Zur's company had to climb down through 550 meters of rock and stone to reach its objective. This was "The Serpentine," after the long, winding road leading up from Arna. Because it was on the eastern slope, away from the sun, the Syrian position already lay in darkness, which covered Zur's approach. The Israelis were right on top of the Syrians when the shooting began. The vanguard platoon leader was shot dead as he personally led his paratroopers into The Serpentine.

Uri Zur's company worked with caution to avoid further loss, so took two hours to secure The Serpentine. Only the one Israeli died in the effort. His comrades found seven dead Syrians after the shooting stopped.

No sooner had the position been secured than the patient paratroopers were rewarded with the arrival of a Syrian truck convoy, which obligingly slowed before the guard shack. One of the drivers must have recognized the shape of an Israeli helmet, for he raised the alarm and ran away downslope with most of his comrades. Only the last of the six vehicles managed to turn back toward Arna. The trucks were filled with heavy mortars and ammunition and equipment for them.

Next up was Captain Shai Lyn's company, which passed through The Serpentine on the way down another 550 meters to The Crevice, which overlooked a particularly difficult turn in the Arna road. Since there was no possibility of achieving surprise in the wake of the Syrian convoy flap, Lyn requested that artillery salvoes be placed on the approaches to the objective. The fresh company moved very slowly as the heavy rounds were walked down the roadway and its shoulders.

The bombardment had all the desired effects: Lyn's company was not molested, and the Syrians holding The Crevice were easily cowed. The Israelis pulled a dozen dead Syrian soldiers from the wreckage of their fighting position after the briefest of close-combat encounters. Among the dead was the position commander and two soldiers who had succumbed to a direct hit by an Israeli heavy mortar upon their pillbox. Many Arabic oaths could be heard as the former defenders scattered downslope.

Israeli casualties to this point were negligible, but the advance was running behind schedule. Even while Lyn's company was moving on The Crevice, Lieutenant Colonel Elisha Shelem climbed down past The Serpentine with his battalion and prepared to pass through Lyn's company as soon as The Crevice had been secured. This he did without incident at 0200 hours on October 22. He was on his way to the main position on the Syrian Hermon behind another rolling artillery barrage.

Shelem had no opposition; the entire Syrian Hermon had been abandoned. At 0330 hours, the 317th Parachute Brigade commander radioed General Hofi with news that the Syrian Hermon was securely in his hands. Only one Israeli had died in this brilliantly executed operation.

As Shelem's battalion was passing The Crevice, the Golani Brigade assault force was completing its advance toward the former Israeli Hermon, to the south, following an arduous eight-hour climb.

The lead Golani battalion assault force nosed into the advance Syrian defenses at 0200 hours. The Syrians spotted the Israelis first because they were equipped with infrared spotting scopes, the latest equipment from the Soviet Union. Twenty-eight superbly trained Syrian snipers allowed the Israelis to reach a tiny ridge just in front of the Hermon bunker. Backing the snipers was a reinforced commando battalion equipped with still more nightscopes and infantry and antitank weapons of every description.

The Syrian snipers had first crack at the attackers. Within a minute, Israelis near the front of the column were falling to the deliberate fire while their own fire passed over and around the well-emplaced enemy snipers. These were the best troops the Syrian Army had to offer in battle; the only way the Israelis could overcome the widely dispersed commandos was literally to walk up to their foxholes and blow them away, no mean feat. On occasion, patient Israelis managed to spot Syrian muzzle flashes, which resulted in showers of hand grenades being hurled at the unlucky sniper.

The Israelis quickly lost the initiative.

At first the Israeli wounded were carried downslope for treatment. But each casualty required at least four able-bodied soldiers to carry him, so the strength of the bogged-down assault force rapidly diminished. This is a classic dilemma in combat, particularly in difficult terrain. Since ironclad tradition placed Israeli officers in the forefront of the assault, inevitable officer casualties had a severe, negative impact on the conduct of the attack. Colonel Amir Drori, the Golani Brigade commander, was himself wounded and evacuated. By the time Drori's assault battalion commander also was wounded, there were not enough infantrymen to be spared for helping get him back to the aid station.

Two infantry companies had to be flown to a nearby landing site from the base of the mountain. Without them, the attack simply would have petered out. As a further precaution, elements of 317th

Parachute Brigade were ordered to move down from the Syrian Golan, though it would be hours before the parachutists could position themselves to take the Syrian-held compound from the rear.

Bravery and motivation simply could not be made to overcome the material advantages afforded the Syrian snipers by their infrared nightscopes.

In the wake of the tiny infantry advances at the Israeli spearhead there were powerful formations of armor and armored infantry. The first contingent of eight Centurions was in the care of Major Yosef Nissem, who had fought ferociously as deputy commander of Yair Nofshe's 74th Tank Battalion until placed in command of the Golani Brigade's organic tank unit on October 10.

At about 0300 hours, Nissem's eight Centurions rounded a particularly difficult curve in the road. According to a Syrian commando, "We heard the tanks approaching us and, in the moonlight, saw [them] making their way up the mountain. We felt this was a golden opportunity as the enemy focused mainly on the road. . . , [When the enemy had closed] to one hundred meters, the captain said, 'Open fire!' At that point, the doors of hell opened."

Seven of the eight tank commanders, including Yosef Nissem, were wounded in the ensuing fight, and the uninjured commander's tank detonated a mine in the roadway. Command of the surviving tanks fell to Sergeant Natan Nagar, a gunner. Nagar calmly selected targets and directed his fellow gunners.

The tank column got under way again at 0520 hours.

Sunrise found the Golani infantrymen still pinned down. The predominant Hebrew word heard that sunrise at that place means "medic." The sun rose in the east, as always—right into the faces of the attackers. The sun also brought out the first Syrian fighter-bombers, but these turned back in the face of awesome Israeli aerial countermeasures. The opposing sides were intermingled, which ruled out bringing the superior weight of Israeli artillery or tactical air to bear.

The operations officer of the leading Golani infantry battalion, a captain, was the senior man on the spot. Calling encouragement to his exhausted, crestfallen infantrymen, he oversaw the painstakingly slow reduction of first one sniper position, then another and another. The momentum shifted, imperceptibly at first, then amid rising waves of enthusiasm. Tiny flanking movements carried individual Israelis—pairs at the most—to better positions. The Golani captain stood up and advanced into the enemy fire, drawing many of those who could see him into the desperate, last-gasp assault.

The shift in momentum became obvious by 0900 hours, and the Syrian officer in command of the sniper-infested approaches to the Hermon bunkers surrendered. According to his testimony, "The Israelis gave me a loudspeaker and asked me to call on my comrades to surrender, for there was no point [fighting] anymore. That was true. The battle was lost. I called to my comrades to stop fighting, but a friend raised his rifle to aim at me. I called out, 'Don't shoot,' but he did—and hit me in the stomach."

Still, other Syrians did surrender, and many others died under the weight of the Israeli attack. No one knows precisely how many retreated.

At 1053 hours on October 22, the Israelis raised two flags over the Hermon bunkers. One was the national colors of the State of Israel; the other was the battle pennant of Golani Brigade, proudly numbered "1st" in the IDF order of battle. The raising of the battle pennant was in immediate honor of the sixty-one Golani infantrymen who had died on the Hermon since October 6.

The last scenes in the drama were played out on the eastern and western slopes, where Israeli parachutists were hunting down isolated and retreating Syrians. One Israeli paratrooper was killed in one of many fire fights on the Syrian Hermon. Downslope, members of Major Yoni Netanyahu's climbing parachute company encountered other Syrians, and most of these were killed at no further loss to the Israelis.

Those Syrians coming off the west slope of the Hermon into Lebanon were given a cool reception by the Lebanese Army forces they met there. The Lebanese even refused to provide medical assistance to the wounded as they directed the survivors of Assad's War to a central collection point for repatriation to Syria. The attitude of these Lebanese toward their fellow Arab soldiers, as much as anything, underlined the utter bankruptcy of Syria's war aims.

* * *

At 0005 hours on October 23, Syrian General Headquarters informed the Iraqi high command that President Assad had accepted the terms of United Nations Resolution 338, which called for the cessation of hostilities by the warring nations. Egypt and Israel had acceded to the resolution as soon as it had been adopted—even as the final assault upon the Hermon bunkers was under way. Jordan, the last of the "front line" Arab powers, followed suit at 0200 hours on October 23.

Thus ended the duel for the Golan.

The Syrians lost 1,150 main battle tanks, and their Iraqi and Jordanian allies lost about 150, respectively. Of all the Arab tank losses, the Israelis counted 867 Soviet-provided main battle tanks on the Golan itself; many of them were found to be in good running and fighting order. Those that could be repaired and refurbished were absorbed, along with captured former Egyptian equipment, into new IDF armored units commissioned in the wake of the war; the rest were used for spare parts or, most insulting, sold to Romania in the wake of a Soviet arms embargo against that Eastern Bloc state. The Syrian Air Force lost 222 aircraft in the war; 167 were destroyed in air combat, and the rest were destroyed on the ground. It is estimated that 3,500 Syrians died in Assad's War, and it is known that 370 were taken prisoner by the Israelis.

It is amazing to note that every Israeli tank committed to the Golan fighting was hit by hostile fire at least once during the war. Of the approximately 250 Centurions and Super Shermans hit badly enough to be considered "knocked out," over 150 were returned to battle (at least once) by IDF ordnancemen, who often undertook refurbishings under Syrian guns.

Israel lost 772 of her sons killed, 2,453 wounded, and 65, including pilots, taken prisoner.

APPENDIX A

ISRAELI BATTLE UNITS AND COMMANDERS

NORTHERN COMMAND	Maj. Gen. Yitzhak Hofi
Corps Artillery	Brig. Gen. A. Bar-David
317th Parachute Brigade	Col. Chaim Nadel
50th Parachute Battalion	Lt. Col. Yair Yaron
18th Parachute Battalion	Lt. Col. "Ilan"
71st Armored Infantry Battalion	Lt. Col. Yoav Vaspe
Northern Command Tank Battalion	Lt. Col. Uzi More
Armor School Tank Battalion	Lt. Col. Memshalom Carmel
36th ARMORED INFANTRY DIVISION	Brig. Gen. Rafael Eitan
188th Armored Brigade ("Barak")	Col. Yitzhak Ben Shoham
7th Armored Brigade	Col. Avigdor Ben Gal
1st Infantry Brigade ("Golani")	Col. Amir Drori
240th ARMORED DIVISION	Maj. Gen. Dan Laner
679th Armored Brigade	Col. Uri Orr
4th Armored Infantry Brigade	Col. Yaacov Pfeiffer
146th ARMORED DIVISION	Brig. Gen. Moshe Peled
9th Armored Infantry Brigade	Col. Mordechai Ben Porat
205th Armored Brigade	Col. Yosef Peled
District Brigade	Col. Zvi Bar
70th Armored Infantry Brigade	Col. Gideon Gordon

NOTE: The above divisional organizations changed radically during the course of battle. Most notably, 188th Armored Brigade reverted from its parent 36th Division to the newly created 240th Division. Numerous ad hoc units, such as Sarig Force, are not listed here. As divisional sectors were created and as divisional boundaries shifted, brigades and battalions—and parts of brigades and battalions—fell under new commands.

APPENDIX B

1st TANK DIVISION   Col. Tewfiq Jehani
  4th Tank Brigade
  91st Tank Brigade
  2nd Mechanized Brigade
  64th Artillery Brigade

3rd TANK DIVISION   Brig. Gen. Mustapha Sharba
  20th Tank Brigade
  65th Tank Brigade
  15th Mechanized Brigade
  13th Artillery Brigade

5th INFANTRY DIVISION   Brig. Gen. Ali Aslan
  112th Infantry Brigade
  61st Infantry Brigade
  132nd Mechanized Brigade
  50th Artillery Brigade
  47th Independent Tank Brigade (attached)

7th INFANTRY DIVISION   Brig. Gen. Omar Abrash
  68th Infantry Brigade
  85th Infantry Brigade
  121st Mechanized Brigade
  70th Artillery Brigade
  78th Independent Tank Brigade (attached)
  Moroccan Brigade (attached)

9th INFANTRY DIVISION   Col. Hassan Tourkmani
  52nd Infantry Brigade
  53rd Infantry Brigade
  43rd Mechanized Brigade

(Continued)

89th Artillery Brigade
51st Independent Tank Brigade (attached)

GENERAL HEADQUARTERS
FORCES   Maj. Gen. Yousef Chakour

70th Tank Brigade
141st Tank Brigade
81st Tank Brigade
62nd Mechanized Brigade
30th Infantry Brigade
69th Rocket Brigade
90th Infantry Brigade
1st Commando Group
82nd Parachute Regiment
Additional artillery brigades

BIBLIOGRAPHY

BOOKS

Ajami, Fouad. *The Arab Predicament.* New York: Cambridge University Press, 1982.

Al Ayoubi, Haytham. "Strategies of the Fourth Round" in *Middle East Crucible.* Wilmette, Ill.: Medina University Press International, 1975.

Albaum, Yacov, and Myron Zur. *Shiron Vi Lev.* The Committee to Maintain Liaison with the Men of the Brigade, 1977 (Hebrew).

Amos, John W. *Arab-Israeli Military/Political Relations.* Elmsford, N.Y.: Pergamon Press, 1979.

Bartoch, Chanock. *Dado.* Tel Aviv: Mariv Book Guild, 1973 (Hebrew).

Ben Porat, Yeshayahu. *Kippur.* Tel Aviv: University Publishing Project Ltd., 1973.

Blow, Desmond. *Take Now Thy Son.* Capetown: Howard Timmins, 1974.

Caroz, Yaacov. *The Arab Secret Services.* New York: Corgi, 1976.

Dayan, Moshe. *Story of My Life.* New York: William Morrow, 1976.

252 ■ BIBLIOGRAPHY

Dupuy, Trevor. *Elusive Victory.* New York: Harper & Row, 1978.

Haber, Eitan. *Barak.* Tel Aviv, 1979 (Hebrew).

Hashavia, Arie. *The Yom Kippur War.* Tel Aviv: Zamora, Bitan, Modan Publishers, 1974 (Hebrew).

Heikal, Mohamed. *The Road to Ramadan.* New York: Quadrangle Publishers, 1975.

Herzog, Chaim. *The War of Atonement.* Boston: Little, Brown, 1975.

Insight Team of the London Sunday *Times. The Yom Kippur War.* Garden City, N.Y.: Doubleday, 1974.

Israel. Ministry of Defense. *Facts and Documents on the Treatment of Prisoners of War, Yom Kippur War, Syrian Front.* Tel Aviv: 1977.

Kahalani, Avigdor. *Oz 77.* Tel Aviv: Schoken Publishing Ltd., 1975 (Hebrew).

Kalmanovitz, Avraham. *Yom Kippur.* Jerusalem: Jerusalem Publishing Co., 1974.

Kibbutz Hamuchad. *The Men of Hagoshrim in the Yom Kippur War.* Tel Aviv: 1974 (Hebrew).

Meir, Golda. *My Life.* New York: Dell, 1975.

O'Ballance, Edgar. *No Victor, No Vanquished.* San Rafael, Calif.: Presidio, 1978.

Ofry, Dan. *The Yom Kippur War.* Tel Aviv: Zohar, 1974.

Palit, D. K. *Return to Sinai.* New Delhi: Palit & Palit, 1974.

ARTICLES

Aliani, Mordechai. *Bamachane,* 7 March 1979.

"Artillery on Damascus." *Bamachane,* 22 August 1980.

Bermudez, Joe. "Syrian T-34/122 S P Gun," *Jane's Defense Weekly,* 15 September 1984.

Cooperman, Menachem. *Bamachane,* 26 October 1979.

"The Journal Interviews: BG. A. Bar-David," *Field Artillery Journal,* May–June 1978.

Lev, Amnon. *Bamachane,* 18 February 1981.

"MAOZ 107." *Bamachane,* 12 May 1976.

Marshall, S.L.A. "Tank Warrior of the Golan," *Military Review,* January 1976.

Morony, T. L. "Artillery Support in the Yom Kippur War," *Field Artillery Journal,* September–October 1975.

Nicolle, David. "The Assault on Mt. Hermon," *R.U.S.I.,* June 1975.

Wakebridge, Charles. "The Syrian Side of the Hill," *Military Review,* February 1976.

· INDEX ·